ARCTIC REVOLUTION

Map 1   The New Canadian North as of 1999

The NWT has been divided into two new territories – Nunavut ("Our Land") to the northeast, the (new) NWT to the southwest. Nunavut contains the Inuit; the (new) NWT contains the Dene, Métis, whites, and Inuvialuit.

ARCTIC REVOLUTION

SOCIAL CHANGE IN THE NORTHWEST TERRITORIES

1935-1994

John David Hamilton

DUNDURN PRESS
Toronto & Oxford

Editor: Dorothy Turnbull
Printed and bound in Canada by Metrolitho Inc., Quebec

The publisher wishes to acknowledge the generous assistance and ongoing support of the **Canada Council**, the **Book Publishing Industry Development Program** of the **Department of Canadian Heritage**, the **Ontario Arts Council**, the **Ontario Publishing Centre** of the **Ministry of Culture, Tourism and Recreation**, and the **Ontario Heritage Foundation**.
 Care has been taken to trace the ownership of copyright material used in the text (including the illustrations). The author and publisher welcome any information enabling them to rectify any reference or credit in subsequent editions.

J. Kirk Howard, Publisher

Canadian Cataloguing in Publication Data

Hamilton, John David, 1919–
 Arctic revolution : a political and social history of the Northwest Territories, 1935–1994

Includes bibliographical references and index.
ISBN 1-55002-206-7

1. Northwest Territories – History – 1905– .*
I. Title.

FC4173.H35 1994 971.9'203 C93-095351-7
F1090.5.H35 1994

Dundurn Press Limited
2181 Queen Street East
Suite 301
Toronto, Canada
M4E 1E5

Dundurn Distribution
73 Lime Walk
Headington, Oxford
England
OX3 7AD

Dundurn Press Limited
1823 Maryland Avenue
P.O. Box 1000
Niagara Falls, N.Y.
U.S.A. 14302-1000

CONTENTS

LIST OF MAPS

DEDICATION

Dedicated in equal measure to the great women of the NWT, such as Agnes Semmler, Nellie Cournoyea, Bertha Allen, Suzie Husky, Elizabeth Mackenzie, Ethel Blondin, Ann Hanson, and Edna Elias ...

... to the outstanding men like James Wah Shee, Georges Erasmus, Nick Sibbeston, John Amagoalik, Tagak Curley, Peter Ernerk, and Rick Hardy ...

... and to dedicated public servants like Stuart Hodgson, John Parker, Gordon Robertson, and Ben Sivertz ...

These people, and many like them, made it possible for the Northwest Territories to evolve from a colony into a vibrant homeland in less than forty years.

THE WISDOM OF OUR FATHERS

The Company have for 80 years slept at the edge of a frozen sea; they have shown no curiosity to penetrate farther themselves, and have exerted all their art and power to crush that spirit in others.

– Joseph Robson, Hudson's Bay Company surveyor, 1752

Canada has administered the vast regions of the North for ninety years in a continual state of absence of mind.

– Louis St. Laurent, 1953

I would be quite willing personally to leave the whole Hudson's Bay Company country a wilderness for the next half century, but I fear that if Englishmen do not go there, Yankees will.

– John A. Macdonald, 1865

If the Americans felt security required it, they would take peaceful possession of part of Canada with a welcome of the people of B.C., Alberta and Saskatchewan.

– W.L. Mackenzie King, 1945

PREFACE

I am a journalist who has been going into the Northwest Territories for half a century. From the very first, the range of things I reported was very wide – from the first stumbling experiments in extracting oil from sand along the Athabaska River to the building of the Alaska Highway and the first hard, all-weather airports. What I mainly reported was the reaction of people to the tremendous changes around them. I watched a canoe carrying two Indians paddling in a leisurely way across the Slave River at Fort Smith while a Norseman aircraft on floats took off past them. I saw the way the people of Edmonton reacted to the American servicemen flooding in from the south in 1942 – and the pleasure Yellowknifers got from the first highway linking them with Edmonton in 1961. I flew in bush planes and helicopters, filmed bull moose plunging through mountain snowdrifts and barges floating down the Mackenzie loaded with tightly canvassed oil drilling rigs. I was present (an exciting moment) when the five Indian nations of the NWT held their first successful Grand Assembly of Chiefs and Elders in Fort Rae.

I went north first as a reporter, but as I watched and recorded events, I soon found I was unable to shed the fact that I was also a man, a Canadian, and a human being. Unlike some of my colleagues, I found it hard to separate my professional and private roles, a troublesome dilemma because the functions of journalist and human witness sometimes come into moral conflict.

Here is an example: At the start of the 1970s, the search for oil and gas on the remote frontiers was one of the great preoccupations of both Canadian business and the Canadian government. Prime Minister Pierre Trudeau made a speech in Edmonton that envisaged a vast northern development with all-weather ports on the Arctic and Hudson Bay, an "energy corridor" along the Mackenzie River to the Beaufort Sea, and new industrial towns in the Delta.

I was a film documentary maker then, and I sold my superiors at CBC on making a program about the first stage of Trudeau's vision, a new highway down the Mackenzie toward Tuktoyaktuk: it would let 18-wheelers travel from Calgary to the Beaufort Sea all year round.

Soon my film crew was fighting black flies and mosquitoes with the bush cutting crews north of Wrigley. We travelled by van as far as the road would take us – to Fort Simpson where the Mackenzie turns north. Already we were seeing what a simple thing like a road could do to the Dehcho (South Slavey) Indians, who had been reasonably well insulated from white culture since the first Nor'Westers came 200 years earlier. My job as a film journalist was to portray as honestly as possible the scenes and events and life going on around us at that specific moment in history. I felt no obligation to do more, nor was I involved in any special interest such as the welfare of the native people or the long-range profits of a petroleum company.

One summer afternoon we were driving around the town of Fort Simpson filming the life of the Slaveys and their Métis cousins. We came back to our motel and my cameraman reloaded as we sat in the van. An Indian girl staggered out of the beer parlour and vomited on the wooden sidewalk, dragged herself erect and wove along, falling down and vomiting again. She was dead drunk; she was about fourteen. My cameraman raised his eyebrows and lifted his Arriflex, mutely asking whether I wanted him to film the girl. I hesitated. It was a dramatic scene and my journalist's instinct told me it would be a shocker in the finished documentary. Professionally, I knew I should shoot the scene even if I didn't plan to use it, "just to be on the safe side." But I knew from experience that if the film clip was there, it would be used even if I decided against it: my superiors were sure to insist on featuring such marvellous "human interest" material. But I remembered the night before, when I opened the door of my motel room and saw the local helicopter dispatcher lurching along the corridor. He was in his forties, white, and he was propped up by two teenaged Indian girls as drunk as he was. One of them was the girl on the sidewalk. The TV audience would just see another drunken Indian; the white man who bought her the booze would not be in the scene. In its own way, the scene would be another lie about the North and its people. Well, if I didn't have the film, my bosses couldn't make me use it. I shook my head at Bob and he put down his camera. Instead, I did an on-camera commentary describing the problems of the whites with booze and drugs in the North.

All through that shoot I ran into similar moral dilemmas. In fifty years of reporting on national and international stories, I've often been offered the cheap shot and cliché, the resort to romanticism. Far too often I've failed to make the right decision and the result has been another stereotype. As I matured and learned more, however, I began to accept the fact that I was on location not only as a journalist but as a human being as well. Dennis Mitchel, the great English documentary maker, told me he had faced similar dilemmas and had decided to make only films that he personally felt were honest. I found that good advice and began to reevaluate everything I was seeing and hearing. Earlier, I had prided myself on my objectivity, but I found it became the objectivity of a man who knows that in the end there is no such thing as objectivity.

In this book, I am trying to follow through on these principles. My text is mainly about change – social, political, economic, and moral – and how that change has affected the people, white and native, who live in the NWT. I am a witness and I am reporting what I saw, heard, and read in the recent history of the NWT. It has been an extraordinary half-century, as the south is now coming to realize. The establishment of self-government in the North belies every colonial and imperial put-off that "it takes time" to make the aboriginals ready to handle their own affairs.

In little more than a dozen years, the position of government leader has moved through white man, Indian, Métis, white husband of an Inuk, to Inuvialuk. The territorial commissioner is a Métis; the deputy commissioner is an Inuk, and a large number of the top bureaucrats are aboriginals. Nellie Cournoyea, the government leader, MPs Ethel Blondin and Jack Anawak, along with other stalwarts like Agnes Semmler, Edna Elias, and Ann Hansen, were all born "on the land" in tents. That is the true measure of the pace of change. I was present at some of the major events during this half-century, trying to make human sense of it. I watched the white residents of Yellowknife stumbling toward democratic government in the 1960s, and I became a friend of the young native leaders who were soon to replace the whites.

One other feature of this half-century has struck me as worth reporting: the role of aboriginal women, who came out of patriarchal Indian and Inuit societies. It seems incredible to me that some 35,000 people should be represented by a far higher per capita percentage of talented, concerned, responsible women leaders than all the rest of Canada. What is it about the people north of 60 that makes them so much more resourceful and adaptable than anybody else on the continent? But then, the North often does remarkable things to whites who move there: opportunities for the native women and their aboriginal male counterparts were vastly enhanced by the presence of half a dozen white men who showed enormous statesmanship in deliberately handing over power to the natives. In particular, I am astonished at the character and sheer size of two commissioners, Stuart Hodgson and John H. Parker. They did something almost unprecedented in history: they deliberately chose to give up colonial power and to hand over authority. That is what makes the NWT so strange and wonderful.

ACKNOWLEDGMENTS

I would like to thank the many individuals who graciously agreed to be interviewed, sharing their memories and opinions. They are too numerous to mention here, but the Bibliography contains the names of all those who assisted me in this way. In the pages that follow, those quotes without a bibliographic source named can be assumed to have been drawn from these personal interviews.

I also want to thank the following organizations for their assistance in the writing of this book: the Canada Council, the Government of the Northwest Territories, Pacific Western Airlines, and the Yellowknife Inn.

Part One

BEFORE THE REVOLUTION

Map 2   The Northwest Territories in 1994, Unchanged Since 1920

Chapter 1

Setting the Stage

The Arctic Revolution: Yesterday, Today, and Tomorrow

The Northwest Territories, which makes up 37 percent of Canada's land mass but has a total population about the size of Lethbridge, Alberta, is in the midst of a social and political revolution. By the end of the century this may well bring constitutional developments as significant in their own way as the formation of the provinces of Saskatchewan and Alberta in 1905.

Yet the revolution only started forty years ago, in 1953.

This historic land mass of *taiga** and tundra, the homeland of the Inuit and several hardy Indian tribes who now call themselves the Dene, "The People," entered European consciousness 400 years ago as the centre of the fur wars between the French and the English. Later it was the fiefdom of the Hudson's Bay Company (HBC), known as Rupert's Land, and east and west, it was the playground of explorers, whalers, and prospectors.

Since 1870 the NWT has been part of Canada.

In 1993, the federal government signed agreements which will divide the NWT into two new territories, one of which will be called Nunavut ("The People's Land") and will be governed by the 20,000 Inuit who form 80 percent of its population. They will also be given ownership of 350,000 square kilometres of land, 36,257 square kilometres with subsurface mineral rights, and $580,000,000 (1992 dollars), which will amount to something more than $1.15 billion by the time payments are completed. Other provisions involve wildlife and environmental controls.

Nunavut, to come into being in 1999, will occupy more than 2,000,000 square kilometres, one-fifth of the land mass of Canada.

---

*A partially forested area lying between the treeless tundra and the boreal coniferous forest.

Yet the cautious term "may happen" must be applied, even though two bills have been passed by Parliament and the one settling the Inuit land claims went into law 9 July 1993. Prime Minister Brian Mulroney handed the Inuit a cheque for $70,000,000 as a down payment. Before the land deal is completed, fourteen years from its passing, it will have paid the Inuit $1.4 billion.

But many things may happen before Nunavut becomes a separate territory 1 April 1999. A whole new government framework must be created from scratch, and the shrunken NWT of the Mackenzie Valley must be restructured. The assets and liabilities of the two territories must be shared. Differences over the boundary between the Inuit-occupied Nunavut and the Dene-occupied area east of Great Bear and Great Slave lakes must be settled.

In the case of Nunavut, the six years between proclamation and implementation of the act must be used to train Inuit to take over the bureaucracy on several levels. The complexity of the problem is illustrated by the fact that the Nunavut Act provides for a ten-member Nunavut Implementation Commission to "provide advice to the parties on the creation of" the new territory.

Three members of the commission will be nominees of the government of the present NWT, three nominees of the Tungavik Federation of Nunavut, and three nominated by the federal government. Ottawa will appoint a chief commissioner. The commission will provide a time-table for the creation of Nunavut and the transfer of powers to it from the NWT and the federal government.

Federal officials say Nunavut Territory may not be ready to assume all of its duties until about 2010, eleven years after it comes into being. In such a case, the GNWT (Government of the Northwest Territories) and the federal government would continue some functions until they can be transferred.

Truly, it is "many a slip"!

Nothing in either the Nunavut (political) Act or the land claims deal provides for negotiation with the federal government for "self-government," although the land claims settlements with the Gwich'in Dene of the Mackenzie Delta and the Sah'tu Dene of the Great Bear Lake region both had such clauses.

The Nunavut Act specifically says that both the future Nunavut Territory and the restructured NWT will be territories similar in function and authority to the present NWT, with an Ottawa-controlled commissioner and a legislative assembly with strictly limited powers not quite up to the level of provincial governments. The new territories will have, to quote the act, "such modernization as may be appropriate."

The great practical leap forward is that Nunavut will be in the political control of the 80 percent Inuit population, whereas the Mackenzie Valley NWT will be divided among non-Natives, Dene, Métis, and Inuvialuit.

Considering that the Inuit will dominate Nunavut for the foreseeable future and the Dene/Métis are still clamoring for some form of self-government, autonomy, or both, the division of the Territories will have a profound effect on both the area north of the 60th parallel of latitude and the future of aboriginal peoples across Canada.

With the exception of the problems outlined, the future of the divided-up NWT is a done deal. When Prime Minister Brian Mulroney signed the Nunavut agreement in Iqualuit 25 May 1993, he marked the high point – so far – of a continuing Arctic revolution that has been going on for forty years. It has drastically changed the lives of all the aboriginals who live north of the 60th parallel. It may have an equally profound effect on the constitutional and structural make-up of Canada. The creation of Nunavut is partial compensation for their bitter disappointment with the failure of federal-provincial conferences on native affairs and the defeat of the Charlottetown Accord, which promised a new deal for all Canadian aboriginals.

The Nunavut agreement brings into focus one of the most serious, ongoing problems with the native population all over Canada. The Inuit, like the Dene of the Mackenzie Valley and, indeed, like the Indians and Métis in the south, are still heavily dependent on white administrators and "experts" – doctors and nurses, teachers, engineers, administrators, sociologists, even lawyers. Jack Anawak, the Liberal member of Parliament for Eastern Arctic, said after the signing: "Our main job in the years running up to Nunavut will be to find a way to train our own experts to replace the kabloonat.* We have a lot of education to do."

What one scholar calls "the indigenization of the public service" has been going on since 1986 when Government Leader Nick Sibbeston, a Métis, started an affirmative action program that was accelerated in the old NWT by his successors.

In Nunavut, the Inuit have an advantage over the Dene of the

---

*Kabloonat is the Inuktitut plural of "kabloona" or "white man."

Mackenzie Valley: they literally speak with one tongue, Inuktitut, and make up 80 percent of the population of Nunavut. Apart from some regional cultural rivalries, the Inuit form a cohesive unit. Symbolic of this is the Inuit Broadcasting System, which broadcasts television programs in Inuktitut by satellite to all regions of the eastern Arctic.

In contrast to the eastern Arctic, the future of the Mackenzie Valley was cloudier in the early 1990s, largely because of racial differences. Six communities in the Beaufort Sea/Mackenzie Delta region are occupied by the Inuvialuit, a sharply distinct branch of the Inuit. Two of these communities, Inuvik and Aklavik, are shared with the Gwich'in Dene, and there is a substantial white population in Inuvik. The Inuvialuit broke away from Inuit land claims negotiations in the early 1980s to make their own settlement deal with Ottawa. This 1984 agreement was the first in the NWT and marked the crumbling of unified native negotiation.

The political arm of the five Dene tribal groups, the Dene Nation, sometimes in alliance with the Métis, for a time presented a fairly united front to the federal government. Had they managed a deal, they would have headed a powerful native confederation with a large land base from which to negotiate an autonomous state. In 1990, however, the Dene Nation rejected the terms offered, and Ottawa promptly switched to negotiations with regional Indian tribal groups.

The Gwich'in (formerly known as the Loucheux or the Loucheux Kutchin) of the Mackenzie Delta signed their own deal in 1992. The Sah'tu (North Slaveys, Hareskin, and Mountain People from around Bear Lake) signed a deal 4 March 1993. The Dog Ribs north of Great Slave Lake, the Dehcho (South Slavey) of the Upper Mackenzie, and the Chipewyans and Cree from south of Great Slave were all proposing individual settlements.

The Dene Nation faded into irrelevance as a political force, though it stayed in existence, hoping to play a major role when negotiations begin on native self-government. The Dene dream of a kind of federated Indian state, which developed in the mid-1970s, seemed far away and unlikely.

All this leaves the creation of Nunavut, the Inuit territory, the most exciting news north of the 60th parallel. It has all the fantasy of a butterfly emerging from a chrysalis, and that is proper because it is part of one of the oddest revolutions in political history – a revolution that grew out of a long Rip Van Winkle–like sleep and quite suddenly became a pell-mell procession from colonialism to emancipation.

Forty years ago, Canada's Eskimos – as they were known then by everybody except themselves – were living their nomadic, heroic lives along the shores of the Arctic Ocean. Few in number, resourceful and inventive, they stoically faced the hardest environment on earth.

Until the 1950s, the Government of Canada scarcely recognized the indigenous inhabitants of the eastern Arctic as human: they seemed like mysterious denizens of some Norse legend transplanted to America. In 1993, exactly forty years later, Prime Minister Mulroney went to Iqaluit, the Baffin Island capital, to sign a deal with the Inuit. He brought with him hope for the first aboriginal self-government in Canada.

~

The various Indian tribes or nations of the political unit known as the Northwest Territories negotiated their first treaty (Treaty 8) in 1899 and their second, Treaty 11, in 1921. They were never confronted with the disasters of the Plains Indians, whose food supplies were destroyed and whose land was occupied by hundreds of thousands of white settlers.

NWT Indians, in fact, were little affected until white gold miners flooded into Yellowknife in 1935 and began demanding the political, legal, and taxation rights of Canadians south of the 60th parallel. Since then, the life of the Indians – now the Dene – has changed as much as that of the Inuit. From Fort Smith on the Alberta border to Tuktoyaktuk on the Beaufort Sea, the Mackenzie Valley became occupied by a mixed bag of Dene, Métis, Inuvialuit and non-natives.

For the past twenty-five years, the residents of the Mackenzie Valley have been trying to escape from colonialism while at the same time finding a formula that will enable them to get along together and solve their myriad problems. What they are pinning their hopes on is consensus government, a political system adapted from Indian tribal tradition, which seems to be the antithesis of the political party system everywhere else in Canada.

Following a series of shattering setbacks to the economy and to the aspirations of natives across Canada in the early 1990s, it is far from clear that consensus government will work. What keeps its supporters trying is that, judging by the experience of the Yukon, the partisan system might fare just as poorly.

~

If any date can be selected to mark the start of the Arctic revolution it is 1953 when Prime Minister Louis St. Laurent announced that Ottawa would adopt a new, hands-on policy. Almost immediately, there was tremendous activity throughout the NWT, and the pace accelerated over the next twenty-five years. The Americans built the Distant Early Warning (DEW) Line to protect North America from Soviet attack. Airports and radio stations led to the founding of brand-new towns; schools and nursing stations were built; starving Inuit were fed and sometimes transported to far-off Arctic pioneer settlements; nomadic Indian and Inuit hunters were encouraged to move off the land and into the new towns. Everything was centralized, administered from Ottawa by white civil servants.

At the same time, there was a move toward local political representation, and Ottawa began to give the NWT's residents a little freedom. The administrative headquarters was moved from Ottawa to Yellowknife, and a new commissioner with some powers of his own was appointed. By 1979 the commissioner's advisory council had become a legislative assembly, and elected representatives of the aboriginal peoples were starting to take the reins of government. By 1993 the all-powerful white commissioner had been replaced by a figurehead rather like a provincial lieutenant-governor – but he was a native. So was the deputy commissioner. The power formerly wielded by the white commissioner was now in the hands of the Legislative Assembly, and the government leader was a native, along with most of her cabinet.

Both NWT members of the House of Commons were native – a far cry from the days when Jean Chrétien, as minister for Indian affairs and northern development, boasted that he was "the last emperor in North America" – and even farther from the era when all of the NWT (and more) was the fiefdom of the HBC.

The extraordinary thing about the movement of the federal government from conventional colonialism to a progressive devolution that handed many functions over to the indigenes, was that it was totally voluntary: the commissioner's arbitrary executive powers remained in the NWT Act but he (with the benign agreement of the all-powerful federal cabinet) deliberately handed over much of his power to the elected representatives of the voters, a majority of whom were aboriginals.

But why did this enormous, remote, and forbidding territory become the centre of pell-mell change? A brief tour of NWT history and geography will set the scene.

The Land and Its People

There are various ways of defining "the Arctic." In the first place, the Arctic is the land and water within the Arctic Circle, 66 degrees, 32 minutes, north latitude. Second, scientists define the Arctic by its complex characteristics involving temperature and weather, which need not concern us here. Third, the land part of the Arctic is generally treeless – the tundra or Barrens – as contrasted with the boreal forest or *taiga* of other parts of the Far North.

Distances are deceptive and sizes hard to estimate because of the curvature of the globe, which becomes smaller as one approaches the North Pole. The best way to visualize the territory is to remember that one degree of latitude is 115 kilometres. Thus the distance from the southern boundary of the NWT (60 degrees north latitude) to the North Pole can easily be calculated. It is about 3,458 kilometres.

Longitude is harder to calculate quickly because each degree varies in width, depending on whether it is on the equator or somewhere nearer either pole. It should also be noted that the Mercator projection familiar to every schoolchild seriously distorts the size and shape of the NWT. The Arctic tends to be smaller and more crowded than one might think.

Such basic geography is needed to understand the Canadian North, which is divided into two immense segments. The tree line runs diagonally from the Beaufort Sea in the northwest to a point on Hudson Bay just north of Churchill, Manitoba, in the southeast. It continues on through the Ungava Peninsula in Quebec and Labrador.

West of the tree line is the Mackenzie Basin, and because the river valley, the lakes, and the various mountain ranges protect the land, a forest of varying size and density flourishes almost to the ocean. It is in this basin that all of the NWT's Indians have lived for many hundreds (or thousands) of years. East of the tree line is the tundra – that is, the Barren Lands – the Arctic coast, Hudson Bay, and the Arctic islands. This is the habitat of the Eskimos, about 15,000 Inuit plus 2,500 Inuvialuit who live in the general territory and islands around the mouth of the Mackenzie River, sharing parts of the treed Delta with the Gwich'in (formerly known as the Loucheux or Loucheux Kutchin) Indians.

These simple facts of topography and climate have affected every bit of history in the Canadian North. Until the airplane and radio were invented, the Inuit were the only people well enough adapted to survive permanently in such a severe environment as the tundra.

European outposts faced almost as much difficulty as would a human colony on the moon. The west, or Mackenzie Basin, was, by the standards of the Far North, a relative paradise in which the rivers and lakes abounded with fish and muskrats and the forests with moose, caribou, and fur-bearing animals. True, the climate was severe, but the Indians had a far easier time of it than the coastal and inland Eskimos of the eastern and central Arctic.

There was another great difference between the Indian and Inuit ways of life: in the short summers, the rivers could be used to transport all kinds of supplies and trade goods over immense distances – linking the Far North with the Far South, in fact. Between winter and summer, during freeze-up and break-up, both aboriginal races found travel impossible.

Environmental differences were responsible for the diversity of development. In the east, the HBC fur traders huddled on the edge of Hudson Bay and let the aboriginals come to them. In the west, the Nor'Westers went after the furs themselves and opened up the whole continent.

The Ancient Feuds

The forest-dwelling Indians and the Eskimos of the treeless tundra were traditional enemies. This was particularly true in the Mackenzie Delta, where both the Gwich'in, originating in Alaska's interior, and coastal Alaskan Eskimos, moving slowly eastward into areas formerly occupied by another Eskimo culture, were competing for the food- and fur-rich territory.

The HBC, the missionaries, the North-West Mounted Police (NWMP), and early anthropologists all relate many incidents of bloody clashes between indigenous peoples. These conflicts were eliminated only after the police established law and order.

Similarly, the Chipewyans along the southern shores of Hudson Bay were traditional enemies of the eastern Inuit. Samuel Hearne recorded a horrendous massacre of Eskimos by Indians near the mouth of the Coppermine River. In more recent times, the Dog Ribs fought long territorial wars with the Yellowknife, finally exterminating them.

In contrast to the south, where intertribal feuds were often a result of the struggle for supremacy between the French and the British, who enlisted aboriginal allies and turned them against each other with results that were often disastrous for the natives, the northern indigenes were contending for territory long before the white man arrived.

Atavistic fears die hard: when the Arctic Games were held in Coppermine in the late 1960s, one of the competitors was a Chipewyan woman from Fort Resolution on the south shore of Great Slave Lake. She was terrified of being killed and eaten by the Inuit, though she actually was treated with great hospitality.

~

Nothing demonstrates the variation in cultural attitudes more clearly than the way the indigenous peoples look on themselves and one another. The white man – kabloona in Inuktitut – called the Inuit "Eskimos," from a Chipewyan word of contempt meaning "eaters of raw flesh." Many Inuit resent being called Eskimos, though most Alaskan Inuit refer to themselves either as Yupik or Inupiat Eskimos, depending on the part of Alaska they come from. One Copper Eskimo elder from the central Arctic told me gently that it was quite true his people were "eaters of raw flesh" because "in an iglu there was no way to cook meat." He saw nothing shameful in the appellation.

The word "Inuit" means "the people" or "the human beings" in the Inuktitut language, and traditionally the Inuit considered all other races to be mixtures of human beings with either animals or demons.

In Canada, the Inuit are divided into two groups – the indigenous Inuit of the eastern Arctic and the Inuvialuit of the Mackenzie Delta and Beaufort Sea. There are considerable differences between the two. Originally, the Mackenzie Delta was occupied by the Mackenzie Inuit, closely related to the Baffin Island and Copper Inuit. They were wiped out by disease, however, from 1880 to 1912 when American whalers operated out of Herschel Island in the Beaufort Sea.

The Mackenzie Inuit were partially replaced by Inupiat Eskimos from Alaska's North Slope, who intermarried with the white whalers and other Europeans. Today's *Inupialuit* provide something of an Inuit parallel to the Métis.

Many Inuvialuit speak a jargon of English, Inupiat Eskimo dialects, and Inuktitut, which itself has several distinct dialects from South Baffin to the central and High Arctic.

The Delta was a battleground for the Gwich'in and the Mackenzie Inuit until the NWMP established a post in 1903 at Fort McPherson on the Peel River. In 1912 the NWMP and the HBC set up a post further down the Peel River. This was Aklavik, an Inuktitut word meaning "the place of the barren land grizzly." Aklavik had long been the place where the Mackenzie Inuit and the Gwich'in met to trade rather than to fight.

Inuvik, founded in 1955 on the east channel of the Mackenzie not far from Aklavik, was conceived as a meeting place for the various races in the NWT. The word means "place of man" in Inuktitut.

⌇

In the Mackenzie Valley the Indian tribal groups call themselves collectively "the Dene" and the region they live in "Denendeh." The word also means "People's Land" in Chipewyan, but the Dene do not consider themselves part of the same group as the Inuit. The word "Dene" means "people" or "human beings" and "Inuit" has the same translation but there is an implication that the human beings are Inuit – or, if you are a Dene, Dene.

Of the tribal groups – some Indians prefer to use the word "nations" – the farthest north are the Gwich'in. These Indians pushed into the Yukon and the NWT from Alaska and were bitter territorial rivals of the Mackenzie Inuit.

In the area around Great Bear Lake and the middle Mackenzie River lived the Hareskin, the Bear, and the Mountain tribes, collectively called the North Slavey. Today, they call themselves the Sah'tu Dene – Sah'tu means "bear." The South Slavey occupy the upper Mackenzie, the Liard, and the Nahanni rivers and call themselves the Dehcho – a word that means "Great River."

North of Great Slave Lake live the Dog Ribs, most numerous and aggressive of all Indians in the NWT. South of Great Slave are the Chipewyans and some Northern Cree. Their traditional territory stretched all the way east to Hudson Bay, and they were rivals of the Dog Ribs.

Today, the place names of the territory are gradually changing. Frobisher Bay on South Baffin was founded by the U.S. Air Force during the Second World War, and now it is Iqaluit, capital of the eastern Arctic. The tiny Chipewyan community of Snowdrift recently changed its name to Lutselk'e, and as the various Dene groups in the Mackenzie Valley win land settlements and self-government, there are bound to be many more changes. Only predominantly white settlements such as Yellowknife and Pine Point are likely to keep their English names.

Use of the collective word "Dene" would appear to be much more politically expedient than warranted on a historical basis. In some cases, Indian tribal groups have one word describing themselves and another, more collective term to apply to their neighbours.

Of course, such ethnocentric nomenclature appears to be universal among the races of humanity and carries over into advanced civilizations with their variations of "the chosen people" and "herrenvolk" theme.

~

For nearly 200 years after the HBC arrived, the Inuit were almost untouched by Europeans. They had brief meetings with explorers, but it wasn't until the American whalers arrived in the middle of the 19th century that they were seriously affected.

The ancestors of the modern Inuit, those of the Thule culture, were great whale hunters – big whales, such as bowheads. They lost the art during the "Little Ice Age" from 1650 to 1850, but the whaling legends remained part of their culture. When the English and Yankee whalers arrived and invited them to participate, the Inuit were delighted. They liked the excitement of whaling and they liked trading meat, ivory, furs, and carvings to the kabloonat for steel axes, traps, needles, guns, ammunition, and a few commodities like tobacco, salt, and flour.

The whalers, of course, met the Inuit only at their annual camps at Lake Harbour and Cape Dorset on Baffin Island and Marble Island and Southampton Island in the northwestern corner of Hudson Bay. There were also Inuit with different cultures: the Netsilik and Igloolik peoples of North Baffin and the Boothia Peninsula; the Caribou Inuit who lived inland in the Barrens; the Copper Eskimos of the central Arctic; the Mackenzie Eskimos of the Delta. Franz Boas, the German-born anthropologist, made the first serious white study of the Eskimo when he lived among the Netsilikuit from 1882 to 1884.

Lack of regular trading between the HBC and the Caribou Inuit arose from the company's longstanding trade relationship with the Chipewyans, who lived at the edge of the tree line around Fort Churchill and operated as middlemen with the Inuit in the north and the Cree and Ojibway in the south. The Bay gave the Chipewyans guns and ammunition, and for a long time they dominated their neighbours. Firearms also made the Chipewyans more effective hunters than aboriginals who used bows and arrows, spears, and harpoons.

There still is controversy as to the relationship between the

Chipewyans and Caribou Inuit. Knut Rasmussen, the Danish explorer and ethnologist, himself a Greenlander with an Inuit mother, claimed that the Caribou Inuit had always lived in the Barrens. But more recently other anthropologists say that the Chipewyans once lived on and dominated the Barrens, and that they only retreated to the boreal forest during the Little Ice Age. According to this view, encroaching ice on Hudson Bay interfered with seal and whale hunting, forcing the coastal Inuit to move into the interior after caribou.

A smallpox epidemic in 1781 almost destroyed the Chipewyans, and they lost their dominance in the territory beyond the tree line. It was at about this time that the HBC began sending a trading ship around the bay every year, and relations were established with both the coastal and the Caribou Inuit at Marble Island (near present-day Rankin Inlet) and Chesterfield Inlet, the entrance to the lakes and rivers of the interior Barrens.

European whalers entered Arctic waters at a surprisingly early date. By 1650 English, Dutch, and Basque whalers were killing sea mammals in Davis Strait between Greenland and Baffin Island. They found favourable anchorages at Lake Harbour and Cape Dorset on the southwestern tip of Baffin, and these positions opened the way to Hudson Strait and Hudson Bay. It was not a coincidence that such places had been centres of the prehistoric Dorset culture, which preceded the Thule culture.

The peak of the whaling industry came in the middle of the 19th century, and Americans dominated it. Their relationship with the eastern Inuit was, on the whole, happy, and there were few instances of the debauchery that marked the Herschel Island whalery at the end of the century. As in the Delta, there were many sexual relationships between the races, and the Inuit adopted fiddle and concertina music as part of their culture.

But the introduction of European diseases was catastrophic – scarlet fever, measles, diphtheria, smallpox, and a host of respiratory ailments. And then there was the impact of modern weapons and steel traps on the Arctic's fauna. The whalers introduced repeating rifles, and by 1917 the muskox were nearing extinction. During the 1920s, caribou were so reduced (according to anthropologist Eugene Yarima) that hundreds of Inuit starved to death. He estimated that only 500 Caribou Inuit were left, and in 1925 Knut Rasmussen said of white influence: "The clocks cannot be turned back. In most sections the young men are familiar with firearms and have lost their ability to hunt with bows and arrows, kayaks and spears."

Ottawa, still paying little attention to the area, was all but unaware of the diminishing food supply and the threat to the Inuit way of life. The worst areas, in the Barrens, were hardly ever seen by white men, even missionaries. To the infrequent visitor from Ottawa, there seemed to be no change. There was no overall federal administration or policy – no public schools, no health care, no social welfare program. Day-to-day control was left to the Bay men, the missionaries, and a few Mounties. The Indians – even those in the NWT – had an identity under their treaties and the Indian Act: the Inuit had none. When Ottawa began to take notice of them, it was because they figured in the sovereignty picture.

The Coming of the White Man

Much of the history of the area of Canada north of the 60th parallel depends on geography and climate. The Northwest Territories looks like one piece of land stretching across the top of the map from the Yukon to Greenland. This is an illusion: the treeless tundra of the east is different from the green *taiga* with its stunted evergreens in the west. The indigenous Inuit, Inuvialuit, and Dene are as different as chalk, cheese, and soap.

When the Europeans started arriving 400 years ago, they were blinded by simple greed. They never really understood the land or its peoples. Even when the whites based in Ottawa and Washington launched an overwhelming social revolution a little more than a generation ago, they had no clear idea of where they were headed. Joseph Robson in 1752 accused the Hudson's Bay Company of sleeping by the bay while raking in its profits. Two hundred years later, Prime Minister St. Laurent talked in the Commons about the government's neglect of the same Arctic North.

It has only been in the years since that speech that the entire fabric of the Canadian North has been altered beyond recognition. The policies St. Laurent introduced in the 1950s were often contradictory and counter-productive. It's a wonder they worked at all – let alone provide the basis for a fairly workable society.

Almost by chance the federal government gave the native peoples of its gigantic colony a chance to participate in their own destiny, and with an element of desperation young native leaders seized the opportunity and scored remarkable achievements.

Perhaps the social revolution of the NWT has worked because the incoming whites were even more confused than they were greedy. Canadians have always prided themselves on having a relatively benign policy toward indigenous peoples in comparison to Spaniards, Americans, and Australians. Canada had no U.S. Fifth Cavalry massacres, although white men's diseases were just as destructive.

Still, especially in the NWT, the most striking element historically was not malignancy on either side but lack of understanding. The aboriginals for a long time felt secure in their frozen principalities and were confident that the white visitors would go away without causing much damage. The whites, on the other hand, seemed to have had no awareness of native ways of life, let alone native rights. They genuinely thought that once they had arrived the land belonged to them, to be used as they saw fit. This, of course, involved taking natural resources such as gold, or oil, or furs, and harnessing the native population for the task.

For example, consider the fur trade, the industry that brought the white man to the Territories in the first place. Neither the Indian nor the Inuk was a commercial fur hunter before the white man came. They hunted for food and for skins to keep them warm or to use in building shelters and boats. Bones and teeth might be useful weapons or tools. A small surplus became largely symbolic trade goods exchanged between family groups or tribal bands. The white man turned the killing of animals into a highly organized industry, the price of furs set by laws of supply and demand in far-off London or Paris. The trapline with iron traps was a white invention, a variation of the assembly line in an industrial factory.

It took more than a century for the HBC to move inland from Hudson Bay: Samuel Hearne built the first inland post on the Saskatchewan River system in 1774 to counter the spreading success of the Nor'West partners from Montreal. By 1800 the fur-trading concerns were locked in bloody battle from the Beaufort Sea to the Red River, where the first large white settlement in the West would soon be founded.

The Indians and the Inuit became extensions of commercial policy, but they appeared to be living the way their ancestors had. Through the 200-year tenure of the HBC and the Nor'Westers, there was no government in Rupert's Land or the wider drainage basin of the Mackenzie River, and none was needed. The indigenes governed

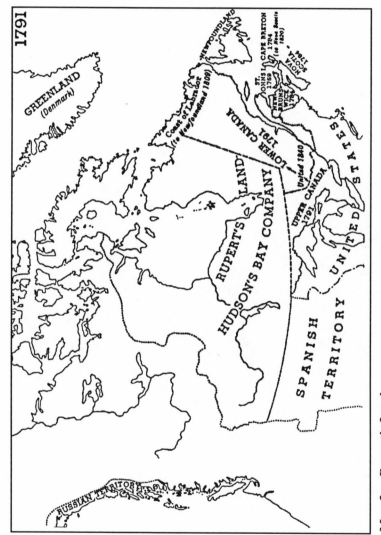

Map 3   Rupert's Land

Rupert's Land was the domain of the Hudson's Bay Company from 1670 to 1870, when the territory became part of Canada.

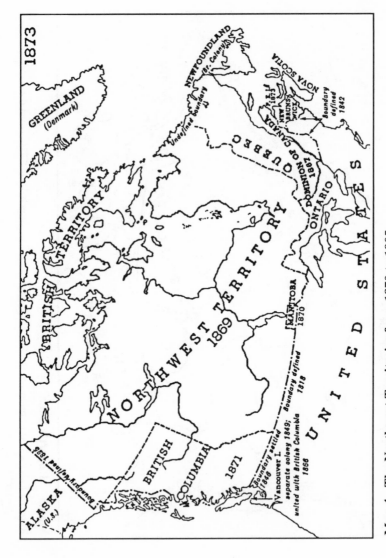

Map 4   The Northwest Territories from 1870 to 1905

In 1905 Alberta and Saskatchewan became provinces and Manitoba was enlarged.

themselves. The fur traders were accountable to the rules of their companies, formulated in London or Montreal. Relations between whites and aborigines were governed by self-interest. As the French discovered earlier in the Mississippi Basin, the most warlike Indian tribes could be kept friendly through control of the supply of firearms and gunpowder. For their part, the HBC traders learned not to cheat their native partners too much lest they lose part of the fur harvest to the Nor'Westers or American independents. In cases of violence or theft, the companies imposed their own penalties on natives and employees alike.

After the HBC lands became part of Canada, little changed until the 1950s. Scattered police posts were set up and occasionally demonstrated white man's justice by arresting, trying, and punishing an aboriginal murderer. Tribal feuds between the Gwich'in and the coastal Eskimos in the Mackenzie Delta were suppressed, but for the most part the Indians and Inuit were left to administer their own affairs.

Without any pressure from white settlers as in the south, the NWT indigenes developed slowly, learning the devastating power of firearms against game and, when so choosing, adapting their lifestyles to the requirements of the fur trade. A relatively few Indians and almost no Inuit settled permanently around the HBC posts. Many were converted to Christianity by Roman Catholic and Anglican missionaries.

In only one area, the Mackenzie Delta, was the impact of the white man devastating, over the very short period from 1890 to 1914. There was a good reason for this. The Delta, separating the wooded Mackenzie Valley from the Arctic Ocean and tundra, was nearly 150 kilometres wide and a little less deep, drained by two mighty branches of the Mackenzie and the Peel River, which joined them, and by countless small streams. The rivers teemed with fish and muskrat. The land was dotted with moose, caribou, hare, and other animals. The sea had thousands of bowhead whales and myriads of seal.

This rich treasure house north of the Arctic Circle was repeatedly invaded by migrating peoples. The coastal Inuit were challenged by the aggressive Gwich'in from Alaska and also by the Inupiat Eskimos, also from Alaska. As late as the middle of the 19th century, Indian and Inuit killed one another on sight, and only the arrival of the NWMP stopped the aboriginal blood-letting.

But those clashes were nothing compared to the arrival of

American whalers in 1890. They set up a wintering base on Herschel Island just west of the Delta and welcomed the indigenous hunters and trappers. In return for fresh meat and furs, they gave the natives trade goods, booze, venereal diseases and influenza, measles and tuberculosis.

The impact was catastrophic, bringing the original population to the verge of extinction and wiping out a whole regional culture. The Inuvialuit who today inhabit the Delta and adjoining islands and coast are not the descendants of the original Mackenzie Inuit, but rather of the Alaskan Inupiat and white whalers. Anthropologist Diamond Jenness and several Anglican missionaries reported the degradation of Herschel Island in detail, and the Canadian government, fearing an outbreak of violence which would bring in American forces and thus threaten the sovereignty of both the Yukon and the NWT, established the first North-West Mounted Police post in the Arctic at Fort McPherson in the Delta.

Fortunately for Ottawa, whaling in the western Arctic ended in 1914, and the ships returned to Seattle and San Francisco. Gradually, the indigenous population revived. The Inuvialuit learned to live in peace and sometimes intermarry with the Gwich'in. In 1970 the two races joined with local Métis to form the Committee for the Original People's Entitlement (COPE). It sought a political and land settlement with Ottawa. The Gwich'in and Métis soon pulled out and made the newly organized Dene Nation their bargaining agent, leaving COPE to negotiate the first NWT land claims settlement on behalf of 2,500 Inuvialuit from the settlements of Inuvik, Aklavik, Tuktoyaktuk, Paulatuk, Sachs Harbour, and Holman.

～

By the 1920s, it was apparent that the fur trade, firearms, and Christianity were having a major impact on the indigenes throughout the NWT. Although the overwhelming majority still lived on the land, spoke their own languages, and followed traditional customs, both Indians and Inuit were adapting themselves to a trading economy.

On another level, the airplane would radically alter all of the North. For the first time, people could move long distances in a hurry, summer and winter. The land was opened to prospectors and white trappers to an unprecedented extent, and the minerals discovered by the prospectors began to be mined, thus bringing in long-term white settlements on a relatively major scale. For 250 years, whites had

been confined to tiny trading posts, dependent on the rivers, lakes, and coastal waters for transportation. A typical white settlement had consisted of a couple of HBC clerks, a Mountie, and a missionary.

But with the airplane making mines commercially possible, white settlements became inevitable. The first was Imperial Oil's Norman Wells, halfway down the Mackenzie. The next was the gold camp at Yellowknife. Later, during the Second World War, thousands of American and Canadian soldiers and civilians arrived in the western NWT as part of the CANOL Project, the Alaska Highway, and the Royal Canadian Air Force's (RCAF) Northwest Staging Route. In the east, a lesser number came to build airports and weather stations. Most whites left when their jobs were done, but Yellowknife became a substantial permanent settlement and by the late 1940s its residents were demanding self-government in the southern style.

This push toward white democracy was to have incalculable effects on the native population even though Ottawa at first seemed blissfully unaware. Up to the 1960s, Indians had virtually no political rights anywhere in Canada: conventional wisdom was that they had given up citizenship rights in return for the benefits of reserves and the Indian Act. The Inuit were even worse off, not covered at all by any kind of treaty or concession. Until the Second World War, Ottawa gave them no identity of their own, tossing them into the orbit of Indian administration. They were identified not by names but by numbers on a metal disk. When Canadians as a whole were granted family allowances during the war, the Indians and Inuit benefited economically, but they had no say in their own destiny.

So it was that when democracy came to the NWT, it was a totally white movement and entailed no machinery to cover either Indians or Inuit. As had happened in the thirteen American colonies, in Upper and Lower Canada, and in those parts of the NWT that became the provinces of Alberta and Saskatchewan in 1905, the new settlers of Yellowknife began in the late 1930s to demand municipal services and a hand in spending the taxes they paid. Mr. Justice M.M. de Weerdt of the NWT Supreme Court says today that the most effective revolutionaries were not the noisy weekly newspaper editors and public-spirited business people — rather they were the first wave of young housewives. Mr. Justice de Weerdt said in an interview:

> The big change came in Yellowknife when miners and businessmen started bringing in their families to live in the New Town which

replaced the old gold camp and seaplane base. Young housewives began asking for cement sidewalks so that they could push their prams easily when they went to the stores.

So husbands began pushing the town council for everything from sidewalks to sewers and that bulwark of democracy – the right to levy and to spend taxes – came to Yellowknife. The next step was an elected Territorial Council that had some clout. It was followed by the Carrothers Commission which changed everything: the Commissioner became a full-time resident of the NWT, Yellowknife became the capital and the bureaucrats began preaching political democracy to the natives in their own communities.

Mr. Justice de Weerdt puts his finger on one of the keys to NWT development: until the governmental commission chaired by Dean A.W.R. Carrothers in 1965, the Inuit and Indians had no part in decision-making; what money and services they were given came directly from Ottawa in traditional colonial style. There were no native political organizations in the white sense. A few token natives were appointed to the commissioner's advisory council. Indians negotiated annually with agents of the Department of Indian Affairs through their tribal councils and chiefs. The Inuit were helpless wards of Ottawa, without recognized spokespeople. If an Inuit family needed help, it had to go to the HBC trader, the Mountie, or the missionary.

This situation changed dramatically between 1953 and 1967 when two totally different revolutions struck the eastern Arctic and the Mackenzie Basin. In their early stages, they were almost unrelated to one another, and they affected the Inuit of the east and the Indians of the west in profoundly dissimilar ways. Their roots lie not in the long, Rip Van Winkle–like dozing of the Hudson's Bay Company, nor in the first eighty years of Canadian colonial government, but in the restless intrusions of surveyors and prospectors looking for mineral wealth.

Chapter 2

Early Boom Years

Petroleum and Mineral Development

The first Arctic explorer, Martin Frobisher, set the patter discovered what he thought was gold on his first voya. . He floated a stock company and led a large expedition nn Island, but the "gold" turned out to be iron pyrite and hire the first of hundreds of Canadian mining fiascos.

As the country opened up, Canadians contind to look for precious minerals. Samuel Hearne and Alexander Mackenzie reported copper and petroleum. By the late 19th century, the occasional tourist was likely to stumble on a geologist anywhere from the Yukon to Labrador. The search was thorough: as early as the 1880s, a wide variety of metals had been mapped in northern Ontario; the Temiskaming and Northern Ontario Railway was built in anticipation of the gold and silver rushes of 1905.

In the NWT, the problem was that it was too expensive to build railways to the numerous mineral strikes. While the fur trade had adapted itself to seasonal water transport, hard-rock mines needed continuous supply and delivery routes. It wasn't until the airplane appeared that mines became feasible. Take petroleum, for instance: geologist R.C. McConnell found a sizable deposit in 1889, and fur trader J.K. Cornwall reported oil seepages at Fort Norman in 1911. These discoveries came at exactly the right time. The world was being revolutionized by the internal combustion engine. In 1914 P.O. Bosworth staked three oil leases on the northeast bank of the Mackenzie near Fort Norman. There were only a few thousand Indians, fur traders, and missionaries in the whole of the Mackenzie Valley. Imperial Oil and the North West Company ed up Bosworth's leases and sent in Ted Link with a drilling v. They struggled with black flies and muskeg and wintered over 1 9 before drilling their first well – a gusher. In 1921 Imperial buⁱⁱt a small

steam-powered gasoline and diesel oil refinery.

So began a momentous new epoch. Imperial, with astonishing foresight, chartered two German Junkers aircraft to haul men and equipment from Edmonton. There had been bush flying in northern Ontario and Labrador during and after the First World War, but the Junkers were designed to carry freight as well as passengers. They marked the first regular industrial air service anywhere in Canada.

The Junkers were far ahead of their time. They were single-engined, low-winged planes with corrugated aluminum skins. The NWT pilots and mechanics adapted them to northern conditions by putting them on floats or skis. It took a while to learn how to use them, and both Imperial planes were damaged in bad landings. On one occasion, mechanic Bill Hill worked a near-miracle when he carved a propeller out of wood to replace a broken one. It worked, flying the Junkers back to Edmonton.

There was no denying that Imperial's achievements were milestones in the history of the NWT, but logistic problems were still too great to turn the Norman Wells field into a major producer. Although the little refinery was able to supply the needs of the Mackenzie for generations, the tiny white industrial community remained an unknown frontier outpost until the United States entered the Second World War at the end of 1941.

Imperial Oil was only one of a number of visionary companies dreaming of huge industrial developments north of the 60th parallel. The businessmen, in turn, acquired their visions from the bush pilots, most of whom had learned to fly during the First World War. The bush pilots flew from Montreal, Toronto, Winnipeg, and Edmonton, and soon they were reaching Aklavik in the delta and Repulse Bay on Hudson Bay. Apart from the rugged Junkers, their planes were usually small, high-winged, single-engined craft designed or modified by the pilots themselves. Skis and floats were first used in northern Ontario and soon spread everywhere. If necessary, pilots could quickly switch to wheels in order to land on conventional airfields.

Their exploits were legendary. J.W. Thompson, the mining promoter, crashed in northern Ontario and was rescued in one of the first mercy flights by "Wop" May, already a hero who had survived aerial combat with the great Baron von Richtofen. Like his fellows, May had a reputation for imperturbability. In the late 1920s, he caught the tip of a ski in a root while taking off from Flin Flon. When he arrived at Stevenson Field in Winnipeg, the control tower signalled to him that one ski was hanging downward at a right angle. May told his pas-

senger, a prospector, to climb out the door and stand on the back of the ski while clinging to a strut. The ski straightened out and May landed safely.

So routine was the event that the *Winnipeg Free Press* dismissed it with a single paragraph on the front page: much the same kind of thing was happening regularly in Edmonton, Norman Wells, or Aklavik. On the ground or in the air, ingenious Canadian farm boys could adapt anything capable of flight to northern conditions.

In 1927 two brothers, Gilbert and Charlie LaBine, enrolled in the School of Mines at Haileybury, Ontario. They were not youngsters but experienced prospectors and promoters who had caught the gold bug from their Uncle Jim, a crony of Benny Hollinger and Noah Timmins in the Porcupine gold strike of 1909. In the early 1920s, the LaBine brothers developed the Eldorado gold mine in Manitoba, and when it petered out they became Toronto stock salesmen. Their dreams took them to Haileybury to study the findings of earlier prospectors. There they found Macintosh Bell's dusty report of a trip he took through the Great Bear Lake country in 1900.

Bell and his young companion, Charles Camsell, were typical of the Canadian wilderness men who grew up in the second half of the 19th century. Bell was a nephew of the famous Dr. Robert Bell, chief of the Geological Survey of Canada and an explorer of the NWT in his own right. Camsell, twenty-four at the time, was born at remote Fort Liard in the mysterious Nahanni country, the son of a legendary HBC factor for whom the Mackenzie's Camsell Bend was named. If ever there was a wilderness man, Charles Camsell was it. He was a deck-hand on Mackenzie River barges when he was a teenager and later went to Harvard to study geology. Ultimately, he became deputy minister of mines and NWT commissioner.

In that summer of 1900, Bell and Camsell paddled into the rivers and lakes southeast of Great Bear Lake and found cobalt, silver, and, near Great Slave Lake, traces of gold. They weren't much surprised: Yukon-bound prospectors had found gold colour there in 1896.* Bell's geological report was published in a mining journal, but no one

---

*Camsell has left us a record of the trip in his autobiography, and it provides us with insight into standard white attitudes toward aboriginals at that time. At one location, Camsell wrote, he and Bell left the trees east of Great Bear Lake and journeyed out into the treeless tundra. With their field glasses, they spotted an Inuit camp and observed its occupants for a time. (Camsell said he and Bell were fearful of the aboriginals because they had heard reports of the murder of white men in the area.) Later, they cautiously approached the camp and found it abandoned. In examining

paid any attention because of the Klondike gold rush. When the LaBines read it, the Klondike was long past and the airplane had opened new prospecting possibilities. The brothers raised money from their moribund Manitoba mine and Gilbert sought a pilot. In 1929 he found Leigh Brintnell working for James Richardson, Jr.'s Western Canada Airways based in Winnipeg. Brintnell had been an instructor with the Royal Flying Corps.

LaBine and Charles St. Paul, another prospector, were dropped off on the eastern shore of Great Bear Lake, and Brintnell flew on to Aklavik, Whitehorse, Prince George, Edmonton, and then back to Winnipeg. All in a day's work: 15,000 kilometres. LaBine found enough colour to verify Bell's findings and then returned to Toronto. In 1930 he hired Punch Dickins to take him back. Dickins had made his first trip to "the Barrens" in 1928. He told his friends years later about that historic flight with LaBine: "We were flying over the east end of Great Bear when I saw a bright blue bay that was quite different from the rest of the water. I pointed it out to Gilbert and he nodded and put a mark on his chart. He told me blue meant cobalt and cobalt meant silver and maybe gold. We flew on to Fort Smith."

In Smith, LaBine outfitted himself and went north again. This time he located not only cobalt and silver but gold and pitchblende. He knew it was the big strike and headed for Toronto to raise development money.

Now the LaBines had a delightful dilemma: gold, silver, or radium? Gold, of course, was the basic lure, but it brought only $18.50 a troy ounce in those days. The price of silver was much lower than that. But radium now ...

In the 1920s and 1930s, radium was the world's most glamorous mineral, selling for $75,000 a gram. Almost the only known deposits of pitchblende and uranium were in the Belgian Congo. The LaBines

---

(continued)
the belongings left behind, Camsell found no weapons or tools that might indicate these Inuit had ever been in contact with whites. He felt they were totally Stone Age people.

The anecdote illustrates the complete ignorance of whites in regard to the Inuit, though, of course, Camsell had lived all his life among Indians. He does not mention that the Inuit may have been equally fearful of them and may have abandoned their camp in terror. From Camsell's report, it appears that Inuit in 1900 knew as little about whites as whites did about them. His fears about murderous savages illustrate well the traditional mindset of many white men in the North.

reasoned that it wouldn't take a very big mine to make a lot of money. They soon found their angel – Bill Wright of the fabulous Wright-Hargreave gold mine. He became their partner in Bear Explorations, and on his third visit to the NWT, Gilbert LaBine staked out a major uranium deposit. The Port Radium mine was operational by 1933.*

The prospecting fraternity didn't miss the LaBine strike, and soon every available plane and canoe was criss-crossing the sparse forests and granite outcrops between Great Bear and Great Slave lakes. It soon became obvious that the searchers needed a base closer than Fort Simpson or Fort Smith. This was found at Yellowknife Bay on the north shore of Great Slave, where huge rocks formed a sheltered anchorage. The country was harsh but beautiful, part of the Canadian Shield that stretched from Labrador to the Mackenzie.

Yellowknife

The float-plane base at Yellowknife Bay was fine most of the year, but it didn't encourage town planners. A low, rocky promontory thrust out from swampy ground covered with scrub willow. At the tip was precipitous Latham Island, and another massive rock, Jolliffe Island, rose on the open bay side. Six kilometres across the bay was the seasonal fishing camp of the Dog Ribs. Before the prospectors came in 1933, there had never been any permanent settlement, white or native.

The bush pilots and mechanics threw up makeshift hangars, and the independent traders built log-cabin warehouses. Walled tents and cabins perched on the rocks behind. There was little shore room, but the single-engined bush planes had plenty of space on the water or ice. There was no need for a land airport. As prospectors. miners, and merchants flocked in, a portable sawmill was barged across Great Slave Lake to cut lumber for hotels, restaurants, and more warehouses. Hookers and bootleggers pitched tents along "Glamour Alley" in the willow flats.

From 1933 there were strikes everywhere. Major Lockie Burwash discovered an open vein of gold at Burwash Point, across the bay

---

*When Gilbert LaBine made his strike, uranium was used to produce radium for medical purposes. But soon it was to become the element used for splitting the atom. Uranium mined in Port Radium and refined in Port Hope, Ontario, was used in the Hiroshima atomic bomb in 1945.

from the camp. Other strikes were by James Fox and T.H. Potter and by Jack Baker and Herb Dickson. Fox and Potter staked the original claim that became the gold mine of Consolidated Mining and Smelting. Consolidated later paid $500,000 to Tom Payne and Micky Ryan for a 60 percent interest in another claim. The Con mine soon became a major force in the creation of Yellowknife as a permanent town.

In his history of those early days, the publisher Duke DeCoursey wrote: "Hundreds arrived looking for work. The well-to-do flew; others used everything from rowboats to stern-wheelers, steamboats and barges."

In the midst of the Great Depression, gold booms provided hope all over Canada. Promoters ran telephone bucket shops in Toronto. Kids out of grade school became prospectors in the bush. Hard-rock miners hitched rides to Rouyn, Quebec, Kirkland Lake, Ontario, or Yellowknife. Carpenters came into the Territories looking for building jobs. Adventure-seeking schoolteachers and nurses flew in from Edmonton. Everybody met and talked deals in Pete Racine's Corona Hotel or the Wildcat Cafe, then owned by Willy Wylie and Smoky Stout. By 1935 Yellowknife's population was 400, and the Con mine was being built across the bay, half an hour away by boat (or by dogsled over the ice in winter).

Vic Ingraham started out as a bootlegger in the Willow Flats, then built his Yellowknife Rooms and the Old Stope Hotel on Latham Island. The Con mine was a town in its own right, where 200 miners lodged in bunkhouses and were fed in a mess hall. There was a management housing row and offices, and there were accommodations for the small army of construction workers. Dr. O.L. Stanton and his wife, a nurse, were brought in to run the mine's three-bed hospital. Within a few years, it had twelve beds and also served the town of Yellowknife. All this was a far cry from a company town like Norman Wells, which existed only for the needs of Imperial Oil. If the Con mine was the first and one of the biggest, there were rival promoters in Yellowknife, and the camp and town were never dominated completely by any one corporation.

Nevertheless, the big boys did their best to get a lock on the best claims. When W.M. Archibald got into town, he wasted no time in buying out the Ryan Syndicate. Fred Thompson, veteran of a hundred high-rolling adventures across the continent, met pilot Glyn Burge in the Old Stope and set up the Thompson Prospecting Syndicate. One day, the story went, Thompson and Burge flew into the bush to meet a couple of sourdoughs. Over a pot of campfire coffee, Thompson offered $50,000 for a half interest in their claim. One of his new partners asked how much it would cost to develop a mine.

"Hundred and fifty thousand," Thompson said.

"You got it?"

Thompson turned out his pockets and produced fifty dollars. He shrugged and grinned. "Don't worry – I've got friends," he said.

The promoter shook hands and climbed into the plane. In New York he had no trouble raising the money for a mine called Sunset Yellowknife. It never produced much gold, but that too was the luck of the draw. Thompson was a veteran, a famous man in the camps, but there were youngsters just starting out who would make Thompson, Archibald, and even Gilbert LaBine look like pikers.

The most famous of them all was Jack Gallagher, who arrived as a University of Manitoba student looking for gold. Gallagher, his billion-dollar exploits with Dome Petroleum thirty years ahead of him, arrived in Yellowknife on one of the famous Junkers "flying boxcars." From Yellowknife he went by canoe to Great Bear Lake and then on to Coppermine on the Arctic Ocean. That trip produced no gold for Gallagher, but it did awaken in him an interest in the Arctic, which saw its fulfilment when he drilled oil and gas wells farther north than anyone had before.

$\sim$

The first successful mine was Con, the next Negus; then came Giant Yellowknife, developed by Bear Explorations, the joint venture of Bill Wright and the LaBine brothers. Giant became a huge success in the boom that followed the Second World War. Giant sank its first shaft some kilometres from Con. Early on, a cat skinner tried to move a boulder to the dump but found it solidly embedded. He got off his cat and discovered the "boulder" was an outcrop of bedrock laced with gold veins. Giant moved the shaft instead.

But that was to come later. Before war broke out, there were two distinct communities – Yellowknife and the Con mine. As Yellowknife bulged, it became obvious that it would have to expand somewhere with reasonably level land. There was a rough path through the willow flats, which ambled around the rocks and ultimately ended at the Con mine, but there was no road of any kind until local business people blasted and dug out a tote road to carry supplies.

Things were happening so fast in the early days that few records were kept, and much of the history of the period is anecdotal. Many of these anecdotes were collected by Ray Price, a Baptist minister and schoolteacher who wrote an entertaining and useful history of the early town. Price recalled that in 1939 there were 1,000 residents in what was beginning to be known (after five years of existence!) as Old Town. In the surrounding district, including the mining communities, there were 2,000 more people. Residents were demanding everything from more beer to movies and dental services. In July 1938 the first soft drinks and ice cream arrived, and the Pioneer Theatre opened with *The Charge of the Light Brigade*, starring Errol Flynn.

The mine managers were kings of creation: James Warren, son of the Con president, brought his pregnant wife to Neilly Lake, fifty kilometres from Yellowknife, and hired a sixteen-year-old half-breed girl to housekeep. May Rice flew in once a week and later got her own plane and became "the Flying Housemaid."

There were many other signs in the wind showing that the freedom of the frontier mining camp was dying almost before it began. Two young women opened a beauty parlour. Miners and businessmen formed an athletic association and built a hockey rink. When wives and children arrived, the need for a school became evident, and when there were twelve children, one was built. The first tourist was – who else? – a female schoolteacher from California. It was no wonder that the *Toronto Star*'s globe-trotting reporter, Gordon Sinclair, said the gold fields were a cross between a three-ring circus and a Sunday school picnic. Old-timers couldn't decide which offended them most.

By the summer of 1939, boosters were predicting 3,000 permanent residents. There was a good deal of talk about moving the whole town to the flatlands beyond Willow Flats in the direction of the Con mine.

The Legends

There were men and women as legendary as the mines. Without any question, Vic Ingraham was the leading citizen. Born in 1895 in Minneapolis, he had been a logger and winter mail runner around Fort McMurray and in 1932 was supplying prospectors with illegal booze and operating a Great Bear Lake freight service on the side.

When the Port Radium mine was being built, Ingraham's boat brought in supplies. Late in the season, a squall upset his boat's galley stove and started a fire. The burning vessel was driven on the rocks and swamped. Ingraham and his two crewmen were badly burned, then frost-bitten during a snowstorm. The others died; Ingraham survived with the loss of both legs and several fingers.

Almost anybody else might have turned into a helpless cripple: Ingraham was just starting his career. He moved to Yellowknife and built two hotels. The Old Stope was a famous watering hole, and its proprietor was the first one to put his hand in his pocket when Old Town needed a sidewalk or a garbage service. Among his many other functions, he served on the first school committee. Ingraham was also one of the prime movers in the shift to a bigger townsite, and he sank $200,000 into the new Yellowknife Inn, then and now at the hub of Yellowknife activity. Only after the new town was well established did Ingraham seek a warmer climate. He owned more hotels in British Columbia's Okanagan and died at Victoria in 1961.

Much of the drive for expansion came from the first newspaper editor, Larry Alexander, who was brought in from Alberta in 1935 by the pioneer publisher C.A. "Chuck" Perkins. Their newspaper, *The Prospector*, was put together in a walled tent under an oil lamp, run off on a mimeograph machine, and peddled from the doorsteps of Weaver and Devore, General Merchant, and the Yellowknife Coffee Shop. Alexander set up the first telephone service linking Old Town with the Con mine: it consisted of an old army field system with wires strung from tree to tree. It was free, but service was so unreliable that few people bothered to hook up. But one improvement led to another. By 1939 Con mine needed electricity so badly that it built a 4,500-horsepower hydro plant at Prosperous Lake. The town reaped the benefit.

Because there was no municipal structure, there was no way to collect taxes for public improvements. At first, residents managed on their own. When a plank sidewalk was needed between "downtown" and the Wildcat Cafe and Old Stope on the top of the hill, the hat was passed and Swede Erickson was hired. It took him two days to sink piles along the rock wall of the harbour and lay down a wooden walkway. In 1939 a wagon road was built to the Con mine, and the merchandising firm of Frame and Perkins charged a quarter for a bus ride.

The big spring event was the arrival of the first barge-load of supplies – especially if it contained beer. The Old Stope was the first and only legal beer parlour, but there were always the Willow Flats bootleggers. When Larry Alexander headed an editorial "Liquor

Problem," he meant a liquor shortage, not a need for prohibition.

Unlike gold rushes in California and Australia but very much in the tradition of the Klondike strike of '97, the Yellowknife boom was marked by very little crime. This was partly because there was no placer mining and therefore little loose gold on the surface to be stolen. Con, Negus, and the other mines bored deep into the hard rock of the Canadian Shield and brought the gold up in chunks of ore, which were then refined and turned into bricks. Theft was not quite impossible but it was difficult and very rare. The sole policeman, Corporal Bing Rivett of the RCMP, was not overworked. *The Prospector* reported that the worst violence was when a drunken miner slugged Fred Fraser, the stipendiary magistrate. The "criminal" was fined $50.

A lawyer who flew in to draw up contracts in 1938 described the scene in Pete Racine's Corona Hotel: "Two exhausted priests lay sleeping in one corner; there was a 24-hour poker game in another; boozers grumbled happily; promoters were cutting deals with prospectors; a dentist was filling teeth with a treadle-powered drilling machine." A colourful scene but not in the tradition of the Malamute Saloon in Dawson City. Most of the Yellowknife miners were glad to have steady work and regular paycheques. In Depression terms, they made fabulous wages: $1,600 a year!

Fighting for Democracy

Once the mines were operating, the corporations had little concern with Yellowknife's municipal problems, though mining executives were among the most active community leaders. Everyone shared a single nightmare: Ottawa's remoteness and lack of interest. Newspaper editors like Larry Alexander, Chuck Perkins, and Jock McMeekan led the howls of rage and impatience in *The Prospector*. McMeekan was the very prototype of the "Disturbed Citizen" one encounters in Letters to the Editor everywhere. He came to Yellowknife as a prospector, became a miner and then a journalist, publisher of the town's second newspaper, *The Blade*. McMeekan's wife, Mildred Hall, was the first schoolteacher.

The angry editors spoke for the whole town. Yellowknife needed every conceivable municipal service and had no way of raising the money for them. As in the case of the prairie settlers of Saskatchewan and Alberta in 1905, residents of the 1939 NWT demanded that

Ottawa set up a suitable democratic structure, one that would have, among other things, the right to levy property taxes.

But it was hard to get Ottawa's attention. When provincehood came to Alberta and Saskatchewan in 1905, the feds continued their meagre responsibilities to the Indians and Métis in the remaining NWT, but since there were no reserves to administer, the task was a minor one. Ottawa's main interest in the North was not its people but its mineral resources, and neither the indigenes nor the few whites in the NWT got much attention.

One of the problems was that the NWT commissioner's job for many years had only been a sideline for the RCMP commissioner; later, it became an extra chore of the deputy minister of the interior or, still later, of the Mines deputy. Perhaps once a year the commissioner paid a quick visit to the Territories. The NWT Council was an appointed body made up of senior bureaucrats, also based in Ottawa. In theory, its function was legislative and advisory, but hardly any regulations were passed and the deputy minister/commissioner needed little advice. The council seldom met and when it did, members could be gathered together in a few minutes and seated in any handy committee room. Indian concerns were handled in an equally off-hand way by a totally separate branch of the federal government, though, of course, members of the territorial council might have a nodding acquaintance with Indian Branch mandarins.

The Inuit, or Eskimos as they were universally called in white circles, had no identity of their own and were not administered at all. If they got into trouble with the law, the police and courts treated them like other Canadians, which was highly destructive to the Inuit, and if they happened to come under other federal regulations, the Indian Branch might pay them a little attention. Otherwise, they were forgotten people. The sole attention the NWT got in the 1930s was the annual visit – regarded as a kind of holiday outing – by the commissioner. Ottawa's chief interest in the NWT appeared to be the fact that mining was booming there during a period of country-wide depression.

In 1938 the commissioner (and deputy minister of mines) was Charles Camsell, the same man who had accompanied Macintosh Bell on the surveying trip that turned up gold and pitchblende in 1900. His chief administrator of the Territories was the deputy commissioner, R.A. Gibson, who ran the NWT like a feudal fiefdom. When the two men arrived in Yellowknife in 1938, they were met by an indignant delegation headed by Fred Fraser, a mining company executive who in his spare time was the stipendiary magistrate. The Yellowknifers asked for a town council and municipal structure. The astonished Camsell said he would study the petition and returned to Ottawa. It was a year before he replied, and then Yellowknife was granted only an advisory committee on local affairs. John McNiven, manager of the Negus mine, was named chairman. Four years later he was named to the NWT Council, the first territorial resident given that honour.

The feds did give some financial support to a local school, to medical service, and to public works. But there was little understanding of Yellowknife problems. At one stage, Fred Fraser shot off a wire to Ottawa, saying the town was endangered by "filth." Ottawa rushed police from Fort Smith to clean up the underworld. They discovered Fraser had literally meant filth in the streets. An embarrassed federal government supplied enough money to build a four-hole wooden toilet in the centre of Old Town. Unfortunately, as *The Prospector* complained, no money was supplied for a custodian. The building soon fell apart.*

In the struggle for self-government, NWT natives had no part. Except for a few Métis who lived like whites, Yellowknife was a totally white town. The only time *The Prospector* mentioned Indians was when the village of Detah celebrated Treaty Day and miners canoed over to watch the native drumming. Yellowknife was a white enclave, the only one in the NWT except for Norman Wells, where the oil-well community was tiny by comparison. Elsewhere, Indians and Inuit lived much the same lives they always had – or at least since the HBC and the Nor'Westers had established trading posts 150 years earlier. The needs of the aboriginals were the concern of the HBC trader, the missionary, and the Mountie (probably in that order).

However, within a generation, Yellowknife's drive for democracy would alter the fate of everybody. Although the burgeoning gold community covered a tiny area, its residents were so restless, so dynamic, and so self-reliant that they finally awakened even the sleeping mandarins in far-off Ottawa.

---

*There is no public toilet in the centre of Yellowknife, and for many years the Yellowknife Inn kept its toilet locked against native use.

Links to the South

A good example of Yellowknife's determination to solve its own problems involved transportation. As the town grew, air supply became totally inadequate, and the marine shipping season was far too short to supply fresh food and other luxuries. Enterprising citizens put their minds to solving the problem.

Although the North American continent is vast, both the aboriginal residents and the European intruders established effective trade routes along the rivers and lakes. Even in the Arctic, the Eskimos were accustomed to move enormous distances over snow, ice, and water. When the fur trade flourished, traders and trappers maintained regular freight routes that linked the Arctic and the Pacific with the Atlantic. So Yellowknifers were not dismayed by their remote position. The nearest railway terminals were on the Peace and Athabaska rivers in Alberta, and the only problem was creating a water and/or land route that would cut across those hundreds of kilometres.

In 1937 Earl Harcourt, Bert Neeland, and Stuart McLeod decided to find the best way to get from the railhead to Yellowknife: would it be overland and by river from Fort McMurray, or by water from Taylor Flats on the Peace? The three pioneers set up the Yellowknife (YK) Transport Company and opened a boatyard at Taylor Flats, which was located on one of the classic fur-trading routes. There was a major portage of twenty kilometres in the swampy country between the Peace and the Slave heading north out of Lake Athabaska, but the HBC had taken its big York boats across the portage by log rollers. YK Transport felt it could do the same thing.

The partners built a scow and an eighteen-metre tug, the *Little Chieftain*, and followed the HBC route to Fort Resolution on Great Slave Lake. From there it was an easy run to Yellowknife. After unloading supplies, the *Little Chieftain* continued to the headwaters of the Mackenzie, then to Fort Simpson and the turbulent Liard. The epic voyage continued up the Liard to Fort Liard and Fort Nelson, B.C., one of the grandest voyages in Canadian history. Unhappily, the voyage proved to be unique because costs were much too high to make it a regular trade route.

Harcourt, Neeland, and McLeod were not discouraged. They immediately began work on an alternate route: a winter road from Fort McMurray/Waterways, Alberta, along the valley of the Athabaska system to Great Slave Lake. This was another classic fur-trading route started by Peter Pond in 1788. YK Transport planned to haul freight by sixteen sleds pulled by T-40 caterpillar tractors. As soon as the muskeg froze, Indian guides blazed a trail among rock outcrops and clumps of trees. This first winter trail was blazed more than twenty years before John Denison developed the "ice road" linking Yellowknife with mines on Great Bear Lake. It was almost as historically important as the arrival of the first airplane.

Harcourt, Neeland, and McLeod faced horrendous problems. On the first trip in February 1939, one of the four cat trains went through the Athabaska River ice and much cargo was lost. Other tractors broke down, and frost-bitten crews quit in minus 40° weather. But the train went through to Yellowknife. The partners proved that cat trains would work, though they were slow and prohibitively expensive. The ice had scarcely melted off sled runners when a dozen competing firms began scheming cheaper ways of hauling goods.

Frank Sedore and Red Hamilton believed that ordinary trucks could do almost everything crawlers could, and a lot faster and cheaper. In January 1939 they drove a Chevrolet truck across Great Slave Lake from Fort Resolution, taking eight days. Then the brothers Alex and Babe Feldman drove a Fargo truck with a caboose from Grimshaw, Alberta. YK Transport itself put two trucks and a Model A Ford car into its cat train in 1939, and all vehicles got through. In 1940 YK Transport moved a full cat train of four crawlers and sixty-four sleds from High Level, Alberta, to Yellowknife in the period from late January to 10 March.

That was the start of new transportation connections between the Mackenzie and the south. In 1942, when the U.S. Army started to build the CANOL Project at Norman Wells, Harcourt showed the Americans how to move 7,000 tons of supplies from Fort McMurray to the Mackenzie. The Americans, guided by Harcourt, made their land terminal at Hay River on the south shore of Great Slave. Very quickly, Hay River became a major marine centre with docks, warehouses, and shipping facilities. Ultimately, it was the main northern terminus of the Great Slave Lake Railway extending from Peace River, Alberta.

The Mackenzie Highway linking the NWT with the south reached Yellowknife in 1961. It spelled a psychological as well as a physical escape from isolation. As one resident of Yellowknife told me in the late 1960s: "When you know you can get on a bus and twenty-four hours later be in Edmonton, you feel far freer than before." There were to be other links with the south and civilization – and also with the North. The Dempster Highway from the Yukon ultimately linked the Beaufort Sea with Whitehorse, Alaska, and the south. And John Denison's famous ice road opened up the tundra east of Great Bear Lake to heavy-duty land transportation.

By 1939 Yellowknife was starting to be a real town in the southern sense, with all the institutions, amusements, and challenges of any other town of its size in the country. There seemed to be plenty of gold in the ground, and the town was growing steadily.

But it was about to suffer a setback that couldn't be foreseen by town dreamers like Larry Alexander and Jock McMeekan. Alexander warned in August 1939 that if a European war broke out, Yellowknife would die because it was built on gold – and gold does not have a high priority in wartime. A week after he wrote that editorial, war was declared. Alexander himself folded *The Prospector* and headed south to enlist. Scores of other young men did the same thing. Some mines started cutting production, and by 1942 most had shut down as Yellowknife became a ghost town. It would be 1945 before Yellowknife would see its second boom, one that hasn't yet ended.

Chapter 3

Sovereignty and Defence

Although the Inuit often seemed invisible to Ottawa and the rest of the world, the resources of the Barrens, the Arctic islands, and the Arctic Ocean were far from invisible. From the time of Frobisher, Hearne, and Mackenzie, Europeans sought their furs, whale oil, ivory, gold, copper, and petroleum. In 1877 enough was known for Sir John A. Macdonald to say of the Arctic islands: "They are rich in mines of iron, copper, gold, silver and large deposits of mica." This wealth inevitably brought up the question of sovereignty in the new Dominion of Canada.

As far as the continental land mass was concerned, the HBC's title to Rupert's Land seemed impeccable (except, perhaps, to its inhabitants). The Arctic islands were a different matter. True, some of the earliest explorers had been British, but in the 19th century Americans, Danes, and Norwegians were finding whole new archipelagos. In 1880 Britain turned its claims to the islands over to Canada, but the legality of the claim was far from clear. The matter was further complicated by the European passion for polar exploration.

In 1879 delegates to an Arctic conference in Germany decided to set up scientific stations around the globe. Canada wasn't even there: her interests were looked after by Britain, which agreed to set up a station on Great Slave Lake. Other nations involved were Norway, Sweden, Denmark, the Netherlands, Russia, Finland, the United States, Germany, and Austria. The Germans were assigned a station on Baffin Island, and it is significant that the first serious anthropological work in the Arctic was done by the German-born Franz Boas among the Netsilik Inuit in North Baffin during 1882–84.

The United States had two stations: at Point Barrow, Alaska, and another under Lieutenant Adolphus Greely in northern Ellesmere Island. His work prepared the way for the North Pole expeditions of Americans Captain Robert Peary and Dr. Fred Cook. Simultaneously, the Norwegian explorers Otto Sverdrup, Fridtjof Nansen, and Roald

Amundsen were making important discoveries in the waters west of Ellesmere. Rasmussen, the Dane, was mapping Greenland. In 1903–1904, Amundsen was the first man to sail the Northwest Passage, in the sailing ship *Gjoa*.

Canada finally became alarmed. A.P. Low, a geologist, was sent to Ellesmere twice, in 1903 and 1904, to find a way of establishing sovereignty. Meanwhile, Canadian-born Vilhjalmur Stefansson was spending a great deal of time in the Arctic and from 1913 to 1918 commanded the Canadian Arctic Expedition. More than any other modern explorer, he lived among the Inuit and learned their ways. Unlike the British from Sir John Franklin to Robert Scott, Stefansson learned from the Inuit. He once quoted – with amusement – the advice given to Sir Ernest Shackleton, the British Antarctic explorer, by a desk-bound member of the Royal Geographical Society: "Of course, anybody can succeed if he is willing to go native." Stefansson's books and lectures helped make Canadian administrators aware of the reasons that the Inuit did things the way they did in their native environment. However, increasing Canadian attention did not solve the sovereignty problem.

During the First World War, Ottawa heard rumours that Denmark was planning a major expedition to Ellesmere that might topple the fragile Canadian claim. In response, the Department of the Interior in 1919 formed an advisory technical board under Dr. Edouard Deville, the surveyor general, to find out whether it was worthwhile to claim the Arctic islands and, if so, what steps should be taken to establish title. Within a year, the board recommended occupation by the Royal Northwest Mounted Police, who would also act as immigration officers, customs collectors, justices of the peace, coroners, and postmasters.

The board feared that Knut Rasmussen might arrive on Ellesmere at any time, and it seriously suggested that Canada should borrow a dirigible from Britain. Mounties would board it in Scotland and a course would be set for the North Pole. Over Ellesmere, the "redcoats" would be dropped by parachute in time to challenge the invading Vikings. Luckily, Denmark abandoned its plans.

In 1922 the Canadian government sent the wooden-hulled vessel *Arctic* north with nine mounties under Inspector C.E. Wilcox, two years' supply of food, fuel, and building supplies, and plans to build police posts at Craig Harbour on Ellesmere and Pond Inlet on North Baffin. J.D. Craig of the Department of the Interior was commander and Joseph E. Bernier was ship's captain. Squadron Leader Robert A. Logan of the RCAF was to study flying conditions and recommend suitable aircraft for the Arctic. Throughout the 1920s, Ottawa probed the North with repeated expeditions into Hudson Bay and some voyages farther north. Ellesmere and North Baffin were secured by the Royal Canadian Mounted Police posts (their name had been changed in 1920), which guarded against future molestation of the Netsilikuit by marauding foreign anthropologists.

The HBC got into the spirit of the times when it moved its Coats Island post to Southampton Island in the northwestern corner of Hudson Bay. The original Inuit population had been wiped out by disease, so the HBC brought in Inuit families from Repulse and Wager Bay on the coast of Hudson Bay and from the Ungava Peninsula. The HBC was interested in opening new trapping grounds, but the experiment was not very successful because the Inuit did not adapt well to conditions around the new community of Coral Harbour. Nevertheless, the HBC scheme provided an example for similar transfers of population by the federal government thirty years in the future. In the 1950s, for example, largely for sovereignty reasons, Ottawa established Inuit communities at Grise Fjord on Ellesmere and at Resolute on Cornwallis Island, thus creating the farthest north communities in North America.

With the whole world avidly reading about Arctic and Antarctic expeditions by dog team, airship, airplane, and even submarine, the Ottawa mandarins pressed ahead with moves to open the North to industrial development. The long-dreamed-of railway to Churchill was finished in 1929, opening up Hudson Bay to the grain trade. Radio stations were built, and in 1927 and 1928 the Department of Marine and Fisheries sponsored a voyage to build airfields at Wakeham Bay, Nottingham Island, and Port Burwell. The first aerial survey was made, and in 1930 the icebreaker *N.B. McLean* began annual patrols. Most of this activity ended with the Depression. The Arctic was again left to the Inuit and to a few HBC and independent traders, the missionaries, and the Mounties.

Air Power

One of the most remarkable things about the 20th century's conquest of the skies was the almost instantaneous understanding of the commercial and military value of the airplane. As early as 1919, the

Advisory Technical Board on the Canadian Arctic said: "It would be undesirable and dangerous to allow another nation to get a foothold in the North now that aerial navigation has become so far advanced."

In 1922, on the *Arctic*'s first voyage, Squadron Leader Logan warned of the possibility of "hordes of Slavs" attacking Canada over the pole. In his study of Canadian northern defence, Kenneth Eyre notes: "It was perceived in Canada that unlike the other armed services, military aviation could be adapted to fulfill a wide range of civil support functions in peacetime." These included exploring for natural resources, police travel, and surveys of caribou and muskox population that might be useful in establishing a herding and meat industry. Logan predicted a northern oil strike in which workers would be fed from herds of caribou.

Such thinking was certainly in step with the rest of the world. In 1923 the American Lincoln Ellsworth flew as far north as 80 degrees, and in 1926 he was on the polar flight of the dirigible *Norge* with Amundsen and Italian explorer General Umberto Nobile. The Americans Richard E. Byrd and Floyd Bennett flew over the pole itself in 1926, while Hubert Wilkins, an Australian, made the trip from Point Barrow to Spitzbergen in 1928. Arctic travel was almost becoming a tourist excursion. In 1931 Wilkins travelled by submarine to the polar vicinity and predicted great cargo-carrying subs sailing the Northwest Passage under the ice, surfacing only to load grain or oil, or to discharge and pick up tourists. (The atomic-powered USS *Nautilus* reached the North Pole in 1958 and the USS *Skate* surfaced there in 1959. The Soviet sub *Leninsky Komsomol* arrived in l962, while HMS *Dreadnought* made the trip in 1971. For a time in the 1980s, Canada talked of buying a whole fleet of atomic subs to police the Arctic.)

～

The Depression ended the light-hearted excursions to the Arctic. The next development, which prepared the way for the social revolution, was the Second World War. From 1935 on, President Roosevelt took a keen interest in the defence of Canada. His actions involving Canada's eastern Arctic and Atlantic coast came long before the U.S. entered the war.

In 1941 FDR acquired air and naval bases in Newfoundland (Stephenville, Gander, and Argentia) from Britain and made arrangements with Canada to share air facilities at Goose Bay and Gander.

The same year, his son Elliott, then a captain in the U.S. Army Air Force, led an Arctic survey looking for suitable sites for airfields and weather stations that would ensure a safe air route for lend-lease aircraft being flown to beleaguered Britain and, after Hitler's eastern invasion, the Soviet Union. As a result, airfields were built at Cumberland Sound and Frobisher Bay on Baffin Island, at Churchill, Manitoba, at Fort-Chimo (now Kuujuaac), Quebec, on Southampton Island (Coral Harbour), and at Goose Bay.

Meanwhile, FDR was preparing to build a large number of military stations in Greenland. Such was the start of the so-called "Crimson Project" or Northeast Staging Route. Airfields and radio stations had to be built less than 800 kilometres apart because warplanes, particularly fighters, had short ranges and little navigational gear.

Several routes were devised linking North America with Britain. The most important went through Gander or Goose Bay, while a second started in Winnipeg and went through The Pas, Churchill, Southampton Island, Frobisher Bay, Bluie West 10 and Bluie West 1 in western Greenland, Ammassalik on the east coast of Greenland, then across the north Atlantic to Iceland and Scotland. The third route started in Montreal and went north via Fort-Chimo to Frobisher Bay, then followed the second route.

Washington had grandiose plans for the routes, but Canada felt from the start that the three-pronged project would be much too expensive to build and operate. The effervescent American generals were cooled down, and only a few bases were actually built. As it happened, the Crimson route was hardly needed and little used. It was only after the war and during the Cold War that Frobisher, Goose Bay, Churchill, and Thule in northern Greenland took on real military significance.

But even the half-finished aerial defence network had an almost immeasurable influence on the social development of the Arctic. The permanent, all-weather airfields with their companion radio stations made settlement and supply of the Arctic feasible. Because of the Cold War, they were not shut down in 1945 with the coming of peace: the Pentagon began promoting the building of new or enlarged military bases or, later, rocket-launching pads as soon as they discovered in 1946 that the USSR had a long-range bomber. This was a year before the Soviets exploded their first atomic bomb.

One may well ask why the Americans were so obsessed with the

Canadian North when their own Alaska was only a few sea miles from Siberia. But Alaska and Siberia are far from the heartlands of their respective countries. The shortest way to the steel mills of Chicago or the hydroelectric plants of the Donbas is over the pole. Thule, the farthest north American SAC (Strategic Air Command) base, is at 77.29 degrees north latitude, and Russia's Franz Josef Land is even closer to the pole.

Canada was a moderately reluctant participant in this "cold war" but realized it was as much part of U.S. defence as Panama or Hawaii and so became an active partner in the 1950s. The smoke had scarcely settled over ruined Berlin before the Americans and Canadians began to learn how to defend the Arctic. Working out of Churchill, Canada staged a large military exercise, "Operation Muskox," in 1946 on the assumption that the Soviets might drop paratroops on Canadian and American airfields. Muskox and an unsuccessful smaller exercise in 1950, "Operation Sweetbriar," showed that it was virtually impossible to either attack or defend the Arctic on the ground.

Muskox had other important effects. Baker Lake in the Keewatin became a staging base and a LORAN (Long Range Navigation) station was built at Cambridge Bay on Victoria Island. The LORAN tower remains the highest landmark in the central Arctic. Churchill became a key military installation for both Canada and the United States, and for a time there was talk of stationing 50,000 American troops permanently at the joint base at Goose Bay, once the biggest SAC base in the world.

When Russia exploded its atomic bomb in 1949, Washington became paranoid, and Canada responded cautiously by building the Pinetree Line and McGill Fence south of the NWT. It was not until the 1950s – after the triumph of Red China, the Korean War, and the Soviet H-bomb – that our Far North became a really major defence zone. Until then, many Canadians considered Americans in the North to be blundering clowns. There were countless stories about foolish American experiments: they were said to have developed explosive capsules for individual Arctic soldiers, which could be used to blast one-man latrines in the ice. Or, American scientists were freezing barrels of water, then chipping all the ice out, on the assumption that there always would be a cup of water left at the centre of the barrel. The tales were worthy of Jonathan Swift.

But the Canadians who worked with Americans found their allies highly adaptable. Working from Thule, the allies built the weather

stations at Alert and Eureka on Ellesmere Island. The Americans
wanted and got further stations at Isachsen on Ellef Ringness Island
and Mould Bay on Prince Patrick Island. The countries also teamed
up to build the important exploration station at Resolute on
Cornwallis Island. Such tiny stations became outposts of Canadian
sovereignty but soon were to be dwarfed by a major American presence stretching from Alaska to Greenland – the DEW Line. Over five
years, it employed 25,000 workers, and vast quantities of equipment
and supplies were flown in by Hercules and Globemaster transports,
or shipped by barge during the short summer.

There were twenty-two DEW Line stations requiring small permanent staffs, airfields, support services, and fuel dumps. Between
each two manned installations was an unmanned station. For most of
the Cold War, the DEW Line stations were commanded by American
officers, though at least token Canadian officers shared the duties.
The stations were built at least five kilometres from civilian communities, and some Inuit were hired as construction workers or on a permanent basis. Building the DEW Line created the facilities that
would make possible the social revolution and the nucleus of several
new high-tech Inuit communities.

The Defence of the West

The NWT and the Yukon might have slipped completely out of
Canadian consciousness during the Second World War if it hadn't
been for President Franklin Roosevelt's determination to keep Britain
in the fight against Hitler and his lesser fear that Japan might cut off
Alaska from the rest of the United States. The United States was
extremely isolationistic in the 1930s, but the president was alert to the
Nazi threat to American security and well aware of Japan's expan-
sionistic policy in the Far East. He feared Hitler more and made several overtures to Canada, seeking a defensive military relationship. At
first, he was greeted with reluctance by Prime Minister Mackenzie
King, who was not anxious to enter military alliances with either
Britain or the United States because of his recollections of the con-
scription crisis in Quebec during the First World War.

In spite of King's hesitancy, Canada was drawn into the bigger
military game. As Hitler's power grew, Canadian and American military planners began quietly to plan air and naval bases along the
Atlantic and Arctic coasts. In the west, the question of Alaskan

defence had been long on American military minds. In 1929 President Herbert Hoover proposed a military highway through Canada to Alaska. B.C. politicians welcomed the idea, but it was turned down by Mackenzie King. In 1934, with R.B. Bennett in office, Washington asked for permission to fly military aircraft over Canada to Alaska but was again refused.

In 1937 President Roosevelt paid a state visit to Victoria on a destroyer and once again brought up the idea of an Alaska highway. He got enthusiastic support from B.C. Premier T.D. Pattullo, who represented Prince Rupert and had spent ten years in the Yukon. Like his predecessor, S.F. Tolmie, and a successor, W.A.C. Bennett, Pattullo favoured almost anything that would open up northern British Columbia. Mackenzie King, back in power again, vetoed the idea.

FDR's overtures to western Canadian politicians were only a tiny part of his overall defence policy. Because of the economic crisis, his first term was overwhelmingly concerned with domestic matters, but in 1935 he proclaimed his "good neighbor policy" to the twenty Latin American r   'ics. As soon as he was re-elected in 1936, he began to show ala   the rise of Hitler. On 14 August 1936 Roosevelt said in Chautauc   .Y., "We can and will defend ourselves and defend our own neit   orhood."

This declaration updated the Monroe Doctrine, which had established America's hemispheric dominance more than a century earlier. It also passed a pointed message to Canada. Mackenzie King felt Roosevelt's statement was a warning to Japan and noted in his diary that Canada could remain neutral in a U.S.-Japanese war. He was silent on FDR's greater fears of an aggressive Hitler.

With American isolationism as strong as the British and French desire for appeasement, Roosevelt's policies were often tortuous and confusing, and Hitler completely misinterpreted them. Roosevelt failed to get Congress to expand the army and army air force but in 1938 managed to win congressional support for a two-ocean navy.

In August 1938 Roosevelt and King met at Kingston, Ontario, and the president said: "The people of the 'S. will not stand idly by if domination of Canadian soil is threaten . by any c' empire."

"We recognize our obligations as a good, fri   ' neighbour," replied King with his usual extreme caution.

One year later, with war about to break out, FDR took one of his celebrated ocean vacations — aboard a cruiser. It just happened to take him along the Labrador coast, where he looked over potential naval bases. At that time, Newfoundland was a colony of the United Kingdom not subject to Canadian influence, although Canada, like the United States, was aware of Newfoundland's strategic importance in the Gulf of St. Lawrence. As early as 1935, Canada joined with Newfoundland to build the great transatlantic airport at Gander. It opened in 1938 and was one of the keys to the Royal Air Force Ferry Command's vital route to Britain during the war.

In 1940, eighteen months before the United States entered the war, FDR signed an agreement with Britain to create a huge new naval base at Argentia, on Newfoundland's south coast, and military air bases at Torbay, near St. John's, and Stephenville, in western Newfoundland. At the same time, Roosevelt persuaded Canada to permit a joint military survey of Labrador and the waters around Hudson Bay and Greenland. This resulted in a large number of American-built and manned weather stations and military airports on Canadian soil. Another joint venture was the gigantic air base at Goose Bay, Labrador, which was also valuable in Ferry Command's flights of bombers and transports to Britain and later became, for a time, the United States' number one SAC bomber base.

When Denmark was occupied by Germany in 1940, FDR sent troops into Greenland on the basis of an agreement with the marooned Danish embassy in Washington. German weathermen were already in Greenland when the Americans arrived, and it took until 1943 to drive them out. After the war, the great American SAC base at Thule became one of the most important U.S. defences of the Cold War.

On 17 August 1940 FDR met King at Ogdensburg, New York, and proposed a Canada-U.S. permanent joint board on defence. This time King agreed. The board wasted no time. In October 1940 it recommended that the military take over a string of rudimentary civilian airports linking Edmonton with the Yukon: Grande Prairie, Alberta; Fort St. John and Fort Nelson, B.C.; and Watson Lake and Whitehorse in the Yukon. The Royal Canadian Air Force was to upgrade the fields and supply radio links for what was called the Northwest Staging Route (NWSR). The U.S. military would be allowed to use the route to supply Alaska. The five stations were opened in September 1941, four months before the attack on Pearl Harbor.

Here was an example of "nick of time" foresightedness, but the military facilities were inadequate. Shortly after the U.S. was attacked by Japan, it rushed squadrons of bombers north. Many crashed in the mountains because of poor radio facilities and inexperienced air crews. The Americans bitterly criticized Canadian equipment and demanded the right to take over the airfields. In typical Canadian style, Ottawa allowed the Americans to rebuild the fields, then took over the refurbished stations and ran them.

Alaskan defence was still far from secure after the Japanese attacked the Aleutians early in 1942. It was clear that there must be a military highway as well. The airfields themselves would be supplied by the road, while ammunition, fuel, and troops could be trucked all the way to Alaska. Above all, there was need for a new supply of petroleum to keep the warplanes flying and the trucks rolling.

So the oft-rejected American plan for an Alaska highway was back, and even Mackenzie King was silent this time. As he saw it now, his job was to maintain Canadian sovereignty while persuading the Americans to pay most of the costs and do most of the work. Even though he considered himself a close and trusted friend of FDR, his misgivings about Washington never faltered.

When the Americans proposed a joint study of territory being opened up by the highway, King told the cabinet's war committee that he was against it and darkly predicted in his diary that "efforts will be made by the Americans to control developments in our country after the war." He was so determined to make sure that impatient U.S. officers should respect Canadian rights that he made Brigadier-General W.W. Foster special commissioner for defence projects in the NWT. Foster made Edmonton his headquarters and got along fine with the Americans.

CANOL

There were three parts to the defence of Canada's northwest: the air route, the military highway, and the CANOL (Canadian Oil) Project. The last part was the most controversial.

Lieutenant-General Brehon Sommervell was head of U.S. Army Services and Supply, and he was in charge of the Alaska highway and the expansion phase of the NWSR (along with hundreds of other schemes, including the Manhattan Project, which built the atomic bomb). He was concerned about finding a new source of petroleum and learned of the Norman Wells field. On 1 May 1942, Sommervell telephoned Imperial Oil in Toronto and found that only four holes had been drilled, of which one was in production. Imperial expressed modest confidence that the field could be expanded and on Sommervell's insistence agreed to a new exploration program.

To Sommervell, the deal was a natural: after all, Imperial had been owned and controlled by Standard (New Jersey) since 1898 and thus was an American firm. The American-born Canadian minister of supply, C.D. Howe, announced the Norman Wells expansion program to the House of Commons several days after it had gone into effect. One month after Sommervell cut his deal, the Japanese attacked Dutch Harbor, Alaska, and invaded the Aleutian islands of Kiska and Attu. Already, more than 15,000 U.S. troops were stationed in the Yukon and NWT, many of them engineer troops working on the Alaska Highway and the RCAF airfields. A year later there were 33,000.

Sommervell rushed 3,000 black engineer troops by rail to Fort McMurray Waterways in northern Alberta and prepared to ship them to Norman Wells by boat. The CANOL Project was under way. It included plans for a major oil field at Norman Wells and a three-inch pipeline 1,700 kilometres across the Mackenzie Mountains to Whitehorse in the Yukon. There the crude oil would be refined and sent by tanker truck to Alaska. Earl Harcourt of Yellowknife Transport was hired as a consultant, and the Americans stormed north over muskeg, rock, and rapids. Canol Camp on the banks of the Mackenzie was about to be born.

The various northwestern projects were started secretly in late 1941 and early 1942, but they soon had an impact on northern Alberta and a much greater one on the environment and peoples of the NWT and Yukon. Many far-reaching effects came about casually, as a by-product of global strategies which seemed to dwarf the local problems of the Canadian North.

For instance, military considerations changed the way that airplanes were used. Up to 1941, business on the frontier could be handled by float or ski planes, and all-weather landing strips were not necessary. However, fighters, bombers, and big transports could not be effectively converted to floats and skis, especially when they had to be put to use immediately on arrival at their destinations. Second, military pilots had to have dependable weather forecasts and radio reports. So networks of all-weather airports with long, solid runways and twenty-four-hour radio stations were built. The Northwest Staging Route thus provided a pattern for the whole of the North: airports were soon being built along the Mackenzie, the Slave, and the

Athabaska in the northwest and at many locations in the eastern Arctic. The first Canadian public awareness of American troops occurred in Edmonton, jumping-off place for Alaska and the CANOL Project. Jasper Avenue soon was full of American uniforms, and many of these young soldiers had little awareness of where they were. One teenage private was asked if he would like to "go overseas" and replied in bewilderment, "But I am overseas!"

It was entertaining in those days to go to the Edmonton airport (then the city's only such facility but today the downtown industrial airport, largely supplanted by the international airport south of Edmonton) and watch planes coming in from Great Falls, Montana: clusters of fighters escorted by four-engined Liberator bombers acting as mother ships. It was for all the world like a goose teaching goslings to fly. Each Liberator carried spare parts and mechanics. Flights from airstrip to airstrip were short because the fighters' range was limited and they had primitive navigational equipment. Even so, many crashed, and so did B-25 medium bombers headed for Russia's battlefields. Dawson Creek, B.C., was mile zero on the Alcan military highway, and its streets were knee-deep in dust or mud, depending on the season, as hundreds of trucks roared northwest.

There were two aerial workhorses – the twin-engined C-47, which was the military counterpart of the DC-3, and the single-engined Noorduyn Norseman, the legendary bush plane that could go anywhere and carry amazing amounts of freight. Such planes took men and supplies everywhere along the northern supply routes. Soon many places had two airports – an old seaplane base and a new all-weather strip with a met tower. For the first time, large-scale civilian air service became feasible. Edmonton and Vancouver grew much closer. The military installations, many of which remained long after the war, ranged from the U.S. bomber refuelling base at Frobisher Bay to remote strips in the High Arctic and along the Mackenzie.*

---

*The American intrusion into Canada early in 1942 frightened Prime Minister Mackenzie King, and he may have been aware of the dreadful lack of planning that was involved in the U.S. military's precipitate moves. It has only recently been revealed (by history professor Shelagh Grant of Trent University, an authority on Canadian sovereignty in the Arctic) that General Sommervell ordered the Alaska Highway, the CANOL pipeline, and a working refinery all completed by the end of 1942. This showed a stunning lack of knowledge of the climate and terrain involved. The preliminary survey of the CANOL route through the Mackenzie and Selwyn mountain ranges wasn't finished by the end of 1942, and completion of the highway and the pipeline didn't come until 1944.

The CANOL Project was different from anything that ever had been attempted in either the Canadian or the American North. The nearest practical railway ended at Fort McMurray, Alberta, and the bush trails of YK Transport had to be vastly expanded. A visitor to Fort McMurray in 1942 had to be sharp-eyed to detect any sign of activity. Here was the old transportation and fur-trading post of the Nor'Westers and the HBC, and it remained a sleepy bush community. Bush planes on floats landed and took off from the Athabaska River, and an occasional canoe carried an Indian or Métis trapper.

Visitors were taken to a tiny Rube Goldberg machine on the banks of the river, where a professor of geology was boiling up black sand. He said the sand was full of oil and that one day millions of barrels would be produced in the area. It seemed most unlikely. Unless visitors scurried around the river to nearby Waterways, they might miss seeing hundreds of black American troops waiting to go north by boat. They arrived by train from Edmonton, along with mountains of equipment and supplies earmarked for far-off Norman Wells.

In Fort Smith on the Slave, the story was similar. The major sign of change was a brand-new airport with a hard black tarmac. The reason for the airport was obvious to a discerning visitor. Hadn't Canadian Pacific Airlines just been formed? Wasn't CPA using modern airliners that needed smooth, well-maintained runways? Such aircraft would be flying into the long-established airports at Winnipeg and Edmonton as well as the new fields in the NWT. One had only to talk to CPA's general manager, Grant McConachie, to realize that he was dedicated to opening up the North to Bay Street brokers and California tourists. The wheeled, twin-engined CP airliner sitting on the Fort Smith airfield was the symbol of the North's future.

In that summer of 1942, the NWT and the Yukon were poised on the brink of enormous change. A visitor might fly over hundreds of square kilometres of silent forests, but at the end would descend at Norman Wells on the turmoil of the mighty Mackenzie – the river sprinkled with islands, full of barges, tugs, and water taxis, all carrying soldiers and civilians from the airfield on the east bank above the original town to the sprawling military base on the west bank. No troops or civilian workers were housed in town: the U.S. Army built its own town on the west bank and another one at Dodo Canyon, far to the west across the Carcajou Flats in the first range of mountains. To Canadians, Indians or whites, the most astonishing thing was the mass of black faces: there were several thousand U.S. Army Engineer

Corps soldiers, and in America's segregated forces that meant black. All the officers were white, of course.

The new tote road stretched west across the flood plain to Dodo Canyon, a spacious pass that provided a level gravel beach for the big staging camp. Ten-ton trucks loaded with lumber, generators, culverts, pipe, gas drums, and food roared across the flats, and everyone was in a hurry. Barges were unloaded on the Mackenzie's west bank, then were pushed upriver to the supply base at Hay River.

The Hay River terminus showed what could be done with a lot of money and plenty of men and machines. After one look at portages, rapids, and muskeg, the Americans decided to improve the existing overland road considerably. Some rapids were blasted out in the terrible stretch between Fort Fitzgerald and Fort Smith. A rough but serviceable road was cut through the swamps and rocks to Hay River, where wharfs, harbour facilities, and shipyards were built. In summer, tugs pushed barges across Great Slave Lake to the start of the Mackenzie, then along the river to the Wells. In the early stages, the Americans imported tugs that weren't up to the job, so a bustling shipbuilding industry developed in Hay River. At freeze-up, essential supplies were hauled across the lake and river ice by tractor train or truck. Other supplies were stored in warehouses awaiting break-up.

∼

The achievements of the soldiers and civilians have never been adequately recognized. In the first year, 35,000 tonnes of supplies were moved through Hay River. Simultaneously, thousands of troops and civilians were driving the Alaska Highway northwest from Dawson Creek, B.C. Another supply base was built at Johnson's Crossing in the Yukon, and from it a third army worked northeast through the Ross River country to link up with the Norman Wells crew. Surveyors on snowshoes laid out the pipeline route across the Mackenzie Mountains in the winter of 1942–43.

All the projects were staggering. At Norman Wells there ultimately were 5,000 black soldiers without winter uniforms or roadside shelters. Their truck cabs were unheated. Bulldozer blades shattered like glass in -50° temperatures. In summer the land turned into a fly- and mosquito-infested swamp. The white officers were good engineers and competent soldiers, but they had learned their trade in Hawaii, the Panama Canal Zone, and the Philippines. They simply could not cope with the North.

In that first terrible winter, the bases were built and the route picked. But it was clear that white civilian workers must replace the blacks. Working in unbearable conditions, the engineering troops were near mutiny. Yet finding civilian workers was almost impossible. Most able-bodied young men were already in the military, and draft-proof construction workers were working overtime in the defence industry.

Recruiting a workforce big enough for the Alaska Highway, the airfields, shipyards and staging bases, and the CANOL pipeline was far beyond the capacity of any individual company. A consortium of three of the biggest U.S. construction firms – Bechtel-Price-Callahan – was formed. It scoured the United States for workers willing to go into the frozen wilderness. Not a few ex-cons and fugitives found a temporary haven there.

The changeover to civilian labour involved a disgraceful episode when the black troops were shipped out in the summer of 1943, packed into the holds of barges as their ancestors had been packed into slave ships. Because of wartime censorship, no one in southern Canada or the United States knew anything about it.

Censorship hid more than the problems of the U.S. Army. Canadian civilians were not permitted to work on the pipeline because Ottawa feared that if the consortium paid Canadians at the same rate as it paid Americans, inflation would ensue and Canadians in the south might become discontented with their low wages. Censorship conveniently covered up discrimination in employment policy as well as racial discrimination.*

To their credit, the U.S. Army and the American contractors made a considerable effort to protect the indigenous population from their presence. Some Métis and a few Indians got jobs in the transportation

---

*In 1942 most Canadians had their minds focused on the dramatic events in Europe, Africa, and the Pacific, and not one in a hundred had any idea of what was happening north of the 60th parallel. For instance, two young reporters for British United Press were stationed temporarily in Winnipeg. Looking for a feature story, Jim Maclean speculated that it seemed all too easy for an enemy to sail into Hudson Bay and thus reach the heart of the continent. The other suggested that HBC traders and Inuit trappers might be effective spotters for the Canadian government. Maclean thereupon "casually" suggested the idea to an HBC official in Winnipeg, and the story that this sort of thing had actually been going on poured out. Maclean wrote it up and by a fluke it was passed by the military censors and created a minor sensation in newspapers from Florida to California. Neither reporter knew anything about the Alaska Highway or the CANOL Project. I was one of the reporters and about to stumble on the story in Fort McMurray. Such fumbling revelations and casual discoveries were typical of the times.

and supply end, but as with southern white Canadians, almost none were hired for the pipeline and tote road crews. The Americans, military and civilian, were kept under tight discipline and lived in compounds far from the native communities. Liquor was rationed, and workers were encouraged to save their recreational energies and money for their return to Edmonton or San Francisco.

∾

The astonishing thing was that the projects succeeded brilliantly in spite of many mistakes. American engineers ignored Canadian advice against laying the pipeline on the bed of the Mackenzie: in the spring, the ice took the pipeline out, and it had to be replaced in a protected trench laid beneath the river bed.

Similarly, Canadians pointed out the need for corduroy roads across the *taiga*. The Americans went ahead and ripped off the peatmoss that covered the permafrost, then laid a conventional road on top. When trucks drove over it, the friction caused heat and the permafrost melted, precipitating the trucks into the muskeg. In B.C., along the Alaska Highway, hundreds of trucks were parked on a low bench of the Peace River. A freshet rushed down from the mountains, flooding over the trucks, then freezing them in for the winter.

Yet the Americans learned quickly and corrected their mistakes. In less than two years, the Alcan Highway* was crowded with trucks heading for Alaska; the skies were swarming with fighters heading for the USSR, and Norman Wells oil was flowing through the CANOL pipeline to the refinery that had been assembled in Whitehorse.

In other epochs, the projects might have been remembered as among the great engineering achievements of history, ranking with Xerxes' crossing of the Hellespont. Instead, the CANOL Project was abandoned as soon as the war ended, and it was many years before the Alaska Highway became a major tourist artery. The airfields of the NWSR were reduced to way stations for local airlines.**

The Japanese did not attack mainland Alaska; they abandoned

---

*The Alcan (Alaska-Canada) Highway was the original name of the Alaska Highway.

**Ultimately, the military airports were taken over by the Ministry of Transport and were essential in the building of new civilian communities made up of Indians and Inuit living off the land, white bureaucrats from Ottawa, and a polyglot mass of white and Métis settlers seeking new jobs and new lifestyles in the mines and other new enterprises.

Attu and were driven out of Kiska. The CANOL pipeline, which cost a quarter of a billion dollars, was left to the caribou and grizzly. The Whitehorse refinery was dismantled and shipped to Alberta, where it helped to launch the new Leduc field in 1947. In a few years, there were hardly any signs of the supply roads and bridges spanning the Mackenzie Mountains. The 10,000 workers of the Yukon and the NWT departed. Norman Wells returned to being a little oil well community dozing along the Mackenzie River.

Part Two

REVOLUTION UNDER WAY

Chapter Four

The Revolution Begins

Nineteen hundred and fifty-three was the year when President Dwight D. Eisenhower stopped the fighting in Korea by threatening to drop the atomic bomb on Red China. It was the year when the USSR detonated its first hydrogen bomb, thus ensuring the United States would build a radar fence in the Canadian Arctic. It marked the beginning of diplomacy termed "the balance of terror."

It was also the year when Prime Minister Louis St. Laurent launched a new and sweeping policy for the development of the Canadian North. The Department of Resources and Development became the Department of Northern Affairs and National Resources. The minister was Jean Lesage; his deputy was Gordon Robertson from the Privy Council Office. Robertson had an executive assistant, Ben Sivertz, who was to have a vital role in changing the Arctic.

St. Laurent told the House of Commons on 8 December 1953 that "Canada has governed the NWT in an almost complete state of absent-mindedness for ninety years," adding that "the centre of gravity is being moved north." There was widening public interest in the North. Yellowknife was one of the world's great gold producers, and it was booming again after being a virtual ghost town during the war. Prospectors were everywhere in the NWT, following a Canadian tradition that had been going on for a century.

It didn't take a genius to tell the Ottawa mandarins that the rules had to be changed to make it easier to develop northern resources. This would involve wider political and taxation rights for whites already in Yellowknife, and there might have to be new rules for the indigenes. And something had to be done to protect Canadian Arctic sovereignty from the Americans, who were pressing for military bases.

Considering that there were no government administrators in residence – just the HBC, the missionaries, and the Mounties – the mandarins had to fly by the seats of their pin-stripe pants. They had foreign examples, of course, but these were mostly to be avoided. The country with by far the most Arctic experience was Russia: it had conquered and colonized Siberia in the 17th century. Archangel, at 64 degrees, north latitude, had been a seaport since 1553; Murmansk (69 degrees, 33 minutes) was a famous Arctic seaport during the Second World War.

The problem with using Siberia as an example was that it differs so much from the Canadian North. Proportionally, it has far more boreal forest and grazing land because the Ob, the Yenisei, the Lena, and several other considerable rivers flow into the Arctic Ocean and provide drainage basins in which plant and animal life flourish. Canada, on the other hand, has only one great north-flowing river in the NWT, the Mackenzie. Siberia, which extends as far south as Canada does, today has a population of 25 million people and a generation ago had 15 million. In the USSR, more than 100,000 lived north of the Arctic Circle in the 1950s, and the number has increased steadily. By the 1980s there were several hundred thousand industrial workers, most of them working in vast mineral, gas, and oil projects. Several sizable cities are mushrooming north of the Arctic Circle.

The Russian example showed what could be done, but Ottawa had somewhat different objectives and, anyway, was in a hurry. The truth was that when the prime minister rose in Parliament, there was a human emergency in the Arctic, postwar entrepreneurs were impatiently waiting for Ottawa to open the mineral resources of the North to them, Washington was pressing Canada for new military defences in the Arctic, and white residents of Yellowknife were demanding the equivalent of provincial rights.

The most dramatic and most immediately pressing of these concerns – though probably not the most important in the eyes of most cabinet ministers and Bay Street and St. James Street businessmen – was the plight of the indigenes of the North. Hundreds of Inuit in the Barren Lands and in Ungava were starving because of the failure of the caribou migrations.

In another time, the plight of the aboriginals might have gone unnoticed, but this was the right period for humanitarian action. As with other people around the world, the war had taught Canadians to share and work cooperatively and to make sacrifices for great causes. In the postwar period, voters had agreed there must be better social and medical services for all Canadians. Family allowances – the "baby bonus" – had started in 1944, and there was growing concern for the poor and unfortunate.

It was during this mood of humane desire for improvement that the northern equation was drastically altered by the entrance of a brand-new player: Dr. Hugh Keenleyside, a professional diplomat who was asked by Prime Minister Mackenzie King to succeed Charles Camsell as NWT commissioner and deputy minister. Many businessmen inside or close to the Liberal government saw the Arctic as a treasure chest ripe for looting, but Dr. Keenleyside was largely concerned with the welfare of the aboriginal peoples.

He completely reorganized the NWT administration between 1947 and 1950 and made a modest start in improving health facilities and introducing public education in the Mackenzie District. Ultimately, he clashed with the business-oriented Robert Winters, who became minister in 1950. Keenleyside went to a high post in the United Nations, while many of his NWT reforms were put on hold until the era of Jean Lesage. Winters was primarily concerned with resources – there was good reason for the ministry now being called the Department of Resources and Development. However, Keenleyside's reorganization and his fledgling social program made the St. Laurent-Lesage-Robertson revolution of the 1950s much easier to accomplish.

For instance, it paved the way for Ottawa's intervention when the long-developing famine emergency reached a head in the Keewatin District in 1953. The Caribou Inuit desperately needed help. They had recently become visible to southerners, but only after a whole series of blood-chilling incidents.

The supply of game had been declining from about 1910 onward, and traders had reported changes in caribou migration patterns during the 1920s. To make matters worse, the fur market collapsed in the 1930s, wiping out the only source of cash money for both Inuit and Indians. (Ironically, the Inuit had only just accepted the trapline as a way of life.)

There were many grim tragedies, though at first few of them were heard about in the south. How many knew the fate of the man who played the hero in Robert J. Flaherty's great documentary film, *Nanook of the North*? Nanook's face was familiar to the thousands who saw it on a movie screen in 1921, and he was guest of honour at the movie's opening in New York. A year later Nanook and his family starved to death in Ungava.

Another Inuk, Nuligak, wrote a beautiful book about his life in which he described how, one winter, he found himself with eleven 22-calibre rifle bullets – and no way of buying more. He killed ten meat animals and only missed once. His written account expressed great pride at his success in keeping his family alive. Ironically, Nuligak wrote the book while dying of tuberculosis in Camsell Hospital in Edmonton.

In the mid-1920s a trader for Révillon Frères, the French fur company, travelled across the Barrens with two Indian guides. They came upon an Inuit band of about twenty people, men, women, and children. An Inuk hunter told them he had missed the caribou migration. He asked for nothing, but the white man gave him as much as he safely could – enough to feed the Inuit group for a few days. The hunter said he believed there were caribou two days' walk to the northwest and started after them. The trader and his guides went on to Baker Lake.

A year later, the trader and the Indians were in the same area and decided to see whether they could find any trace of the Inuit. The trail was pitifully easy to follow – discarded belongings as people became too weak to carry them, then bodies: the old first, then the babies, then the children. At last there were only two sets of tracks left, and soon the Indians discovered the picked-clean bones of the hunter. He had no rifle. Casting about, the Indians found another trail and followed it for a few hours. At the end of it were the remains of a twelve-year-old girl. She was carrying the rifle, which had one bullet left.

These true tales of the Arctic were far from unusual at any time, but in the early 1950s they reached a climax that could no longer be ignored by Ottawa. In the winter of 1949–50, four Canadian soldiers were manning a Signal Corps radio station at Ennadai Lake at the edge of the tree line just north of the Manitoba border. One day, members of the Kazan Lake Inuit band staggered into the army camp in an advanced stage of starvation. There were forty-five in the group, and the soldiers managed to save all of their lives. They asked the RCMP at Churchill for help, and after a while the Inuit were airlifted to Churchill, then on to Nueltin Lake below the tree line and in Chipewyan territory. The Inuit were given arms, ammunition, and fishing equipment.

Unfortunately, the transfer didn't work out, and the Inuit returned to the Barrens. In the spring of 1954, the soldiers nursed the band through a bout with influenza. The Mounties complained to Ottawa that the problems of starvation and relocation were beyond them. For once, someone heard and was ready to do something. What happened then was the most dramatic part of the Arctic revolution.

∽

Considering the massive changes that have happened in the last generation, it's hard to believe how little attention was paid to NWT aboriginals before 1953. The first federal administrative office opened in 1921 at Fort Smith to serve white, not aboriginal, needs. The main reason for its existence was the oil strike at Norman Wells, but it was also a response to the growing activities of trappers, traders, missionaries, and miners.

In 1923 the Department of the Interior set up a division of its NWT branch called Eskimo Affairs to provide "basic health care and supervision of medical health officers; education; sanitation; arts and crafts; support for mission schools and hospitals, and study of Inuit needs and habits."

But the government never got around to doing anything about these concerns in the 1920s. In 1936 the entire Interior Department ceased to exist, a casualty of the Depression. Its functions – a few of them – were taken over by Mines and Resources, which in 1950 became Resources and Development.

Hugh Keenleyside wrote in his memoirs:

> The awakening general interest in the Arctic was in part the result of political and defence considerations that marked the period of the Cold War. But additional recognition of its importance came also from a new appreciation of the economic possibilities of that region. And the more admirable aspect of humanity's split personality was illustrated by a growing appreciation of the social responsibility of those living in a more favourable environment for the welfare of others of our common destiny who had been existing in half-forgotten isolation beyond the horizon of the North.

Alvin Hamilton, who was minister of northern affairs and national resources from 1957 to 1960, put it more tersely: "The atmosphere of the country and the world was toward hospitals, nurses, schools and co-ops." Under Keenleyside and his successors up to 1967, Ottawa remained the headquarters of the NWT: all decisions were made there. In a conversation with me, Ben Sivertz, who was an assistant to Keenleyside, Major-General Hugh Young, and Gordon

Robertson before he became a leading administrator, defended Ottawa as the NWT capital:

> In those days problems of travel were incredible. Single-engine planes on floats in summer and skis in winter had neither radar nor gyro compasses. Few people realize how difficult it is to navigate with a magnetic compass in the bumpy and swinging cockpit of a small plane near the North Magnetic Pole which makes astonishing angles of variation. Such planes are on visual flight rules which means the pilot must be able to see the ground, and as soon as he is away from lakes and rivers a map is essential for safe flying over the million-and-a-quarter square miles.

Until there were better planes, gyro compasses, and aerial maps, NWT travel between east and west was just not feasible. Ottawa remained the hub from which the Mackenzie Valley and the Arctic were administered: the two parts had almost nothing to do with one another.

Up to 1951, the NWT was run (as much as government had anything to do with running it) by a handful of Ottawa mandarins in their spare time. The commissioner still was deputy minister of whatever department had been given responsibility for the NWT, and the four members of the NWT Council were appointed from the mandarinate except for one or two token white northerners. The council met occasionally, never in the Territories.

When Mines and Resources became Resources and Development in 1950, it was given a Lands Division to look after federal lands, minerals, and timber, and a Northern Administration Service divided into an Arctic Division and a Yukon-Mackenzie River Division. There were promises that something would be done about hospitals, schools, public health, law and order, and so on. There were new regional offices in Smith, Hay River, Yellowknife, and Aklavik – but none in the eastern Arctic.

In 1951 the NWT Council was expanded to eight members, three of whom were elected, all from the Mackenzie District and all white. For the first time, the council was ordered to meet in the Territories once a year, with a second meeting in Ottawa. The first meeting outside Ottawa was in Yellowknife in December 1951.

Until 1948 the deputy minister/commissioner administered the NWT with the advice of his NWT Council and also with regular advice from the RCMP, the Anglican primate of Canada, the Roman

Catholic archbishop for the North, and the HBC. But in 1948 the Advisory Committee on Northern Development (ACND) was set up. According to Gordon Robertson, "its mandate related to the North and especially to the coordination of the activities of the various departments and agencies there." Robertson added: "The committee did not deal with the policies of defence, or of transportation, or of foreign relations (in the sense of 'policy'), but only with the fallout of ministerial policies decided by ministers elsewhere. It also dealt with the plans and activities of the departments and agencies in the North."

Historian Donald Creighton said the ACND was to advise the government on "policy relating to civilian and military undertakings in northern Canada and to provide for the effective coordination of all government activities in that area." There appears to be some conflict between Robertson's and Creighton's view of the committee's functions, and it must be noted that Robertson spoke from the absolute authority of being commissioner at the time. However, considering that some of the main activities of the federal government in the North involved defence, sovereignty, and relations with the United States during the 1940s and 1950s, it must have been hard to keep the ACND deliberations separate from those areas. Robertson says today:

> The minister of northern affairs and national resources as a member of the cabinet would be able to say his piece about policy in any proposal that he thought would be of importance to the North when another minister brought it to cabinet for consideration, but one has to recognize that northern implications would, in most cases, not be seen as decisive or major.

This may explain why Ben Sivertz, in conversations with me, denied that there was any connection between his Arctic program for helping the Inuit and the defence and sovereignty programs that were affecting most of the Arctic during the 1940s and 1950s. Today, more than thirty years later, it is still difficult to disentangle the interlocking mazes along which the mandarins tripped so easily. "The government became aware that the North was in a strategic location," Robertson said in the briefest – and clearest – summation on record.*

---

*Asked about the relationships among the departments during his three years in office, Alvin Hamilton told me: "The [Defence Department] used to lie to us a lot." He was, of course, referring to a department presided over by a fellow Conservative in the Diefenbaker government.

The pitfalls were not only in the possibly conflicting policies of various government departments: there were difficulties in deciding what policies suited the indigenous populations. "We had been charged to look into what should be done about the North," Robertson said of the 1953 instructions he received from his minister, Jean Lesage. "There was not one officer of the department north of the tree line, and no government schools."

In those days, Ottawa had about a score of employees at Smith, but they were only concerned with the Mackenzie Valley. The few schools were run by the Anglicans and Roman Catholics until, in the late 1940s, Keenleyside started building secular day schools. They were all concentrated in the Delta or south of Great Slave Lake, and the program had hardly begun when Keenleyside left. The only educational effort among the Inuit was a residential school run by the Catholics at Chesterfield Inlet.

Robertson had no previous experience in the North and was the purest of Ottawa mandarins. A native of Saskatchewan, he studied at Oxford and Toronto before joining External Affairs. He served the Privy Council from 1945 to 1953 and, by reputation, was eminently qualified to understand the changes in the machinery of northern administration that had been put in place by his predecessors, Dr. Keenleyside and Major-General Hugh Young.

The new department and the new commissioner faced an emergency that had to be dealt with immediately. Reports of Inuit starvation and epidemics had been frequent for thirty years, but now they were getting so bad that serious measures had to be taken at once: human beings were starving at Palai ... Baker Lake ... Garry Lake ... the Thelon River ... on the lower Kazan ... in Quebec Ungava.

The caribou population was declining; proper housing was non-existent for people dying of measles, diphtheria, meningitis, tuberculosis, or influenza in snow houses and skin tents, without medicine or sanitation. "And we were instructed to do something about transportation and communications," Robertson added drily. His summary of the disasters facing the new department was capped by infant mortality: higher than 300 per thousand for the Inuit and 200 per thousand for Indians, compared to 40 per thousand for Canadians as a whole.

Sivertz and Hunt

Robertson's chief administrator in the Mackenzie District, with head-quarters in Smith, was L.A.C.O. Hunt, who had long experience along the Mackenzie, especially in the Delta. Hunt's principal duties involved whites: supervising mining permits, registering claims, issuing business licences, and so on. The Indians were not in nearly as serious a crisis as the Inuit, though health care was almost non-existent, economic conditions were very bad, and secular schools had not nearly fully replaced the missionary schools. While there was poverty, there was no starvation.

In the Arctic, Robertson picked as his chief administrator Ben Sivertz, an assistant to both Keenleyside and Young. Sivertz was from Victoria, a former schoolteacher, merchant marine officer, and navy commander who had been in Ottawa since the end of the war.

"I created the Arctic Division," Sivertz told me in 1989. "We hired six northern service officers and created six divisions. We hired social workers, writers, and Inuktitut language teachers. When there was a report of starvation we sent help: sometimes one of our people chartered a plane and went in with food and equipment; sometimes the police were asked to go by dogsled. No two cases were the same. Health was always part of it, either as cause or effect. Accident or illness to the principal hunter sometimes began a food shortage. Some people would have to be taken to hospital."

Looking back, Gordon Robertson described the scene:

> What has to be remembered is that the Eskimos were, with very few exceptions, hardly removed at all from their aboriginal condition in the 1950s and less so in the 1940s. Almost everyone who had any-thing to do with the policies that were designed to prepare them for the sort of world they would have to face in twenty, forty, or fifty years was desperately concerned that our western life should not crash in on the Eskimos in a way that would be destructive. The Anglican and Roman Catholic churches were strongly of the view that the aboriginal people of the North, both Indian and Eskimo, had a way of life and structure of society that were well suited to the conditions of land and climate. These clergymen agreed that change had to come but they wanted it to be as little destructive of these basic things as possible. Because of these considerations, a deliber-ate effort was made to keep defence stations, airfields, and weather

stations separate from existing or planned communities of Eskimos. When the DEW Line was built, this policy meant that the various facilities, with their airfields and staff accommodations, were located in uninhabited places as much as possible.

While this may have been policy when the DEW Line stations were built, communities often did grow up around them. In Cambridge Bay in the 1980s, for instance, some of the DEW Line staff actually lived in the civilian town and drove out to their duties daily. The commander, or civilian manager, of the station was an important patron of community events, and his staff socialized with local residents, both Inuit and white.

Robertson expressed a comprehensive and far-sighted theory of development. But it was sometimes overwhelmed by uncontrollable events such as the actual building of the DEW Line and the new civilian communities, requiring as they did very considerable semi-permanent facilities for the construction workers. Some of these workers got involved with the indigenous population and even settled down to raise mixed-blood families. The influx of southern teachers, doctors and nurses, and administration employees further complicated the noble goals of the mandarins and the bishops.

It must never be forgotten that the headlong defence program was plunging ahead at exactly the same time that Sivertz and his men were making an equally urgent effort to save the Inuit from starvation and disease. The official history of the hamlet of Broughton Island, on the east coast of Baffin Island nearest to Greenland, tells the story of several communities: Broughton Island did not become a settlement site until 1956–57 when Inuit families moved there from Pangnirtung and Padloping Island to help build the DEW Line station.

In the case of Hall Beach, on the coast of the Melville Peninsula, there were no Inuit camps in the immediate vicinity of the Foxe Main DEW Line station. Construction, as elsewhere, caused a mini-boom, which attracted Inuit to the area and raised the level of employment and income to unprecedented levels. Government installations followed, and even after the construction boom was over, the community retained a relatively high dependence on wage employment. As the *NWT Data Book* for 1986–87 says: "Inuit continued to migrate from the outcamps until, by 1968, the last family had left the land."

While this was happening, administration and policy-making for both the defence/sovereignty and social development programs remained in far-off Ottawa. Robertson said: "We did look ahead. There were serious debates. Some people opposed education on the basis that it would destroy Eskimo culture and character. We had long debates over this. I disagreed because I thought this view was based on keeping the native population down to a level which could live off the land."

The dilemma was not new. At times it had involved the Mackenzie Basin Indians. The oldest trading post on the lower Mackenzie was Fort Good Hope, and the Sah'tu began living around the post in the early part of the 19th century. There were too many of them for the game supply, and soon they became dependent on supplies from the HBC store. In 1844 many starved while waiting for a delayed supply ship.

This was exactly the same problem facing the Inuit who began moving into the white trading posts in the 1940s and 1950s – sometimes even earlier. As early as 1916, the "free" white trader, Charles Klengenberg, reported that the caribou herds were declining around Coppermine on Coronation Gulf. In 1927 half the people of Bernard Harbour north of Coppermine died of influenza. The rest fled to Coppermine. Baker Lake also became a centre to which starving and ill Inuit were brought in the 1940s and 1950s. Whale Cove, on the shore of Hudson Bay between Eskimo Point and Rankin Inlet, was created when 199 inland Inuit were relocated from both the northern and the southern Keewatin. That was in 1959 after a 1957–58 famine. At Garry Lake in 1958, fifty-three people starved to death before the remaining thirty-one were rushed to Baker Lake.

Perhaps the most pathetic catalogue of Job's afflictions occurred at the old whaling station of Lake Harbour. From 1946 to the 1960s, Lake Harbour suffered from plagues of botulism, tuberculosis, and pneumonia. But it wasn't until 1960 that the Inuit were driven to town-living by an outbreak of distemper that killed 80 percent of their dogs and made traditional hunting impossible. The same outbreak killed most of the dogs in Pangnirtung on Cumberland Sound.

Before the Robertson regime, the Mounties (who were the only federal officials in the Arctic) faced other puzzling problems. In 1944 the federal government began paying family allowances to all Canadian mothers with children under sixteen who were in school. But what did one do about the Yukon and NWT Indians and the NWT Inuit, who had no schools?

The situation was handled in a typically paternalistic way. In both the Yukon and the eastern Arctic, native mothers had to go to the police post and choose food and other supplies from an approved list. The police would then sign the list and the HBC store would fill the order. It was not thought wise to give any cash to the natives – a policy approved by the HBC, which had been carrying on the fur trade by barter for centuries. (In the late 1940s, L.A.C.O. Hunt created a controversy when he insisted on paying Indian and Inuvialuit mothers in the Delta in cash.)

The system sometimes broke down because the police were not available to sign food chits. Duncan Pryde, an HBC trader in Baker Lake and Bathurst Inlet, said of family allowances and old age pensions: "I doubt whether the politicians of the South had any idea at the time just how much benefit they were bringing into the Polar country." He had a grim explanation of the reasons that family allowances were so important. Before the white man came in any numbers, Pryde said, Inuit men were extremely violent, prone to blood feuds resulting in murder.

"It was not uncommon during the course of a blood feud for eight or nine people to die in the aftermath of one murder," he wrote in his autobiography, *Nunaga: My Land, My Country*. He said the reason for the feuds was to obtain wives because of a shortage of women. This, in turn, was caused by the regular practice of female infanticide. After the government began paying old age pensions and family allowances, "an extra girl baby suddenly became more of an asset than a debit and was allowed to live." As late as the 1960s, Pryde said, he was withholding welfare cheques at the Perry River post.

The Inuit receiving welfare tended to hang around the post doing nothing, and Pryde said he was instructed to try and force them to go back to the traplines in keeping with longstanding HBC policy. (This was the reason that the HBC didn't heat its stores.) Pryde said that after 1954, when it was noted that the policy was obsolete almost everywhere else, pensions, family allowances, and welfare were administered by NWT or federal officials with regional offices throughout the Arctic. The police and HBC no longer had any authority in that area.

The new administrators changed things considerably. So did the new government schools and nursing stations. Unlike the old mission schools, the new schools were supposed to teach the Inuit how to survive in a white, English-speaking, high-tech world: a wage economy was just around the corner. The nursing stations were supposed to save lives and they really did. Robertson was aware that the ecological balance might well be disturbed: for instance, could a healthier, more numerous population live on available supplies of game and fish?

Aboriginal Policy

Recalling the elements of the new northern policy of the 1940s and 1950s, Robertson said: "The pressure from whites was for the things that would help business – mining, mostly. Other white pressure was from the missionaries, HBC and Mounties not to change things at all. There was no pressure from the native populations because there were no native organizations."

That summed it up. The world had changed dramatically after the Depression and the Second World War. Now the mandarins and the politicians were trying to find a path for the future somewhere between the greed of the northern conquistadores and the colonial conservatism of the old Arctic hands who had been running things for three centuries. It had always been the policy of the HBC and later the Canadian government to leave the Eskimos to their own devices because there were so few of them and their environment was so severe. Unlike the Indians of the western plains, they never were threatened by white immigration.

Canadians have always been pragmatic about the aboriginal population: the policy was not to talk about a treaty until it was needed for mineral development or the opening up of land for settlement. Thus, the numbered treaties in the West were negotiated in the knowledge that the railway would soon be filling up the Prairies with Europeans. As for the North, Treaty 8 of 1899 was chiefly concerned with Alberta and Saskatchewan, but it also covered the southwestern corner of present-day NWT. Treaty 11 was negotiated in 1921 because of the Norman Wells oil strike.

No other treaties involved any part of the NWT – especially not the eastern Arctic, where the very idea of mass immigration was ludicrous. A very few permanent settlers did come after 1900, and they were to have an important impact on the eastern and central Arctic. They were mainly freetraders and trappers who married native wives and settled down to create whole dynasties bearing the names Lyall, Firth, Joss, Carpenter, Ford, Ruben, Steen, Klengenberg, and several others.

Such marriages were successful partly because the Inuit, unlike whites, have never had any serious concerns about racial mixing, and there have been few examples of the complex relationships involving Indians and Métis. By and large, it has been an Inuit tradition to accept any kabloona who wants to become one of them and proves it by living in the Inuit way and perhaps marrying an Inuk. "Living the Inuit way" is, of course, an extremely difficult initiation for a white man to pass.

It's hard to say, in the light of later developments, whether the benign neglect of the Inuit was a good or a bad thing for them. Quite early, HBC men and missionaries reported on the impact of epidemics on the native population. The Inuit and the Indians survived (though not by much – they were always close to becoming an endangered species). For a long time the Inuit way of life made it difficult for whites to discover much about them. Unlike the kabloonat and many Indian tribes, the Inuit (at least in modern times) had no fixed, permanent communities. They were nomadic hunters who followed the game and the seasons. Perhaps twice a year they would gather at the mouth of a river, or in a sheltered cove of the sea, and share a social life with their neighbours. Mostly, they travelled and lived in small family groups.

Unlike the Indians of the south, the Inuit had no tribal or band structure, no chiefs, no elders. The head man of any family group was the man respected as being the best hunter. Sometimes this was disastrous when a hunter grew old and lost his skills but tried to hold on to power. Peter Pitseolak reported one case in which the group had to murder the head man to save themselves from catastrophe. In such a society, there was no need for government in the sense we know it. It was foreign even to the simple commercial rules of the HBC, which depended on a predictable supply of furs each year. How could a factor depend on people who followed the caribou, or the seals, or the run of Arctic char? Perhaps the watershed in Inuit history came when the Bay men or the whalers first gave the indigenes rifles and ammunition. Perhaps it came with the introduction of the steel trap, which revolutionized the catching of fur-bearing animals, or perhaps when the Inuit were introduced to the system of receiving money for services. At any rate, after about 1900, the whole landscape began to erode very gradually, almost imperceptibly at first, then at a faster and faster rate. Under the spur of white greed, the land and sea were methodically stripped of fur-bearing and meat- or oil-producing animals. The enormous caribou herds started to follow the path of the buffalo in the south.

The disease situation became appalling. The Sadlermiut of Southampton Island were wiped out, and when Coral Harbour began in 1925, it had to be settled from Ungava and North Baffin. Gordon Robertson found that 1,600 out of a total Inuit population of 8,000 ended up in southern tuberculosis hospitals within a few years.*

The reasons for the reduction of the caribou have still not been determined with certainty. Farley Mowat, in his 1959 book about the Caribou Inuit, *The Desperate People*, placed most of the blame on white trappers in the late 1920s. He says they didn't use traps: they shot hundreds of caribou and poisoned the carcasses with strychnine; white foxes, wolves, and wolverines ate the meat and died. This was a plausible theory except that the white killers weren't in the Barrens for long: the fur market collapsed in 1932.

Wildlife officials say that aerial surveys show that the greatest caribou decline – 75 percent or more – occurred during the war years when there was no hunting or trapping at all by kabloonat and much less by Inuit and Indians. These scientists believe that the caribou may have been struck by a periodic disease or that the lichens on which they fed were reduced. Whatever the cause, the caribou declined and many Inuit died of starvation.

Saving the Inuit from starvation was one thing; what to do with them was another. Somebody in Ottawa wondered whether two urgent problems could be merged into one happy solution: it was decided to send some of the displaced and hungry Inuit to Ellesmere Island and some to Cornwallis Island. "We wanted to make sure Canada owned the oil and mines in the Arctic archipelagos," Alvin Hamilton said. "Our big secret was to maintain an effective occupation, then get the International Court to accept the Canadian claim to the territory."

The plan was relatively simple and could be explained on humanitarian grounds. Besides, there was the example of the HBC on Southampton Island in 1925. The police post at Craig's Island was moved sixty kilometres to Grise Fjord, becoming the farthest north community in Canada at 76 degrees, 25 minutes, north latitude. Other displaced Inuit, some from Pond Inlet, went to the weather and scientific station at Resolute Bay.

---

*Some returned home, cured. Others were buried in anonymous graves on Indian reserves in the south. Too often, their relatives did not even know their fate. They simply disappeared into the vast fog of impersonal white bureaucracy.

∼

The relative importance of the Canadian sovereignty issue and the sometimes connected question of Canadian Arctic defence – especially insofar as the presence of U.S. troops was concerned – remain an area for sharp debate. Gordon Robertson told me:

> No one who had any knowledge of the law of sovereignty and the facts relating to all land and islands in the Canadian North had, in the 1950s, any worry about "sovereignty." The Norwegian claims to the Sverdrup Islands had been settled around 1928. The Danes never made a claim to Ellesmere Island. There was no possible doubt about Canadian sovereignty over land in the 1940s or 1950s. The straits between the islands was – and still is – another matter.

Ben Sivertz has written that there has been no challenge to Canada's Arctic sovereignty "since Britain and Norway vacated their claims in the last century." Sivertz said that during the time he was an Arctic official and then NWT commissioner, he had no contact with Canadian or American military planners, or with those dealing with sovereignty problems. "I operated under the 'need to know' principle and recommended it to all my employees," he told me.

But the recently revealed record of Canada's defence posture in the Arctic presents a different perspective, especially considering the long American military presence in the Canadian North. Alvin Hamilton says the Defence Department often lied to the Department of Northern Affairs in cases of national security involving the Arctic. Even Robertson admits that Northern Affairs was often ignored by other departments dealing with major issues in a way that might not coincide with Northern Affairs aboriginal policy.

Hamilton, speaking of the time when he was minister of northern affairs in the late 1950s, said that he, personally, was denied landing rights by a U.S. officer commanding a DEW Line station. "He didn't even know he was out of the U.S.," Hamilton said, adding that his protests to the NORAD (North American Air Defence Agreement) commanders quickly opened up the DEW Line stations to him and other Canadian officials. Hamilton said there was no direct U.S. military pressure on him as minister, but "we had no choice because the Russians' main line of attack would be over the Pole."

Apart from the underlying tension between Americans and Canadians, there were a few difficulties involving the relocated refugees. When north Keewatin Inuit were moved to Baker Lake from Garry Lake, they were asked to switch their eating from caribou to freshwater fish. Some refused on the grounds that freshwater fish were fit only for sled dogs.

Duncan Pryde quoted his boss, Sandy Lunan, as saying the reason for periodic starvation was that the Keewatin Inuit refused to catch fish until after the caribou hunt was over. By that time, Lunan said, the lakes were frozen eight feet deep. This would be totally disastrous at a time of diminished caribou herds because a dog team normally eats one caribou in two days, and soon there would be nothing at all to feed either man or dog.

Building a Team

One of Sivertz's problems was finding suitable personnel for administrative posts. Few whites had any Arctic experience, and among Mounties and Bay men who knew the country there were even fewer who understood the new policies of enlightenment. Traditionally, the northern white man was seen in the south as a noble, almost godlike figure, dispensing justice or alms to subservient savages. The exceptions to this fiction were the independent traders who "went native" and married Inuit girls. Yet Sivertz found some remarkable men.

The most famous was James Houston, a Toronto-born artist who went to the NWT as part of Keenleyside's social program. He was fascinated by Eskimo soapstone carvings, and the Eskimos in turn were fascinated by his sketching on paper. He found that they had a natural talent for drawing, and it struck him that they might supplement their meagre incomes through silk-screen prints for southern customers. In 1949 Houston went to Japan to study print-making, then returned to the Arctic, this time to Cape Dorset, traditional centre of the Thule culture. Houston discovered many soapstone carvers and taught others to draw on paper and how to make prints literally "off the stone."

"Eskimo art" was totally unknown to the southern public, though a few mining executives had handsome collections. Houston took a few boxes of carvings to Montreal and dropped into the offices of the *Montreal Standard;* where Helen Gougeon, a staff writer, was deeply impressed. She and a few friends held a public exhibition in her

Westmount home, and the *Standard*'s colour supplement, *Weekend*, gave the carvings a special section. That was the beginning of Eskimo art as an industry.

Houston was living at Cape Dorset and working for the Canadian Handicrafts Guild when Sivertz hired him. He stayed with the Arctic Service for six years and organized Inuit cooperatives. These groups have played an important role in promoting Eskimo art and have also provided competition to the HBC as suppliers of food and consumer goods.

Another outstanding member of Sivertz's team was Peter Murdoch, a Newfoundlander who had spent many years in Baffin Island with the HBC. He had a mystical concept of the Arctic, and his chief pleasure was to take off in winter with an Inuit friend (male) and two dog teams, living off the land and staying out as long as they could. "You don't take any food with you," he explained. "I once stayed out six months and travelled most of the way around Baffin Island." Asked what happened if no game appeared, Murdoch shrugged. "You starve a little," he said. "That's good for a man." He said he married his French Canadian wife because "French Canadians have learned to live in a northern climate."

Murdoch later took over the Eskimo co-ops from Houston and expanded them greatly from a base in Quebec City. His greatest strength was a deep understanding of the Arctic, and ultimately he had considerable power as an administrator. But the North is so complex that the authorities in one area often know little about another.

In the early 1960s, I was present when Murdoch visited the Dog Rib community of Fort Rae, near Yellowknife, which was almost as poor as the Keewatin. Murdoch enthusiastically tried to persuade the Dog Ribs to start making and selling arts and handicrafts to southern whites. He showed them Eskimo carvings and prints as examples of desirable work. The Dog Rib elders listened courteously, and then Chief Jimmy Bruneau thanked Murdoch. However, he added, the Eskimos were traditional blood enemies of the Dog Ribs and it would not be fitting to do the kinds of things that Eskimos did. The Dog Ribs and other tribes did produce their own beautiful beadwork, caribou and mooseskin jackets, and moccasins for the white market.

～

The Eskimo co-ops were a tiny part of the social program launched in the 1950s, which was and is much misunderstood by southerners.

Robertson realized at once that no matter how much food was flown to remote camps, the continuing problem was housing. The Inuit were living on the land, in igloos in winter and skin tents in summer. Such dwellings were wonderfully ingenious and were satisfactory as long as the occupants were healthy, but crowd a big family together in a small, damp igloo, with plenty of germs around, and you literally produce a death trap. Better housing had to be provided and with it medical services to help those already sick and to prevent disease from spreading. That meant nursing stations. Schools were needed, along with police posts, missions, and quarters for the builders of the houses and the administrators who would attend to local needs on an ongoing basis.

From the very start, Ottawa understood the dilemma: leave the Inuit alone to their traditional ways and there would be starvation and widespread death from disease. Save their lives and you made yourself responsible for their future as well. Ottawa decided the Inuit had to be brought into the 20th century and be prepared to live in it. That meant schools that taught English and white men's skills so that the Inuit could cope with a wage economy.

The mandarins had no doubt that a wage economy would ultimately come to the North. They believed the fur trade could not sustain the Inuit for long and that the diminishing supply of land and sea mammals could not feed them. So it was decreed that schools would be built, as well as the support base needed to keep them going. The result was instant towns.

Arctic Towns

Today, the Delta has four important communities: Inuvik, Tuktoyaktuk, Aklavik, and Fort McPherson. Originally, the most spectacular showpiece was Inuvik, which rose like Camelot on the permafrost of the Mackenzie Delta. But its creation has been clouded by misdirection and misinformation. The popular story is that Ottawa made one of its classic goofs, deciding in a panic that the residents of Aklavik were about to drown in a flood and moving them, helter skelter, to a new location eighty kilometres away. And then, the legend went, Ottawa spent millions on this useless white elephant, only to have the Aklavik people move back to their perfectly safe habitat on the banks of the Mackenzie's east channel.

The truth was rather more complex. During the reorganizational

period from 1947 to 1951, it was decided that an administrative centre was needed for the western Arctic. Akalavik had a police post,
missions, an airfield, and the HBC. It was next door to the Yukon,
close to Alaska, and within easy range of the Beaufort Sea. Ben
Sivertz, then an assistant to M.   -General Hugh Young, deputy minister of resources and development, was sent north on a three-month
orientation tour in 1950. Part of his job was to visit Aklavik and study
major building projects. He found that Aklavik had been serving its
administrative function quite well but could not be expanded to
accommodate a much larger resident population. For one thing, the
soft, spongy land of the Delta was not suitable for large-scale building. Also, in such a location, sanitary problems would be a nightmare.

Sivertz asked engineers and town planners to find a suitable site.
The location they chose was on the east channel of the Mackenzie.
Building at Inuvik began in 1955. It was conceived from the first as a
showplace for the latest Arctic technology, as a scientific experimental station, as a military garrison post to demonstrate Canadian sovereignty, and as a regional capital. Residents of Aklavik were invited to
move there and many did, especially after one of the periodic floods
that plagued the older community. Aklavik continued its comfortable
existence and even thrived as prosperity came to the area; it remained
the centre of the muskrat trapping industry in the Delta.

Building Inuvik from the permafrost up was one of the most significant signs that Canada was determined to occupy the whole of the
NWT. Planners envisaged a radically different community, using new
techniques for Arctic survival. The town had to have the potential for
almost infinite expansion, with land suitable for a major all-weather
airport and runways long enough for the new long-range transports
and bombers. It had to have an adequate supply of fresh water and
land solid enough to bear large buildings such as schools, barracks,
hospitals, community halls, skating arenas, and office complexes.
Aklavik was nice but it didn't measure up.

Contractors placed the buildings on stilts that were anchored in
the permafrost. They were laced together with the utilidor, a system
of sewer and hot-water pipes and electrical cables housed in wooden
tunnels on platforms above the ground. This meant that it was easy to
dissipate heat without melting the permafrost. The electrical, fresh
water, and sewage services, all above ground, could be serviced
quickly and easily, even in the coldest months. The town was built
well above the Mackenzie, out of reach of floods, while a nearby lake

supplied fresh water and the airport was a few kilometres away. By 1960 Inuvik was a going concern and a model (some called it a horrible example) for the building of other Arctic communities.

More than any other site in the NWT, Inuvik symbolized Canada's determination to make herself known as an Arctic power. The Russians had been active in their North since the 16th century, and the word Siberia conjured up visions of terrible living conditions and slave camps – under czar and commissar.

It is not surprising that Canada has tried to discover what has been happening in the Soviet Arctic – to learn from the good things and avoid the mistakes. This was one reason that Prime Minister Pierre Trudeau visited Norilsk during his late 1960s visit to the USSR. He found a 19th-century-style city of old-fashioned, multi-storey brick buildings. The labour turnover was 200 percent a year despite high wages and various other perks. The air was full of pollution and the tundra was being seriously damaged. The USSR has been opening up the enormous mineral wealth of northern Siberia since the 1920s. Norilsk, at about the same latitude as Inuvik, today has a population of 180,000 and stands at the hub of a great open pit mining complex as well as oil and gas developments. Unfortunately, the impact of hundreds of thousands of industrial workers on the land north of the Arctic Circle has been disastrous.

In contrast, the U.S. did little with Arctic Alaska until the 1968 oil and gas discovery at Prudhoe Bay. There was an old scientific station at Point Barrow, more like a moon outpost than a working community. The town of Barrow called itself "the largest Eskimo town in the world," but it was badly built and had very few modern facilities. The best model for Canada was Greenland, where Denmark has exercised an enlightened policy for generations. Like everyone else involved in the Arctic, the Danes made mistakes. Their settlements have undergone many changes, but today they appear to be well designed for the environment. Canada could (and did) learn a good deal from Greenland.

Inuvik was built over six years in a classic sequence: first came the machine shop, then a school with attached residence, then a nursing station, then a police post, then a power plant. The utilidor tied everything together. In the early days, the Inuvialuit, Indians, and Métis working on construction lived in wooden shacks called "512s" (because they covered 512 square feet), located on mud flats between the new town and the river. The indigenes were too poor to afford the heat, water, and sewage disposal of the utilidors: human waste was disposed of in the traditional way – in the notorious "honey bags" (ordinary green garbage bags).

Consequently, the flats became a slum, which included the low-rent apartment buildings thrown up in the area to house workers' families. One of the most prestigious native leaders, Agnes Semmler, lived in a 512 because she couldn't afford anything else; she was co-founder of the Committee for the Original People's Entitlement (COPE) and later was deputy commissioner of the NWT.

Like most company and government towns, the planned community was hierarchical. Apartments and individual houses were colour-coded to show exactly what salary bracket the occupant was in.*

The magnitude of Inuvik was impressive. Both the elementary and the high school had residences for students from outlying communities. The military base contained a garrison, and there were two large hotels, the Mackenzie and the Eskimo Inn. The Mad Trapper bar, named for Albert Johnson, the so-called Mad Trapper of Rat River in the 1930s, became a famous watering hole.

Almost from the first, Inuvik was a truly interracial community. One of the best musical groups was led by a young Inuvialuit vocalist and featured both whites and Indians.

As time went on, the early slums on the lower bench became a little less slum-like. In the 1960s the oil rush began, and Inuvik was host to hundreds of prospectors, geologists, riggers, roustabouts, and seismic technicians. The crews flew in from oil camps, then continued on by jetliner to Edmonton and points south. Sometimes the tiny airport was jammed shoulder-to-shoulder with oil crews, bureaucrats, soldiers, muskrat trappers, entertainers, promoters, and hippies.

Although Inuvik was an intended as a model, it was not duplicated, because northern planners found that they had to tailor every community to local climate and terrain, the availability of fresh water, and the size of the population. It was found, for instance, that while the utilidor worked fairly well in Inuvik, it was too expensive and unwieldy for places with a population of up to 1,000. Such settle-

---

*Bob Rhodes, the earthy and talented broadcast executive, was at one time manager of the CBC's Inuvik radio station and as such one of the town's leading citizens. He and his wife, Anne, kept a sled dog team chained outside and hundreds of pounds of fishheads were constantly simmering on the stove. The stench was remarkable, and Bob's peers felt he was letting the side down. But he was brilliantly successful in Inuvik and several other northern posts.

ments came to be served by tank truck rather than sewage and water lines.

Inuvik was the most spectacular of the new Arctic towns, but it was only one of twenty-odd that stretched from Grise Fjord on Ellesmere Island to Eskimo Point in the Keewatin. While the all-weather airport and radio communication made the new towns possible, heavy gear and construction supplies came in by water. The HBC had been supplying its eastern Arctic posts through the annual voyage of the Naskopie. The sailing season was very short: along the Arctic coast it was only about six weeks long. Ships like the *Naskopie* and the *Arctic* brought in lumber, cement, hardware, and furniture, as well as trade goods and food, and took south the furs from the posts. When Ottawa went into the business, the water route was divided in two. Ships still sailed annually from Montreal or Quebec for the eastern Arctic, while in the west, Northern Transportation Company Limited (NTCL) had one barge terminus at Hay River and another at Tuktoyaktuk on the Beaufort Sea. As soon as the Great Slave and Mackenzie broke up, the barges would be towed down the river, supplying each community as they passed.

At Tuktoyaktuk, barges or ice-breaking ships would be loaded to supply true Arctic towns like Sachs Harbour, Holman, Paulatuk, Cambridge Bay, Coppermine, Spence Bay, Chimo, and Pelly Bay. Anything that didn't spoil was shipped by the sea lift, which was absolutely essential for bulk products like prefab houses, heavy machinery, fuel oil, and gasoline. The northern communities could be kept going on a week-to-week basis by plane, but the sea route was essential. With this combination of ocean and river routes, which were closed most of the year, and air service that was able to operate 90 percent of the time, the Arctic towns were built quickly.

In the eastern Arctic there was, from the first, heavy pressure on available housing. Prefab houses, or lumber to construct differenᵗ types of buildings, came by the sea lift but never in sufficient quantᵗ ties. As the Inuit moved in from the land, they were urged to buy houses from the local housing authorities established by Ottawa. There were some – never enough – rental units, and Eskimo families found themselves crowded together in two- or three-bedroom frame houses. When the children grew up and got married, there seldom were houses for the new couples, so they were forced to remain with their parents and in-laws.

Theoretically, the Inuit and Inuvialuit could still live outside town in igloos and tents while they sent their children to school, but Alvin Hamilton said, "Once you get a woman with a kitchen and a fridge you get a contented housewife." Bob MacQuarrie, longtime resident and member of the territorial legislature, recalls that he arrived at Baker Lake in 1966 as a school principal and "that was the last year the people lived outside town in igloos."

Houses and apartments were built by the federal government for the white southerners who served the communities – teachers, doctors, nurses, engineers, bureaucrats, and some construction workers. The government also built schools, nursing stations, community halls, machine shops, garages, powerhouses, and office buildings for the myriad government employees who made it all work.

In a sense, every community needed two complete towns: one for the Inuit and one for the whites serving them. The government was often criticized for not teaching native languages, but Gordon Robertson has pointed out that none of the new teachers spoke Inuktitut or any of the Indian languages: they had to teach in English. Teachers, nurses, doctors, bookkeepers, mechanics, carpenters, electricians were given all kinds of inducements to bring them north: high salaries, hardship allowances, housing supplements. It usually wasn't enough. Most of them left after a year, or perhaps after a single school term.

The government had total power and the indigenes none. The mandarins decided on policy in Ottawa; the northern service officers carried it out with the authority of rajahs. They (or their underlings) decided who would be fired, who would get housing, who could travel – in actuality, who would be allowed to stay in a community or even in the Arctic as a whole. There were virtually no native leaders. Abe Okpik became a hero because he had one cause and one cause only: to get rid of the offensive numbered metal disks by which all Inuit were identified instead of by name.

Aboriginal Employment

The school system was designed to make Inuit and Indians capable of earning their living in a white industrial society. Some 200 Inuit were employed in building the DEW Line, and they were adept at learning mechanical trades. But what next? The government thought of mining. It reasoned that the industry might be the very test the educational policies needed. After all, from 1902 till 1914 there had been a mica mine at Lake Harbour, which employed Inuit as well as imported Scots. And a nickel mine was about to open at Rankin Inlet, close to the HBC's old trading post on Marble Island.

The mining company was not anxious to hire natives, but it bowed to pressure from Ottawa. A 1986 study of native employment by the Arctic Institute said that before the mine opened, no more than ten families lived in the Rankin area, but soon there was an HBC store, a hospital, homes for government workers, three churches, a school, and many individual homes. Sixty-five percent of the trainee miners came from Chesterfield Inlet, 25 percent from Eskimo Point, 7 percent from Repulse Bay, and 3 percent from Baker Lake. Northern Affairs built a second village, Itivia, about a kilometre from the mine, designed specifically for Inuit brought in from distressed areas. It had small houses, a school, a workshop, and quarters for white social workers. But Itivia failed because it never really got started, and most natives and whites settled in Rankin Inlet proper.

Although the mine only operated seven years, from 1955 to 1962, it did show that Inuit could adapt up to a point to industrial life. Within a year, 30 percent of the miners were Inuit, and in the last years the proportion was 72 percent. The Arctic Institute study said men were paid $6 a day and women $4. The report was sharply critical of the government's handling of the project, saying it was based on paternalism and segregation: "At Rankin Inlet, the Eskimo was being trained to be a laborer, not a citizen." Ottawa found that private industry was reluctant to participate in any broad-gauged training of aboriginal workers.*

After the Rankin Inlet mine closed in 1963, the Consolidated Smelting gold mine in Yellowknife agreed to hire some of the laid-off Inuit. The Arctic Institute said Con expected them to pull up stakes immediately and leave for Yellowknife the day after they were interviewed, leaving their families behind. "Neither the company nor the government helped its Inuit workers provide for their families until they were able to relocate in Yellowknife," said the institute,

---

*Since those early days, some progress has been made. The base metals mines at Pine Point and Nanisivik hired natives from the start, and in 1978 mine bosses in Yellowknife and Thompson, Manitoba, told me that they would hire as many qualified natives as they could find. They claimed that they actually were employing natives then, though most held surface jobs because they didn't want to work below ground. The bosses took this as a racial characteristic, but a quick check of the white population showed that few whites wanted to work deep underground either.

that the miners' families were left virtually destitute.

When Inuit miners were sent to the Sherritt-Gordon gold mine in Lynn Lake, Manitoba, "no housing was provided because the mine didn't want any separate native community." The Arctic Institute found that Sherritt-Gordon wanted Ottawa to provide two halfway houses where Inuit could stay until housing could be located, but the government refused and "suggested the Inuit should save $500 and purchase a home with help from the Eskimo loan fund." The institute concluded with damning restraint: "The Inuit felt very ill-equipped to deal with home ownership, maintenance and finance and making sure the properties and payments were attended to."

∼

Overall, the speed of change in the Territories was astonishing. In 1959, after only five years of existence, the Northern Administration and Lands Branch had burst through its bureaucratic framework and had to be reorganized. Its annual report said: "The rapid pace of northern development made desirable a complete reorganization ... to meet changing conditions. Through its emphasis on decentralization it gave much more administrative responsibility to the field." The magic word was "decentralization, which was to be the major drive of Ottawa in the North for the next fifteen years. For instance, the duties and powers of Fort Smith were expanded, and the Mackenzie District now included Coppermine, Tuktoyaktuk, and Cambridge Bay in the central Arctic, and Banks Island in the Beaufort Sea.

The Arctic Division was split into the Keewatin and Franklin divisions and had responsibility for Arctic Quebec. Ottawa remained the capital, though Frobisher Bay was becoming important. Area offices were located at Rankin Inlet, Coral Harbour, Eskimo Point, and Baker Lake, and they all reported to a regional headquarters at Churchill. Cape Dorset, Igloolik, and Hall Beach reported to Frobisher. Arctic Quebec offices were located at Fort Chimo, Sugluk, Port Harrison, and Great Whale River.

A year later came a change that was to have momentous impact. New mining regulations encouraged a much wider range of exploration. The most dramatic symbol of such progress was the drilling of the first oil and gas well in the Arctic Islands by Jack Gallagher of Dome Petroleum and Peter Bawden of Peter Bawden Drilling at Winter Harbour on Melville Island, about as far north as Resolute. The hole was a dry one, but it foreshadowed the age of petroleum exploration in the Canadian Arctic. That exploration was to have a major effect on the political future of the NWT.

Free Whites and Tied Whites

By 1960 the northern revolution had been under way for six years and was rapidly changing the lives of the Inuit. The impact was less visible in the Mackenzie Basin, where it had a different pace and a different direction. In other words, government policies, east and west, were so out of phase that drastic changes were needed to bring them together.

In the mid-fifties there were fewer than 10,000 Inuit scattered over more than a million square kilometres of tundra. A large majority did not speak English and lived a semi-nomadic life hunting and fishing. Because of the emergencies of starvation, disease, and economic chaos, they were being guided – without the slightest input on their part – into an entirely different world.

In the west, the Indians, while far from well-off, were in an infinitely better position than the Inuit and retained a good deal of cultural and economic stability. Well over half the population of the Mackenzie District was white and quite prosperous. Dr. A.W.R. Carrothers, who was to head the Carrothers Commission in 1965–66, called these settlers from the south the "free whites," in contrast to the "tied whites," who were missionaries, police, and HBC employees. Add to these the new administrators and northern service officers who were building the new towns.

The free whites lived principally in Yellowknife, but there were growing numbers in the expanding transportation centre of Hay River, the old administrative capital at Fort Smith, Inuvik, Norman Wells, and mining communities like Pine Point. Most of them arrived after the second gold boom of 1944–46. Like many frontiersmen and women, they were a vigorous lot, independent and self-reliant. They hated absentee government and itched to run their own affairs. As early as 1938, Yellowknifers had been asking for local government.

During the regime of Commissioner/Deputy Minister Charles Camsell the free whites got nowhere in their drive for self-government, and when war came in 1939 the issue was put on the back of the stove to simmer. From time to time, Prime Minister Mackenzie King expressed a little interest, but even when Ottawa began to contemplate progressive changes in 1946, the demands of the

Yellowknife whites were ignored. Dr. Hugh Keenleyside became commissioner and deputy minister in 1947, and he was an outspoken reformer in some respects – he had impressive plans for improving the health and education of the indigenous population. But he was suspicious of what he felt was white prejudice toward the natives, and he was loath to give up any of Ottawa's powers of government. As late as 1948, Keenleyside wrote to Jock McMeekan, the Yellowknife editor and agitator for representative government:

> The NWT are governed by the Commissioner, the Deputy Commissioner, and five Councillors appointed by the Governor General in Council. The Commissioner in Council has power to make the ordinances for the Government of the Territories under instruction from the Governor General in Council, or the Minister of Mines and Resources, subject to the Act of the Dominion of Parliament applying to the Territories. (H.L. Keenleyside, *Memoirs*, 1981–82)

It is relatively easy to strip away the meaningless parts of Keenleyside's careful bureaucratese. Because the NWT Council was only advisory and legislative in its powers, the commissioner was in reality the sole executive, directly responsible to the Department of Mines and Resources, which, in turn, was responsible to the federal cabinet. But as the commissioner was also deputy minister, he had a double clout.

Keenleyside seemed to have no intention of changing the power structure. Professor Shelagh D. Grant says in her *Sovereignty or Security?* that in 1948 the NWT Council investigated pleas for greater representation and "saw the problem as arising from unrealistic expectations of growth which had resulted in the initiation of projects far beyond the requirements of the community. Believing that Yellowknife would likely remain dependent on federal assistance, Council recommended that the request for a fully elected Trustee Board be denied."

In 1950, under pressure from his new minister, Robert Winters, Keenleyside reluctantly recommended that the Mackenzie District be made a separate territory with a fully elected council. The commissioner told his council: "While there are many people in the Territories who would make excellent and responsible members of the NWT Council, there are many others who would behave in an irresponsible and partisan manner."

Keenleyside said he admired the rugged white settlers, but Grant says he felt their attitudes ran counter to his approach to northern government: he thought of northern development in terms of the British tradition of "peace, order and good government," and "his interpretation of democracy and liberty did not include the American right to local self-government and squatter sovereignty or the right of a Euro-Canadian white minority to rule a non-voting native majority." Such arrogant elitism was what both the white settlers and the indigenes had to deal with when they sought some role in their own government.

In spite of, or because of, Ottawa's neglect, Yellowknife flourished. When the young mining engineer John Havelock Parker arrived from Edmonton in 1954, there were 2,000 residents. The Con gold mine was in full operation, and Giant Yellowknife was reaching peak production. John Parker recalls that gold fever was subsiding in favor of uranium. He was hired as a uranium specialist because he had spent three summers around Beaver Lake and Uranium City in Saskatchewan.

When Parker arrived, Yellowknife's Old Town on and around Latham and Jolliffe islands was being moved inland to more level and spacious quarters. Vic Ingraham's new Yellowknife Inn was the centre of New Town, with shops, restaurants, and business premises rising around it. This was a different kind of place from Old Town, which was largely male and temporary, a collection of tents, log cabins, and galvanized-iron warehouses. New Town was actually planned as a proper city, with roads, cement sidewalks, a sewage system, and zoning. The new houses were occupied by families, and the young wives were demanding many amenities.

The prospectors, bush pilots, and hard-rock miners were joined by lawyers, doctors, teachers, pharmacists, nurses, storekeepers, movie projectionists, bricklayers, mechanics, editors, printers, real estate salespeople, and insurance agents – all the inhabitants of the modern world. These were not birds of passage but permanent settlers, looking to the North for their future. Why not? Their grandparents had created Saskatchewan and Alberta from the old North-West Territories; their parents had opened the silver camps in Cobalt and had broken virgin land in the Peace River area. "These people were active, progressive and forward-thinking," John Parker recalls, remembering that he first slept in the back room of Norm Byrne's mining registration office.

The town was white, he remembers, and the Dog Ribs lived across Yellowknife Bay at Detah and spent most of their time in the bush, following game, fish, and furs. When new settlers began to build residential neighbourhoods in New Town, some Indians pitched their teepees among the rocks. There were arguments and talk of racial tensions, and the commissioner reluctantly acceded to white requests to build a new Indian village, Rainbow Valley, at the tip of Latham Island, miles from the centre of New Town. Officially, there was no such thing as a mixed-blood. Individuals of mixed race were either considered Indian – or integrated into the white community.

Yellowknifers were a busy lot, building schools and hospitals, laying sewers, opening new subdivisions, or coping with the eternal "dog problem" which still plagues northern communities. Residents were scarcely aware of the commissioner or his council, but Parker says the town "was a little island of democracy." It was incorporated in 1954 and Jock McNiven was the first mayor. At that time, Yellowknife was the only incorporated community in the NWT, and Parker said he and his friends were aware that every other settlement in the Territories was "very much ruled at the whim of senior government."

Don Stewart, another charter member of the free whites who settled in Hay River, said the territorial settlers didn't even have the vote until 1950. David Searle, who became a prominent lawyer and the territorial legislature's first Speaker, says the first real government was the judiciary. In 1956 Jack Sissons, an Alberta lawyer and politician, was appointed territorial judge and came to live in Yellowknife. "Jack Sissons led the way as far as government on the ground was concerned," Searle says. A veteran Liberal politician from the northern Alberta bush, Sissons was familiar with the isolation and disdain for the city felt by people who lived in the outback.

Instead of setting up his court in Yellowknife and waiting for the Mounties to bring in malefactors, he returned to the ancient British tradition of the circuit judge who held court wherever a few settlers could be gathered. He rightly said he would "bring Justice to every man's door." Sissons's court provided an example for the Carrothers Commission in its efforts to suggest a government suitable for all of the Territories.

∽

In the 1930s, social life in largely male Yellowknife centred around the Old Stope beer parlour and the Wildcat Cafe, not to mention

"Glamour Alley" in Willow Flats, where the whores and bootleggers resided. By the 1950s, the new Yellowknife Inn had a cavernous miners' bar, where a visitor could hear whispers of new strikes or overhear a merchant conspiring with a pilot to bring Eskimo carvings out of the Arctic illegally. There were no Indians until it became legal for them to drink in public in 1960. This – and the racist hiring practices of many bosses – made it popular for many mixed-bloods and Métis to choose the white side of their ancestry over the Indian side.

Many of the Mackenzie mixed-bloods – later commonly known simply as Métis – had worked for wages for generations, as rivermen, oil patch roughnecks, muckers in the mines, heavy equipment operators, and construction crew members. In Yellowknife they rubbed shoulders with European immigrants working underground and with southern Canadian whites who had drifted north.

Most people worked for wages and there were no fabulous gold strikes for them, but there was no unemployment and hourly rates for miners were getting better. The people with real money were the promoters and a very few prospectors able to peddle their claims to the big operators. One of the great legends of the Yellowknife Inn was a beautiful blonde European waitress. She was said to be a $1,000-a-night hooker who only plied her trade occasionally – with "strike it rich" prospectors or lucky poker players. She thriftily saved her money, bought an interest in a hotel across the street, and finally retired to an orchard in the Okanagan. It was the kind of dream anyone could share.

While the NWT's heroic northerners were not as flamboyant as the Klondike sourdoughs, the freetraders who challenged the HBC came close. Their trading methods differed sharply, though the Bay men were not all company drudges.

E.J. ("Scotty") Gall served the HBC all over the NWT before taking over the company's big department store in Yellowknife. He was a humane, thoughtful man, much given to reflection on the fate of the native peoples, but his philosophy was that of an old Arctic hand. He sincerely believed that the Indians had an acute sense of inferiority to whites because they saw the whites doing everything natives could do – and better. This, Scotty felt, led the Indians to despair, confusion, and alcoholism. "They see whites as dominant, even in their own severe environment, and they try to endure more than we can," he said. "The white man, having no sense of inferiority, doesn't try to endure the worst of the climate and takes steps to make survival easier. The sense of inferiority is destroying the Indian from within."

Gall had a deep compassion and liking for Indians: it was just that, like so many other white men from Sir John Franklin on, he felt everything would be fine if the Indians would only accept white moral and intellectual superiority and remain satisfied with their inferior position. Over and over again, this patronizing attitude was expressed by long-term Mounties, missionaries, and Bay men.

However, there were exceptions. Duncan Pryde, like Scotty Gall, was a native of Scotland and came out to the NWT as a young HBC apprentice. He joyously accepted the equality of the Eskimos and boasted of his sexual liaisons, running for territorial council on the slogan: "There's a little Pryde in the best of us." Pryde's conduct and his unembarrassed remarks about both Inuit and whites shocked the tied and free whites alike. At the height of his notoriety, he married an Indian girl who had been chosen princess of the Yellowknife Winter Carnival, though he had often said that he despised Indians. He quarrelled publicly with her and disappeared into the North Slope of Alaska, pursued by legal writs and invective.

Most colourful of the fur traders, Bay or independent, was Pete Baker, who called himself "the only Arab musher in the world." He was from Lebanon, the descendant of generations of pedlars, and worked his way north from Edmonton in the early 1920s. Instead of following the example of the Bay – setting up a post and waiting for the Indians to come to him – Baker loaded a sled with gewgaws and learned how to drive a dog team.

Baker was known in every Indian camp in the southern Mackenzie country. Once, he said gleefully, he bought a ton of oranges and loaded them on a river barge. At every stop along the Mackenzie, he sat on the stern selling oranges at a dollar apiece. NWT residents were enchanted. He opened a post at Fort Rae and was much admired by the Dog Ribs for his low prices, honesty, and supportive advice. In 1951 he was one of the first people elected to the NWT Council. (In 1954, the council was increased to nine, five appointed and four elected, all of them white independent traders from the Mackenzie District.)

~

Nothing illustrated the racial solitudes more graphically than the census. In 1955, when the total population was 26,000, school enrolment was listed as Inuit, 380; Indians, 618; "other," 1,020. Eight years later, after the school-building program in the east, Inuit enrolment was 2,494, compared with 1,187 Indians and 2,560 "other."

Educating the aboriginals would upset the political applecart in less than a generation. The 1955 census showed that the only residents capable of influencing their own destinies were the free whites. In Yellowknife they were levying property taxes, building their own schools, and running local affairs. And they were hollering louder than ever for a voice in the running of the entire Territories.

Another free white town beginning to expand was Hay River, for generations a Dehcho gathering place with an HBC post and a couple of missions. The man most associated with its rise was another flamboyant frontiersman, Don Stewart, who came to the NWT in 1940 as a radio operator for Grant McConachie's Yukon Southern Airline. Later, Stewart worked with a crew pumping out an abandoned radium mine on Great Bear Lake and in 1946 found himself in Hay River as agent for Peace River Northern Airways. His wife was the fifth white woman in the area. Only a few remnants were left of the U.S. Army's installations for the CANOL Project.

"Hay River had a bit of a commercial fishery, but anybody could see it would be an important transportation centre," Stewart says. "There was a winter ice road to High Level, Alberta, 200 miles south. It took eighteen hours to drive and after that it took fourteen to eighteen hours to drive to Edmonton. In 1948 we got a year-round road." Cree Métis from Manitoba and Saskatchewan built a fishing village at West Channel where the Hay River flowed into Great Slave Lake. Soon there were eight fish companies, and the lake was producing more than 3.6 million kilograms of fish a year.

As the only port on the lake's south shore, Hay River was a natural shipping terminal for supplies going to Yellowknife and down the Mackenzie. Settlers rebuilt the American wharfs and warehouses, and later Northern Transportation Company and Kap Transport from Edmonton brought in barges and tugs. Northern Transportation, a Crown corporation, served all the communities along the Mackenzie and many along the coast of the Beaufort Sea. Kap Transport specialized in moving petroleum gear and supplies for exploration companies.

By 1954 Hay River's population reached 1,200, half of it white. Stewart became the leading citizen, first mayor and then an elected member of the NWT Council. He had the distinction of being the first white to be defeated by a native – Nick Sibbeston, a Dehcho Métis from Fort Simpson who, in 1986, became the NWT's first aboriginal government leader. By then, Stewart was Speaker of the Legislative Assembly.

"We came up here to get away from civilization," Stewart said to me forty-six years after he first arrived. "We wanted to escape from the government and all the rules and regulations. There was no money to be made in those days but we had a lot of freedom. We didn't even have a post office: you just handed your letters to a pilot and he put it in a bag and took it away with him. Incidentally, the mail always got there – faster than it does today. We didn't really know what was going on in the eastern Arctic. We didn't know what was happening in the west either. We weren't part of Canada: we were owned by Canada."

Stewart shared the views of many of the early free whites as far as the natives were concerned. He believed that there would be no "native problem" in the future because "within three generations the Indians will be assimilated." Yet as the indigenous leadership increased and the territorial government changed, Stewart was able to grow with it. Ultimately, he believed, the NWT could and should be shared on an equal basis by the various resident races – "if only southerners and southern government will keep their noses out of our affairs!"

~

Stewart, Scotty Gall, John Parker, and a pilot named Lyle Trimble from the Delta led the ever more insistent cry for provincehood and/or the splitting of the NWT into two parts. To forward-looking whites in the Mackenzie District, Ottawa's policies were paralysing. At the same time that the new Conservative prime minister, John Diefenbaker, was proclaiming his vision of the North and advocating "roads to resources," the key mandarins were concentrating almost totally on the problems of the Inuit.

The resource boom was continuing. One of the biggest lead-zinc mines in the world was about to open at Pine Point, a few kilometres east of Hay River. The Great Slave Lake Railway to serve that mine and bring cheaper supplies to all of the western NWT was under construction and would be completed in 1964. The highway link was being extended from Hay River around the western tip of Great Slave Lake to Yellowknife on the North Arm. At the same time, the road to the south was being improved so that Yellowknife as well as Hay River would be directly linked with Edmonton most of the year. Still another branch of the Mackenzie Highway was extended in the 1960s to Fort Simpson, where it ultimately hooked up with another highway

up the Liard to Fort Nelson, B.C., on the Alaska Highway. The industrial boom was felt in the eastern Arctic when the Rankin Inlet nickel mine opened in 1955.

Out of this ferment, the movement to divide the Territories
became urgent in 1959. It had no native input at all. As Dean
Carrothers later said : "The Eskimos had no appreciation of what the
issue was about and the Indians simply wanted their treaties to be carried out. After that, they wanted to be left alone."

The division plan was simple. The Mackenzie District woul
become a separate territory with its capital at Fort Smith. The eastern
Arctic would be called Nunassiaq in recognition of its overwhelmingly Inuit population. No capital was suggested because there were
no real towns as yet: the only two with any facilities were Rankin
Inlet, a purely industrial community, and Frobisher Bay, an American
military base.

Commissioner Gordon Robertson proposed that the boundary
should be an extension of the border between Manitoba and
Saskatchewan, extending in a straight line to the Arctic Ocean. The
Mackenzie Delta, Victoria Island, Banks Island, and some of the
Queen Elizabeth archipelago would be in the Mackenzie territory.
Because all of this land was populated by Copper Inuit of the central
Arctic or Inuvialuit from the Delta and Beaufort Sea, there was bound
to be some confusion.*

By 1961 the idea of division had been accepted by many southern
politicians, and two bills were before Parliament. However, Gene
Rhéaume, the Conservative MP for the NWT, found the indigenous
population had no input, and when he took his misgivings to other
members of the House of Commons, there was enough concern to
force the shelving of the bills.

At that stage, in 1963, the Diefenbaker government was replaced
by Lester Pearson's Liberals. Arthur Laing became the new northern
affairs minister and Gordon Robertson became clerk of the Privy
Council, while Ben Sivertz was named commissioner. Policy changes
were under way which would be as important as those launched ten
years earlier by St. Laurent.

---

*The idea of a division following the tree line in a northwest/southeast direction
came later. It had the advantage of separating the Indians from the Inuit, but there
were difficulties in running a boundary line through hunting areas claimed by both
groups. Also, the Inuvialuit and Copper Inuit were not comfortable with the Baffin
Island Inuit.

The first step was to make the commissionership a full-time job, separate from the deputy ministership. Sivertz's office remained in Ottawa, and that made little difference for him because he had been working continuously in the North for a long time. The council had been altered again in 1960. Three of the appointed members came from outside the government and from outside Ottawa as well. By 1964 the only federal civil servant on council was the deputy commissioner, and even that changed in 1967.

The council held its fall meeting in Frobisher Bay in 1964, and one of the newcomers, Air Marshal Hugh Campbell, suggested that it was time to study the political future of the Territories and come up with a practical plan that would look after the needs of the aboriginals as well as the whites. Council passed a unanimous resolution requesting a full-scale inquiry into the political future of the NWT.

No one in the North had yet heard the name Fred Carrothers, but he was about to become a prime mover and shaker of everybody and everything.

Chapter 5

The Carrothers Report

Alvin Hamilton said that when Prime Minister St. Laurent announced his new northern policy in 1953, he made the minister responsible "czar of the North." Hamilton, who became that minister in 1957, relished the title. Later, Jean Chrétien called himself "the last emperor in North America." From 1963 to 1968, Arthur Laing was one of the most powerful and influential of these ministers, yet he probably would not have referred to himself in such terms. He was too wily and experienced a Liberal warhorse to deal much in labels.

Laing inherited from the Conservative Walter Dinsdale a department that needed an infusion of new blood and some new direction. The Arctic revolution, launched by St. Laurent and Jean Lesage and carried on effectively by Hamilton, had run into conflicts of purpose growing out of the program for the Inuit in the east and the lack of program for the free whites and Indians in the west. The Diefenbaker era had begun with great fanfare about northern visions, then flickered out in party quarrels. Hamilton went to Agriculture in 1960, and Lester Pearson scorned Diefenbaker's "roads to resources" as building trails "from igloo to igloo." Actually, the continuation of the revolution depended on the resourcefulness and determination of the deputy minister commissioner, Gordon Robertson.

In spite of Pearson's scorn of Diefenbaker's vision, Laing's Arctic policy was a good deal more vigorous than the Conservative program had been since the departure of Hamilton. Both parties were aware that development of national resources had always been popular with voters; besides, Yellowknife was vociferous about getting a share of the benefits and authority. It was time, Laing realized, to find out whether the Territories should be divided or whether a central policy could adequately cope with more than three million square kilometres and several diverse races. He decided to set up an advisory commission that would look into the constitutional future, as advocated by the NWT Council in 1964. But who would make up the commission?

John Parker was an inevitable choice: he was mayor of Yellowknife and one of the most respected of the free whites. The chairman was not so obvious. On Laing's short list was A.W.R. Carrothers, dean of law at the University of Western Ontario and a distinguished authority on the common law. Laing asked his executive assistant, Jack Austin, what he knew about Dean Carrothers. As it happened, he knew quite a lot because he had been one of the professor's students at the University of British Columbia. He remembered being impressed. Then Laing recalled that he had known Carrothers's father. That clinched it: the dean had a distinguished academic record, solid achievement, a pleasing personality – and he was a member of the old boys' club.

The first choice for third commissioner was Maurice Strong, the maverick genius from Manitoba who was head of the Power Corporation in Quebec and was becoming Canada's first global ecologist. He turned the job down. Laing then selected Jean Beetz, professor of constitutional law at l'Université de Montréal and an authority on civil law. He had served as a consultant when the new African nation of Tanzania had drawn up a landmark constitution. Later, Beetz would become a justice of the Supreme Court of Canada. "Jean was an ideal choice," Dr. Carrothers recalls. "His academic discipline complemented mine perfectly. And John Parker was an equally good selection because he knew so much about the North. We all got along famously." Dr. Walter Kupsch, a Dutch-born geologist and director of the Institute for Northern Studies at the University of Saskatchewan, was appointed executive director.

In the summer of 1965, the commission, plus interpreters and reporters, got into an amphibious flying boat and started visiting Indian villages south of Great Slave Lake. Ten years later the Mackenzie Valley royal commission headed by Mr. Justice Tom Berger made such tours famous, but in 1965 they were unheard of. Distinguished academics and learned judges are no more eager than the average bank president to suffer hardship, risk, and black flies. (The pioneer had been the NWT's Judge Jack Sissons and his travelling circuit court in the 1950s.) Parker and Kupsch were outdoorsmen, but they knew little about the eastern Arctic. The professors had no knowledge at all of the North, either east or west.

Like many visiting the Arctic for the first time, all members of the commission were emotionally affected, and Dr. Carrothers wrote movingly of the human situations he observed. In Cambridge Bay, he

loaded the coffin of a two-year-old on the plane. Storms, fog, and ocean swells prevented a landing at Clyde River. Twice the plane got stuck in the mud, at Milne Inlet and Mary River.

The commissioners learned from personal experience the differences between the free whites, the Inuit, and the Indians. They began their tour at exactly the right time to assess the progress of the revolution, now ten years old. At Bylot Island, across the strait from Pond Inlet in North Baffin, Carrothers observed only one Inuk subsisting on the land: everybody else was in prefab houses in the town; the lone hold-out stayed in an igloo in winter, a tent in summer, using a dog team. Otherwise, the skidoo had already replaced the dogs.

The first of three tours began in the old Chipewyan trading post of Fort Resolution, and the commissioners immediately found they were in foreign territory without maps. At their first community meeting, the commissioners invited Indian bands, non-status Indians, and mixed-bloods. The chief and his elders refused angrily, saying the mixed-bloods had no treaty rights. Two separate meetings were required.

"When we finally placated the Indians, the meeting was arranged in what we thought was a normal way," Carrothers related. "We commissioners sat at a table on a stage in front. After a while, the chief picked up his chair and moved it up on the platform beside me. Only then could the meeting go on." No one had bothered – or was able – to brief the commissioners on the common courtesies expected by the indigenes. John Parker traced the problem back to the first meeting of the commission in Ottawa:

> Instead of dutifully going to the office of the deputy minister as may have been expected, Dr. Carrothers arranged for our own office in Northern Affairs. He asked the deputy to come to us. When we had finished questioning them, Dr. Carrothers thanked them politely and said that would be all. They looked surprised, as if they expected he would turn over the meeting to them. But it was important that the chairman establish our total independence. No one ever challenged it.

Carrothers said wryly that the commission received very little further briefing after that first meeting. "One official gave us some help but didn't seem very forthcoming when we asked him about the Indians. We learned later all his experience had been in Frobisher Bay, among the Eskimos."

The commissioners soon found culture shock worked both ways. "When we set up our meeting at Rankin Inlet, we were told we should be patient with the local people," Carrothers said. "After making our first statement we asked the audience to say anything it felt like. There was a long silence. Then a hunter rose and said, through our interpreter, that he and others were worried as to whether the commissioners would understand what they had to say. We all looked at one another in astonishment because that was just what we had been worried about them!"

In Tuktoyaktuk, an old woman asked whether she could send a letter to the commission. The chairman said of course but asked why she didn't give it to the area administrator. "The area administrator is the problem we have to write about," she said tartly. In Spence Bay Carrothers asked a woman what she wanted in the future and she replied: "I need a mattress." Summing up the attitudes across the NWT, Carrothers said:

> The Mackenzie Valley whites were hollering for their political rights. There was no input at all from the natives. The Eskimos had no appreciation of what the issue was about; the Indians wanted their treaties to be carried out, and after that they wanted to be left alone. In any case, there wasn't even much conversation among the various Indian tribes, who spoke different languages from one another and didn't have much in common. To them, the constitutional issue was a white man's problem.

As he went from community to community, Carrothers found it almost impossible to find a common denominator. He discovered quite soon why political division would be a bad thing: "It would turn the Arctic into a living museum for the Department of Northern Affairs." In the west, he found, "the demands of the Indians were not very profound," while "whites were demanding provincial status: not whether, but when." After the tours were completed, the commission held a three-day conference at Montebello, Quebec. Experts were asked to supply "holistic solutions" that could be applied to the whole NWT. Carrothers recalled:

> After a day and a half, I realized it wasn't going to work. The experts knew only about specific times and places: they knew nothing about any other specific time and place. I could see their advice

would not help solve general problems. Of course, this was a situation I'd discussed frequently with Jean Beetz. As a civil lawyer, his training was to go from broad principles to individual cases, whereas I was just the opposite as a common lawyer who moved from the specific to the general. When we were travelling from place to place, I tried to find a thread suggested by an individual situation which could be applied to the experience of all.

In deep frustration, Carrothers retired to his suite and began drawing up a list of precepts based on the notes he had taken during the tour.

I remembered the Code of Justinian, the Eastern Roman Emperor in the sixth century who codified Roman law. Justinian's scholars had a mountain of conflicting laws, and he dealt with the problem of finding a common base by outlining what he called "generalized precepts." These began: "The precepts of the law are these: To live honestly. To give every man his due ... and so on. That was the beginning of our report.

Beetz, Parker, and Kupsch joined Carrothers in late afternoon, wondering whether he was sick. He read them his notes, and they became excited and began supplying input from their own observations.

The Final Report

The final report, tabled in the House of Commons in October 1966, was exhaustive in its findings and devastating in its conclusions. It listed aboriginal problems as

packing case houses, tents and igloos, primitive sanitation and bad water, pernicious illness, persistent coughing, infant coffins, young men languishing in unemployment, an increase in juvenile delinquency inherited from the urban world of the white man, a demand for a greater police service stemming to a large extent from a liquor problem that may itself be an adjunct of unemployment, and other indications of depression and demoralization.

It added: "The fact remains that the people of the North are economically depressed, virtually to the subsistence level, yet the land

harbours wealth in national resources. This is one of the major para-
doxes of the North." In an uncompromising analysis of the argument
over keeping native cultures intact, the report said:

> If one value judgment dictates there should be a move to decrease
> the high rate of infant mortality in the North, then to attain that end
> the peoples of the North must obtain adequate food, clothing, med-
> ical and para-medical services, and, above all, warm housing. But a
> move to improve housing is a move, depending on the location and
> the nature of the housing, that is likely to entice indigenous peoples
> away from camps and their traditional ways of earning a living, and
> into communities and hence toward a cultural erosion of an indeter-
> minable depth.
>
> Again, a move to educate is a move that is calculated to atten-
> uate a language containing concepts and words which have served
> the culture of nomadic people for thousands of years, yet does not
> serve and probably cannot serve in a 20th century industrial econo-
> my.
>
> A move to introduce responsible government is a move that
> imposes strange concepts of social and political relationships on
> people who did not solicit them.
>
> A move to administer justice according to law – Canadian law
> – is a move that superimposes on indigenous cultures the social val-
> ues which shaped that law.
>
> The precepts, then, are value judgments that were devised in
> order to give direction to our studies and to break into manageable
> dimensions the attack on the vast problems of the North.
>
> They form the foundations of our recommendations.

Carrothers and his colleagues showed a remarkable understanding
of the issues puzzling the aboriginal peoples. For instance, the commission's report defined Ottawa as "an idea which ultimately symbolizes impersonal power."

Taking note of "the abrasiveness in the relationship between
Indian and white," the report gave the following as the causes of
Indian hostility: the failure of Canada to implement some clauses of
Treaties 8 and 11; lack of economic opportunity; social rejection; and
physical isolation in communal enclaves on the edge of white-
dominated communities.

"He [the Indian] lives near subsistence, in a poor white sub-culture, and in an irreversible state of dependence on the white man's way of earning a living, an unwilling ward of the state and victim of custodial care," said the report, which added that the per capita income of NWT Indians was one-sixth the national average. The Indians earned 72 percent of their income from trapping, guiding, and so forth, while 28 percent came from pensions, treaty money, family allowances, unemployment insurance, and welfare. "We expect the Indian will be much more cautious than the Eskimo of any offer from the white man of political opportunity," the report said presciently in a sentence worthy of *Time* magazine in its prolix reversement.

Statistics cited were staggering: one-sixth of the potential Indian-Eskimo labour force were employed, compared with two-thirds of the white force; only 2 percent of NWT management positions were held by indigenes.

> Some young people seem to be educated virtually into a state of unemployability. The white man's education makes them dissatisfied to earn their living in the traditions of their forebears, yet they cannot find or keep employment in the white man's economy.
>
> But the indigenous peoples crave educational and economic opportunity. Parents favor educational opportunities for their children without fully understanding the implications, for at the same time they wish to preserve their cultural heritage. In their representations to us, they asserted a preference for jobs to welfare.

The report hammered home the realities of the tragedy: while native income was less than one-sixth that of whites, the cost of living was "substantially higher" than in the south. "As one writer stated, 10,000 people in the NWT live well; 15,000 live dreadfully," it said. In a passing reference to a phenomenon studiously avoided in Ottawa's ongoing social revolution, the commission said that construction of the DEW Line "influenced the lives of the people more than any other change." Carrothers said scornfully of the NWT Council: "One might find southern city councils more powerful and influential."

The commissioners were unafraid to grasp thorny issues and actually supplied a blueprint for future negotiations with the aboriginals:

> It may well be argued that attaching so much importance to political and economic development is imposing values of the 20th cen-

tury western white man on civilizations whose cultures are antipa-
thetic to those values. But there are a number of reasons for reject-
ing the argument that government policy should be based on this
view. First, contact by the Indian and Eskimo with the 20th century
western white man has long since gone beyond the point of no
return; there is no practical possibility that either ethnic group might
return to the "noble state" he was in before the insurgence of the
white man. The question is not whether the peoples of the North will
move forward under the white man's influence but to what they will
move.

Second, there is no articulate body of opinion – a fact which
admittedly may be argumentative – among the Indians and Eskimos
that they wish to live in isolation, and there is much evidence of a
desire – i.e., in the wants of parents (there are exceptions) that their
children be educated in public schools – to adapt to and adopt at
least some of the white man's values. The white man is now part of
the environment of the indigenous peoples of the North (biological-
ly he has become part of the peoples themselves). There is no escap-
ing that fact.

The commission quoted the Glassco Royal Commission on
Government Organization: "What is needed is a program of economic rehabilitation and social development which the local people
understand and in which they will cooperate – an object more easily
stated than met."

These penetrating comments preceded the commission's recommendations, of which the principal ones were:

1. The NWT should *not* be divided "at this time." (Division might
   come later.)
2. The seat of government should be moved from Ottawa to
   Yellowknife.
3. There should be a commissioner, an executive council which
   would provide ministers for the various departments of government, and a Legislative Assembly with fourteen elected and
   four appointed members.

The recommendations continued:

• The commissioner should have the rank of deputy minister,
  directly responsible to the minister of northern development.

- The deputy commissioner should be appointed by the commissioner and chosen from the elected members.
- The assembly should "have the powers of a provincial legislature, subject to listed exceptions."
- A development board from the federal and territorial governments and the Economic Council of Canada should be set up, as well as a NWT Development Corporation, to attract new industry.
- The territorial government's departments should be Economic Development and Finance, Local Government, Education, Welfare and Social Services, Public Works, Justice, and Lands and Resources.
- Ottawa should continue to hold subsurface land rights while surface rights "in and adjacent to Yellowknife" should go to the government of the NWT
- A review after ten years. (This resulted in the 1978–80 Drury Report.)

Arthur Laing quickly accepted Carrothers's recommendation to move the GNWT to Yellowknife, though Ottawa kept tight control over the only revenue-producing sources available – natural resources. Some recommendations were quietly dropped, postponed, or modified. The main thrust of the report came into effect over the next twenty years but mainly as a process of evolution presided over by two far-sighted commissioners, Stuart Hodgson and John Parker.

The Carrothers investigation had a major effect in another direction: it provided philosophic justification for St. Laurent's northern revolution. It also supplied a well-thought-out foundation for the negotiating positions of subsequent ministers dealing with native claims: Jean Chrétien and John Munro on the Liberal side, David Crombie and William McKnight for the Tories. Ten years later, the whole approach of Carrothers was challenged by Tom Berger's commission into the pros and cons of a pipeline in the Mackenzie Valley, but by Berger's time the face of the NWT had changed. The Indians and Eskimos were serious players, able and willing to outline objectives strikingly different from those of the white settlers.

In 1966, however, the revolution was only getting into high gear, and its symbol was the order to move Ottawa civil servants to Yellowknife. It is extremely doubtful whether they knew what they were getting into. One person benefited directly from the commission's experience – John Havelock Parker, mayor of Yellowknife and mining engineer. What he learned as a drummer for democracy was put to brilliant use when he became deputy commissioner and later commissioner.

Summing up his goals twenty years later, Carrothers said:

> I had three vital steps in mind. The first, and most important, was that local government had to be brought to the people throughout the NWT. When we started, only Yellowknife had any kind of local government structure, with, perhaps, Fort Smith, Hay River, Inuvik, and Fort Simpson moving in that direction. The indigenous peoples had to learn how to look after themselves and be given the government structure to carry out the work.
>
> Secondly, the federal government had to provide financial and economic help on every level so that an infrastructure could be built, and built quickly. Third, there was an urgent need for local schools which would replace the large residential schools located far away from the families of the children. If the educational system was to work, it had to be part of the local communities.

In an aside paying tribute to his commission colleague, John Parker, Carrothers said: "John Parker has behaved in a way that has made all of this possible." The Carrothers Commission paved the way for the first real territorial government. Now it was time to bring it into the NWT.

Chapter 6

Ottawa Arrives:
Thirty Tons of Paper

On 18 September 1967 two DC-7 aircraft landed at Yellowknife. The first one carried seventy-four civil servants and their families; the second thirty tons of files. The capture of Yellowknife by the Ottawa bureaucracy was thus accomplished without a shot being fired.

Actually, the invaders were met with flags and pipers. The newcomers and those who welcomed them were celebrating the birth of Yellowknife as capital of the NWT. Until then, the character of the town had been embodied in the headframes of the Con and Giant gold mines. Now the heart of the community was to centre on a new office building rising across the street from Vic Ingraham's Yellowknife Inn.

The issue of whether Ottawa or Yellowknife should be the seat of NWT government had been briskly debated for years before the Carrothers Commission was appointed in 1965. Ben Sivertz, the first full-time commissioner, appointed in 1963 to succeed Gordon Robertson, felt at home in Ottawa. Yet he also told Northern Affairs Minister Arthur Laing that he intended to resign as commissioner as soon as the Carrothers Report was finished so that he could lobby for a more powerful, better-paid commissioner and council.

Sivertz was the link between two completely different phases of the Arctic revolution, the last of the old Ottawa hands to exert direct control over the indigenous peoples and the free whites. As a key administrator under three commissioners, Sivertz had ushered in Louis St. Laurent's revolution; he had been in Ottawa since 1945 and knew his way around the corridors of power. In the early days, he also found it was physically easier to administer the NWT from Ottawa than it would have been from any point inside the Territories.

However, as Fred Carrothers foresaw and Arthur Laing agreed, the whole emphasis in NWT government would have to change.

From 1905 to 1966, the Territories had been run off-handedly either by senior policemen or by federal mandarins. Theoretically, the minister, a politician, was in charge, but in reality the man in effective control was the deputy minister and his network of civil servants. Like Robertson and Robertson's predecessors, Sivertz was a member of the club. However, as commissioner, he had far less authority than Robertson had: Sivertz was responsible to the deputy minister; Robertson had been the deputy minister as well as commissioner.

Sivertz could see the weakness of a full-time commissioner's position under the new rules, but he did not anticipate the ingenious way Laing would deal with it. The minister decided to go outside the Ottawa bureaucracy to find a new commissioner. Sivertz opened the way for him when he said he intended to resign; Laing now could look for a successor without any restrictions.

Laing found his Conservative predecessor had supplied him with a ready-made tool for his purpose: in 1960 it had been decided to select three of the NWT Council's appointed members from outside Ottawa and the civil service. This opened the political and patronage doors, and in 1964 Laing chose Stuart Hodgson, a flamboyant union leader from Vancouver, as a representative of labour. Hodgson, an official of the International Woodworkers of America, had gone to a Geneva conference as a delegate of the Canadian Labour Congress.

The process of shunting Commissioner Sivertz to the sidelines remains cloaked in mystery. L.A.C.O. Hunt, Sivertz's long-time colleague and perhaps rival, said in his memoirs that Laing fired Sivertz for refusing to move to Yellowknife. Hunt died before Sivertz could confront him. Sivertz says he actually was one of the first to advocate moving the capital to Yellowknife and that Laing asked him to stay on for two years after the Carrothers Report was released in 1966. Whatever the real reasons, Sivertz today admits he was ready to quit. By 1965 Hodgson was the heir apparent. In that year he was named deputy commissioner,* and David Searle, first Speaker of the NWT legislature, told me:

> We all knew the deputy would be named commissioner and there
> was a lot of rivalry between Hodgson and John Parker, who had lots
> of support in Yellowknife. Then Parker went to the Carrothers

*Hodgson says that his selection as deputy was a matter of blind Chance: "In 1965 the deputy, who was a civil servant, had a heart attack. I was asked to prepare the council's budget because I'd been financial secretary of my union local."

Commission and when Stu became commissioner it was natural to
name John deputy. It worked out very well: they were a great team.

By 1967 the NWT had been governed from afar by senior policemen or faceless bureaucrats for sixty-two years. Now it was about to
be governed by a colourful, dynamic individual who was actually
going to live in the Territories and visit all of their fifty-odd communities every year. He was as exotic to the bureaucrats as he was to the
indigenes and soon became a visible presence everywhere: a big,
powerful man with a deep voice and a bristling mustache. In winter
(which meant most of the year) he wore a brightly striped outer coat
made from an HBC point blanket, a voyageur's toque, and an arrow
sash. The Inuit called him Umingmuk – muskox – and the name fit-
ted him well, but he was also as cunning as Nanook the white bear,
as lordly as Aivik the bull walrus.

There is a good deal of evidence to show that the colourful image
Hodgson exhibited was all that he was meant to have, even though the
resident commissioner was supposed to have authority equal to that
of the deputy minister. The civil servants who flew north in 1967 to
start the government of the NWT in Yellowknife were, after all, federal bureaucrats, accustomed to taking their orders from headquarters. From their perspective, the deputy minister was still their boss.
Hodgson's functions were ill-defined, and he was an outsider, the first
commissioner not from Ottawa. It may have been that Arthur Laing
saw him as a useful public relations figure, bustling from outpost to
outpost in his flamboyant costume.

John Bayly, who started as a junior administrator in the eastern
Arctic and rose to be a prominent Yellowknife lawyer and adviser of
native organizations, says that in the early stages Hodgson was given
little authority and almost nothing to do. "He had enough time to sign
everybody's liquor permits when he came to the hamlet I was in,"
Bayly told me. "Ottawa still ran the show and did all the administration through the kabloonat it had sent to run the local communities."

If that was true at the start, Hodgson was smart enough, tough
enough, and ambitious enough to change the situation. He gradually
fought for control of his own civil servants and he did remarkably
well. Looking back on his first days, Hodgson says:

> I found an awesome task. I vowed I would concentrate my efforts
> on the communities, on the people, and I would dedicate myself to
> a group of people who, to me, were living in a stone-age environ-

ment and yet were being compelled to move in one generation into the jet age. Putting the emphasis at the community level was probably the best way to go.

Hodgson and Parker now became a team. Importantly, it was a team that did not originate with the Ottawa civil service and therefore was free of traditional strings.

Great progress had been made since 1953, but the task had just begun. Carrothers had noted that 1,000 houses had been provided for 9,000 Inuit, but housing remained one of the worst problems. There were fifty-one day schools compared with twenty-two a decade earlier, and classrooms had gone from 88 to 321; enrolment from 2,279 to 6,415. But the schools were being run on the Alberta and Saskatchewan curricula: all teachers were recruited in the south; pupils were taught almost exclusively in English; no attention was paid to local or cultural backgrounds. Social welfare payments had risen tenfold, from a quarter million dollars to $2,582,000. This was a million dollars more than the Defence Department spent in the North in 1964–65. Almost unnoticed was the beginning of the CBC in 1959, when it took over several local radio stations and began to upgrade them.

∾

Here are some of the things that were happening across the NWT in the early and mid-1960s:

In Hay River a flood forced the building of a new white community a few kilometres from the old commercial town. All the houses had high, narrow gables like Swiss chalets, and the area was known as "Disneyland."

The high school was painted in seventeen designer colors. In the days before Pacific Western began flying 737 jets into the central Arctic, transportation depended on Single Otters, which landed on skis or floats. For the six weeks of break-up and the six weeks of freeze-up, settlements were cut off completely except by air.

Towns like Coppermine were dependent on the HBC. A visitor was likely to meet Inuit women selling carvings illegally, protesting the Bay's policy of shipping in junk carvings from the south and selling them to tourists at outrageous prices. The Bay paid local artists almost nothing, and even their own co-ops were niggardly because they were marketing most of the local product in Toronto or

Montreal. Profits went into the co-op's general fund. The Bay store hadn't much variety, but its supplies were adequate. The display of hunting rifles was impressive: high-powered weapons with long-range scopes, priced at $400, that could bring down a polar bear or walrus. The Bay manager told me that local hunters took great pride in their skills and demanded the best.

There was no television, radio reception was poor, and there was no recreation centre with electronic games and videos. Once or twice a week, washed-out prints of third-rate movies were shown in the school to a collection of puzzled Inuit children and bored kabloonat. God knows what the Inuit made of the Florida beach scenes and bikinis! A visitor desperate for news could hike up to the Ministry of Transport's radio cabin and talk to the operators. Otherwise one went visiting, dropping in on Father Lapointe and admiring the two-toned sealskin stations of the cross in the Roman Catholic church. Local women did the needlework. Or one might drop into the teacherage and talk books with a middle-aged schoolteacher (the Mounties gossiped that she was always reporting perverts looking in her windows).

There was no restaurant and no liquor or beer – at least not out in the open. With no hotel, tourists dossed down in an abandoned DEW Line barracks. Sleeping bags were borrowable, and food could be bought at the Bay. If canned beans were too prosaic, tourists might beg a frozen char from an Inuk and cook their own meals. There was much visiting and much tea drinking back and forth, and even if a visitor didn't speak Inuktitut and the hosts spoke no English, they always seemed glad to see him or her and showed great hospitality. In thirty Inuit communities from Tuktoyaktuk in the northwest to Pangnirtung in the southeast, life was simple. Most of the Eskimos were beginning to realize that they weren't going to starve or die in an epidemic this year or next. On the other hand, the more perceptive could see their traditional habits disappearing.

Fred Carrothers told of a white missionary he met at Cape Dyer, the easternmost tip of Baffin Island. He tried to hitch a ride, and when Carrothers refused him on policy grounds, the missionary pleaded that he might be stuck for a long time in that remote spot. Later, Carrothers found out that the man had arrived in Cape Dyer only a day or two before the commission: he simply couldn't stand the Arctic.

Carrothers said that the most depressing community he visited was Fort Rae, the biggest Dog Rib settlement: "To me, it symbolizes the impact of economic and social deprivation on the soul of man. A strange town. On an island near the shore of Marian Lake. Foot bridges here and there. Built on rocks. Sewage flows into the water system and pollutes it. Villagers don't want to move."

I was in Fort Rae shortly before Carrothers and found the commissioner's description of the physical town accurate. I came to Rae from Coppermine and noticed that the Bay store carried only the cheapest of single-shot .22-calibre rifles. When I asked the store-keeper why, the answer was devastating: "These people are so poor they can't even afford these rifles. They trap or snare fur-bearing animals, but there no longer is any market for pelts. Most people here live on welfare. A gun is pure luxury."

On that trip, I talked to Chief Jimmy Bruneau through an interpreter. The chief, in his eighties, was against the compulsory public education being brought to his community. He pointed out that the traditional Indian life in the bush involved the whole family and followed the seasons. Boys learned hunting, trapping, and survival techniques from their fathers. Girls learned how to cook, sew, skin animals, and look after the camp from their mothers. If they were forced to attend the white man's school, they would never learn the Indian skills they needed. There had been a Catholic mission and residential school at Rae all of his life. But the new government schools, he felt, would demand that the children go to school most of the year, and that would not work if Indians were to spent their lives in the bush.

Chief Bruneau was dead right in his own terms, yet Rae was one of the first Indian communities to adapt successfully to the changing order. A new town, Edzo, was built across the lake, twenty-four kilometres away by road. It had sanitation and fairly well built houses. The Dog Ribs were the first Indians in the NWT to take over the running of their own school. Today there are classes in the Dog Rib language and training in Indian skills and traditions. The school year is adapted to the seasonal needs of a hunting and fishing people. Some of the most dynamic NWT native leaders have come from Rae-Edzo.

~

In July 1966 the GNWT had sixty employees, but hundreds more were involved with Northern Affairs in Ottawa. The transfer of the capital to Yellowknife would drastically change that proportion as hundreds of civil servants were brought in to every part of the Territories. The men and women who moved to Yellowknife in 1967 formed a cadre that some people thought would take over the majority of management tasks within a few years. A number of talented federal officials transferred to the territorial government to run the various departments and divisions.

Stuart Hodgson says he believed in transferring government to the Territories from the very start, and he set about strengthening it in various ways. First of all, he built a personal base among the people as effectively as a southern senator running for re-election. Everybody but babes in arms soon knew Big Stu personally – and the babies had probably been kissed by him. Second, Hodgson began to press Ottawa to give more power to the NWT Council and urged especially for more elected members. He also advocated putting Indians and Inuit on the council. Third, he took the first steps toward bringing local government to the communities, east and west. Fourth, hardest of all, he tried to get control of his own civil servants and make them responsible to the Territories rather than to the feds. (Gary Mullins, assistant commissioner in the 1970s and one of those who came out of the Ottawa establishment, noted that officials in Northern Affairs "basically treated the GNWT as if it was a subdivision of the ministry." He said the mandarins had fought like tigers to preserve their authority and had tried to change the NWT's four semi-autonomous regions into ten divisions, which could be controlled from Yellowknife and Ottawa.)

Hodgson's long-range dream was to shift power from Ottawa to Yellowknife, from Yellowknife to the regions, and from the regions to the communities. He doggedly opposed the mandarins and at one stage asked the minister to shift him to another government position, far from Ottawa. He managed to keep Arthur Laing's confidence and that of Laing's successor, Jean Chrétien. Gradually, power shifted from the mandarins to the GNWT, thanks largely to the skill and determination of Hodgson and Parker, aided by a little luck.

By 1970 changes in the structure of the GNWT gave Hodgson an edge, and he pushed his advantage by hiring a firm of management consultants from Ottawa (P.S. Ross and Partners) to report on the GNWT's organization. The firm found that the problem was partly a consequence of having a staff of generally competent and dedicated personnel, trained in the federal bureaucracy, whose responses to new challenges and new situations were heavily conditioned by past experience and training.

The way things were run at the GNWT headquarters resembled the practice in Ottawa, with all of Ottawa's appurtenances in terms of ordinances, protocol, structures, attitudes, and other trappings. The basic design of the GNWT was set long before the Second World War. Consequently, the organization was largely vertical while the problems were horizontal, more so, perhaps, in the NWT than in any other area of the Government of Canada.

Noting that half the NWT's population was under twenty-one, the report said few of the senior government staff were under forty. "It's difficult for the senior public servants to see the environment as different from that in which they grew up," it said. "This, in turn, handicaps them in developing new objectives and programs." The consultants found that the number of GNWT civil servants had risen from less than 100 in 1967 to more than 1,500 in 1970 and the budget from less than $5 million to more than $90 million.

There was not one mention of the native population in the report – nor of any need to recruit senior staff from the long-term white residents of the NWT! However, the report recommended a strong search for new, much younger talent to bring in new ideas and shake up the system: "Recruiting is obviously extremely difficult in the North. We believe that consideration should be given to short-term contracts of say two years for a young MBA just out of college."

This savage attack on the Ottawa-bred bureaucracy hardly needed to remind its reader that Hodgson and Parker were the only senior officials from outside the federal government – and that there were many clashes between them and the mandarinate.

What saved Hodgson in the long run was the growing influence of elected members of the NWT Council. They were giving a voice to the various regions and races of the Territories at the same time that the number of GNWT employees was increasing at such a rate that Ottawa found it hard to control them. The first stages of democratic government were beginning to push the absolute authority of the civil servants out of the way. Meanwhile, Hodgson, Parker, and their efficient (though often difficult) colleagues tried to correct early mistakes and improve government generally. Several glaring mistakes had been made, especially in housing and education.

Early on, someone in Ottawa decreed that houses should be uniform through the NWT. This saw Mackenzie Indians living in prefab houses heated by oil furnaces even while fire logs were just outside the door. At Fort Good Hope, originally built of logs, it was decreed that the attractive and efficient log cabins should be replaced by houses of saw-cut lumber.

In education, early thinking was that any schools beyond grade six should be residential, located in the bigger communities of

Yellowknife, Hay River, Fort Smith, Fort Simpson, and Inuvik. Parents hated losing their children for months at a time, and many children lost their language and heritage. But after a while good sense took over, and it was decided to supply all basic education in the communities, no matter how small. The residential schools remained, but they were not compulsory.

Obtaining good teachers who could and would stay the course was always difficult, and the problem still has not been solved. Many teachers were discards from southern systems, misfits or incompetents. Others couldn't stand local conditions and left quickly. All kinds of incentives were offered: well-built, low-rent houses; high pay; numerous vacations and travel allowances. Liquor prices were standardized so that someone living in remote, high-cost Spence Bay would pay the same price for a bottle of Scotch as a resident of Yellowknife. (The incentives applied to other professions and trades, of course, and were not very successful in holding southerners in the North for long.)*

In the health field, doctors, nurses, and bureaucrats did a remarkable job of cutting infant mortality and preventing the terrible epidemics of the past. But with hundreds of patients being moved to extended-care hospitals in the south, some of them literally got lost. Small children with tuberculosis were taken to Edmonton or Montreal and never came back. Some died and were buried in the south. Others disappeared into white society. Grieving parents, many of whom did not speak a word of English, were left totally in the dark.

With the Inuit, one of the difficulties was identification. The first policeman to deal with them found that they had no family names – only individual names. This problem was solved by giving each one a metal disk stamped with the letter E (for east) or W (for west) and a number. Some Inuit and a few whites were outraged by this depersonalization. Gordon Robertson felt, however, that numbering Inuit was not much different from the social insurance numbers of all Canadians. The program had one impact: as I noted earlier, Abe Okpik was so angered that he made it his life's work to have the system abolished. He won, and Stu Hodgson made him the first Inuk on council.

---

*This was why native leaders like Nellie Cournoyea maintained that the white population majority in the Mackenzie Valley was an illusion: she claimed the permanent white population was very small, less than the Dene, the Métis, or the Inuvialuit.

∾

Political development was full of ironies. Under 1967 rules, the commissioner was the sole executive of the GNWT. The council had legislative and advisory functions only. The GNWT administration was responsible to the commissioner. But this was all illusion. The real executive, the real power, rested with the Department of Northern Affairs in Ottawa. And not just with the minister or the deputy minister: the area administrators and the settlement managers took their orders from Ottawa, not Yellowknife.

Dr. Walter Kupsch of the Carrothers Commission wrote of the powers of government in the 1977 GNWT Annual Report: "The NWT Act does not contemplate a fully responsible government inasmuch as the Commissioner, appointed to his office by the Federal Government, is answerable to the Minister and the Governor General." Dr. Kupsch added: "In practice, the Commissioner has always recognized a much greater responsibility to the Council than the Act would indicate." This practice was to have a profound effect on the future of the Territories, as we shall see in later chapters.

For a long time, so many Ottawa departments had fingers in the northern pie that government was a tangle of interlocking authorities. An example occurred at a government meeting in Inuvik in the mid-sixties. At that time, the commissioner and council met once a year in Yellowknife and once in some other NWT community. Each meeting lasted about two weeks. In between, an executive committee travelled to various parts to hear complaints and deal with urgent business.

In this case, the executive committee was led by Air Marshal Hugh Campbell, one of the most effective of the appointed members. The mayor of Inuvik was Dick Hill, head of the government's scientific laboratory there. He carefully prepared a list of fourteen community issues that urgently needed attention. When he presented them, the council members listened impassively. Then the air marshal replied: "The first three belong to the Department of Health. Nothing to do with us. Number five involves education and goes to Ottawa. We have no jurisdiction in seven, eight and nine." The two most minor issues were in the GNWT's jurisdiction and were quickly settled.

That left the most important matter: Inuvik desperately needed fourteen new houses. "Yes, we're involved in housing," said Campbell. He paused: "But we only have $4,000 available."

Mayor Hill looked stricken. "But we badly need fourteen houses. That wouldn't cover one house."

Campbell shrugged. "It's up to you: you can have it if you want. But that's all there is."

"Oh, we'll take it! We'll take it!" Hill said. "Thanks very much!" Such was territorial government in the 1960s.

∼

The way to democracy led through the council, even though Laing hadn't accepted Carrothers's recommendation for a fully elected, provincial-style legislative assembly. Until 1975 part of the council was appointed, and administration was bossed by the executive committee appointed by the commissioner. But progress was steady.

In 1966 elected members were increased to seven, including the first Inuk ever elected, Simonie Michael of Frobisher Bay. Three years later Hodgson appointed the first Indian member, Chief John Tetlichi of Fort McPherson. That was an important year: Ottawa transferred responsibility for education, welfare, economic development, and municipal affairs (in the Mackenzie District only) to Yellowknife. A year later, responsibility for Keewatin and Baffin went to the GNWT.

This was why the civil service rose from 60 in 1966 to more than 1,500 in 1970. The face of Yellowknife had changed, and several regional administrative centres took a leap forward.

Yellowknife's physical changes were remarkable. Headquarters for the GNWT was the Laing Building across the street from the Yellowknife Inn. Soon the one-time mining camp had its own highrise apartment building, and another was built to take care of distinguished visitors like the Queen or the prime minister. Government departments built substantial edifices, and there was a new courthouse and city hall. The luxury Explorer Hotel commanded the highway from the airport, and the Prince of Wales Museum and Cultural Centre rose across from it. There were high-class restaurants and cocktail lounges, a YMCA, and condominiums. The streets saw promenades of pretty secretaries in high heels and bright young men with briefcases.

The transfer of whole divisions of government strengthened the commissioner's power immeasurably. With hope in his heart, Hodgson announced in 1968 that "a program has been established to recruit and train a number of junior executive officers for field and headquarters service. This group will be attached to the Commissioner's office, under the direction of the Executive Assistant." Even before Hodgson's Ottawa consultants reported their findings about the senior civil servants, the commissioner was building his own army to replace them.

At the beginning of 1968, Sid Hancock, director of local government, became chairman of a committee studying the structure of the various GNWT departments. When its report came down, Hodgson had the structural framework on which to hang the various departments when they were handed over to him by Ottawa in 1969 and 1970. Progress continued with the council: in 1970 the number of elected members was increased to ten, among them the first Indian elected to council, two Inuit, and one Métis – Nick Sibbeston of Fort Simpson. Another Inuk was elected from the High Arctic in 1972. Appointed members were reduced to four.

But the milestone year was 1975 when the NWT Act was amended so that all members – fifteen now – were elected. The first Speaker elected by the members was David Searle. Two council members sat on the executive council, "advising the Commissioner on broad policy matters." Three of those elected became ministers in charge of government departments: Peter Ernerk, an Inuk from the Keewatin; Arnold McCallum, a schoolteacher from Yellowknife; and Dave Nickerson, a white businessman, also from Yellowknife. Like its Yukon counterpart, the NWT Council began to call itself a legislative assembly, just as in the provinces.

In theory and in law, Commissioner Hodgson had almost total authority and had to consult no one but the minister of northern affairs, who was his undisputed boss. But in practice, Hodgson had voluntarily handed over many powers to his "advisory" council and to elected members: democracy was getting closer. "I had almost absolute authority in the beginning and almost instantly began to devolve it," Hodgson said proudly, seven years after he retired.

Several major steps remained before the NWT could establish its autonomy: more than fifty communities along the Mackenzie and in the Arctic had to learn how to run their own affairs; the Territories needed to establish financial responsibility; the aboriginals – Indians and Inuit – had to be given a full role in their own destiny.

The native movement toward participating in government – as contrasted with the social revolution, which had been thrust upon them in the 1950s – began in the mid-1960s, almost unnoticed by the white bureaucrats in Ottawa and the free whites in Yellowknife. This native involvement was to change the Ottawa formula for running the NWT beyond recognition.

The Mighty Mackenzie. This is an aerial photograph I took while flying north in the summer of 1972.

The Barren Lands between Coppermine and Yellowknife, the graveyard of explorers from Sir John Franklin's day and of unwary bush pilots even today.

Crossroads of history – Fokker Super Universal bush plane meets
Indian dog team at Fort McPherson in 1930.

Airstrip at Wrigley on the Mackenzie – a traditional supply post by
water or air for the North Slavey, the Dehcho, and the Sah'tu.

Courtesy of National Aviation Museum

Hazards of bush flying: summer (above) – Pilot James Vance's Fairchild has trouble landing on Bear Lake, 1930; winter (below) – Matt Berry's Fairchild gets buried at Coppermine.

Courtesy of National Aviation Museum

Courtesy of Imperial Oil

Workhorse of the North *(this page and top facing)*

The original workhorse *(above):* these German Junkers-Larsen single-engined, low-winged, aluminum-skinned air freighters were leased by Imperial Oil to serve their oil refinery at Norman Wells in 1921.

Courtesy of National Aviation Museum

The Noorduyn Norseman, designed and built in Canada, carried thousands of northerners and their supplies with great dependability. Its successors were the larger, single-engined de Havilland Otter and the Twin Otter. This Norseman is shown coming in to land at Whitehorse, Yukon.

Lockheed Hercules air freighter at Yellowknife.

Gilbert Labine's uranium exploration camp at the eastern end of Great Bear Lake, 1920. Pilot Leigh Brintley flew the Super Fokker bush plane seen moored.

Yellowknife float plane base during the gold rush in the 1930s.

Bush work camp on the Blackwater River near Wrigley during building of the Mackenzie Highway in 1972.

Courtesy of Imperial Oil

Man-made islands on the Mackenzie River at Norman Wells, created by Imperial Oil as platforms for oil drilling rigs.

Photo by John David Hamilton

Christmas tree atop 40-metre drilling rig on Yukon-B.C.-NWT border.

Gas drilling riggers down 5,000 metres at -35°C in Beaver River country in corner of B.C.-Yukon-NWT boundaries.

Jack Gallagher, at his peak in 1972 – the greatest of the oil-gas plungers. He took Dome Petroleum of Calgary to a multi-billion-dollar corporation and then crashed spectacularly.

Photo by John David Hamilton

This man decorated his trusty snowmobile with a muskox skin and head at the Umingmuk Frolics parade in Cambridge Bay.

Photo by John David Hamilton

The turbulent Liard River where it joins the Mackenzie at Fort Simpson. The landing stage sometimes rises 27 feet in 24 hours during floods from the mountains to the west. The ferry links Simpson with the Mackenzie Highway to Edmonton.

DEW Line Station outside of Cambridge Bay on Victoria Island, winter of 1985.

Map room of DEW Line station at Cambridge Bay showing the picket-line of 21 defence bases in 1985. The stations stretched from Alaska to Baffin Island.

Nativity scene, missionary style. An oil painting in the Anglican church at Aklavik illustrates the typical white attitudes toward natives until the last generation.

Spring fish camp at Holman on the Gulf of Amundsen, Victoria Island, an Inuvialuit settlement.

Wildcat Cafe in Yellowknife's "Old Town," where mining deals were consummated in the 1930s.

Downtown Inuvik, 1974. The Roman Catholic "Igloo Church" is seen at right.

Photo by John David Hamilton

Kingalik Jamboree, late May, Holman, 1985. Old ladies lead the outdoor, all-day dancing at the spring games. The community was dry, so the high spirits were natural.

Photo by John David Hamilton

Remote Holman had a population of 400 but its Kingalik Jamboree attracted enough charter planes to cause a traffic problem on its airstrip.

Holman's beautiful harbour on Amundsen Gulf, Victoria Island (1985).

Pond Inlet drum dancers from North Baffin at Expo 87 in Vancouver.

An Inuit television producer prepares for an out-of-doors shoot outside of the Inuit Broadcasting Corporation's production centre in Cambridge Bay. The network broadcasts by satellite to more than 20 Inuit communities in the eastern and central Arctic. All broadcasts are in Inuktitut.

Cambridge Bay's notorious Dome Houses, built to imitate igloos but far from wind- or snow-tight. The author lived in the first one. His wife, Sheila, and Irish wolfhound Queen Morgan le Fay are in foreground.

The last of the absentee landlords, Gordon Robertson, the famed mandarin in the 1950s and 1960s who served as NWT commissioner part time and ushered in many revolutionary federal policies.

Ben Sivertz, Robertson's successor and the first full-time commissioner in 1963. His headquarters were still in Ottawa.

Courtesy of A.W.R. Carrothers

Dr. Fred Carrothers, who chaired the Constitutional Commission of the 1960s that made recommendations to move the nominal capital from Ottawa to Yellowknife and give the residents of the NWT a hand in their own government.

Courtesy of Stuart Hodgson

Stuart Hodgson, the "Umingmuk (muskox) commissioner" who moved his civil servants to the NWT and made Yellowknife the capital in 1967. He started the first decentralization of government program.

Jean Chrétien as minister of Indian affairs and northern development in the Trudeau government of the late sixties and early seventies.

The controversial Tom Berger, whose commission on the proposed Mackenzie River pipeline focused national attention on native rights and land claims in the mid-1970s.

Bob Blair, Calgary petroleum tycoon and Tom Berger's great adversary. He sponsored the Maple Leaf Pipeline proposal.

John Havelock Parker, the mining engineer and one-time mayor of Yellowknife who transferred political power to the NWT natives during his ten years in the commis-sionership. He was the last of the colonial administrators.

James Wah Shee, a Dog Rib from Fort Rae. As president of the NWT Indian Brotherhood, he was the first important Indian leader. He brought in the Dene Declaration but was ousted by his rival, Georges Erasmus.

Georges Erasmus, the radical Indian leader who created the Dene Nation and later became grand chief of the (national) Assembly of First Nations and co-chair of a royal commission on Indian constitutional affairs.

Courtesy of Tagak Curley

Tagak Curley of Coral Harbor, founding president of the Inuit Tapirisat of Canada, and a cabinet minister in the government of the NWT.

Photo by Hans Blohm

John Amagoalik of Grise Fjord on Ellesmere Island, the most northern settlement in Canada. He was Tagak Curley's successor as president of the ITC and one of the most important negotiators of the Nunavut constitutional and land claims agreements.

Andrews-Newton Photographers

Rosemarie Kuptana of Sachs Harbour, Banks Island, president of the ITC during final Nunavut negotiations and the imaginative president of the Inuit Broadcasting Corporation.

Courtesy of the Government of the Northwest Territories

Hon. Nellie Cournoyea, NWT government leader after 1991, co-founder with Agnes Semmler of the Committee for Original People's Entitlement (COPE), and veteran NWT cabinet member. Her father was Norwegian and her mother Inuvialuit, and she was born near Aklavik.

Hon. Ethel Blondin-Andrew, Slavey Dene from Fort Franklin on Bear Lake, who became Liberal secretary of state for training and youth in 1993. She was a schoolteacher and senior NWT official before she entered politics.

A historic moment as DIAND and Inuit negotiators complete the Nunavut Agreements, May 25, 1993.

Kenojuak, an artist from Cape Dorset, created this stoneprint depicting
the four seasons. It is titled *Nunavut.*

Photo by Hans Blohm

Chapter 7

Native Organizations

Fred Carrothers found it impossible to get through to the Mackenzie Indians. He said they didn't seem to grasp the importance of the constitutional change that his commission was signalling. Carrothers was bringing tidings of democracy for all; the chiefs and elders were only concerned with enforcement of their treaties and the way the Indian Act worked (or failed to work).

This failure of communication in 1965–66 got to the very heart of the dilemma of the reformers from the south who wanted to take the NWT from colonial status to self-government in the wide Canadian pattern. Carrothers and his fellow commissioner, Jean Beetz, were steeped in the ancient traditions of British law, justice, and self-government. Their colleague, John Parker, was not a scholar: instead, he was working hard at democracy as mayor of Yellowknife. The three commissioners – and Arthur Laing who had commissioned them – were dedicated to the principle that every Canadian citizen should have equal rights with his or her fellows: the right to vote, to even-handed justice, to travel freely, to own property.

The Indian chiefs and elders met by the commissioners in Fort Resolution, Snowdrift, and Fort Rae seemed unaware of and unconcerned with the whole heritage of British democratic government. Speaking through interpreters because their knowledge of English was sparse or non-existent, the chiefs asked what the commissioners intended to do about Treaties 8 and 11. These leaders of the Chipewyans, Dog Ribs, Dehchos, and, further north, Gwich'in and Sah'tu had no experience with democracy as southerners knew it, but they had plenty with the government that administered the Indian Act and with the only two treaties involving aboriginals north of the 60th parallel.

Treaty 8 had been signed at Fort Resolution in 1900; Treaty 11 at Fort Providence, Fort Simpson, Wrigley, Fort Norman, Fort Good Hope, Arctic Red River, and Fort McPherson in 1921. To the impartial observer reading the treaties today, neither did much for the Indians, and it is difficult for a white person to understand why the NWT Indians clung to them so desperately. The answer to that question goes back more than a century and involves the attitudinal gulf between Indians and whites. From the time of the opening of the West to settlement, the federal government had a policy that treaties with the Indians would be negotiated only when a railway had to be built, settlement on the land was expected, or mineral and timber developments might be in the interests of the country as a whole.

This was the philosophy behind the first seven of the "numbered treaties" in the Canadian West, which started in 1871. The empire builders reached northern Saskatchewan, Alberta, and British Columbia in the early 1880s. In a treaty research report put out by the Department of Indian Affairs and Northern Development (DIAND) in 1986, Dennis F.K. Madill wrote:

> After the HBC surrendered its charter in 1870, the Indians could no longer depend on the Company for social services ... The Federal Government felt no obligation toward those who had not signed a formal agreement, nor did it wish to negotiate a treaty with Indians whose land was not required for settlement or which was of little apparent value.

Madill noted that in the winter of 1887–88 "there were indications that Indians in the Fort St. John area of B.C. were killing their horses for food." As gold rushers began moving north through the Peace River country, NWMP Inspector J.D. Moodie reported that the Beaver and Sekant Indians were "a miserable lot, half starved most of the winter, and utterly unreliable." He added: "There is no doubt that the influx of whites will materially increase the difficulties of hunting by the Indians, and these people who, even before the gold rush, were often starving from their inability to procure game, will in future be in a much worse condition."

Missionaries, Mounties, and the Indians themselves all petitioned Ottawa for a treaty. The Woodland Cree of the Athabaska River and the Chipewyans of the Slave saw with alarm that more and more white and half-breed trappers were invading their territories. Worse, some of the outsiders were using poisoned traps which were illegal but hard to eradicate. Ottawa refused to negotiate for nearly fifteen years, until the Klondike strike brought a rush of miners, prospectors, trappers, and drifters into the upper Peace and Athabaska. It finally seemed to Ottawa that the "true North" was about to be opened up.

The Woodland Indians already knew what was going on: ever since the Red River Rebellion of 1869, Plains Cree and Métis had been moving northwest, to the Saskatchewan, to the Athabaska, to the Slave. The Woodland Cree and Chipewyans, first in line of advance, desperately wanted to protect their own territories, not only from whites but also from other Indians and Métis. The Woodland Cree and Chipewyans knew that without treaties, nothing could stop marauding whites and half-breeds. Treaties would at least regulate the invaders and provide some protection to traditional tribal lands. Besides, there was a desperate need for food and medical treatment.

Treaty 8 was negotiated and signed in 1899–1900 with the Woodland Cree, the Beaver, and the Chipewyan, Yellowknife, Dog Rib, and Dehcho – all of whom lived south of Great Slave Lake. The only real sticking point was the insistence of these forest Indians that they did not want reserves like those given to the Plains and eastern Indians: they wanted guarantees that they could continue trapping, hunting, and fishing in small family groups across the territories they had occupied for many generations.

This was hard for the white negotiators to comprehend and ran against the whole history of treaty-making: the idea had always been to give treaty signers small reserves and encourage them to abandon hunting and gathering in favour of agriculture. Victorian whites were convinced that hunting and trapping weren't proper "work" (they were more like "fun") and that the Indians should settle down to planting crops and tending cattle on small plots of land. There was almost a note of distaste in the tone of J.A.J. McKenna, treaty commissioner at Fort Resolution, in reporting to the Privy Council: "The Indians of the North Country act rather as individuals than as a nation and any tribal organization which may exist is very slight."

The chiefs and elders were verbally assured that Her Majesty's Government would guarantee their way of life. They believed such guarantees were being written into the treaty. No such luck. Treaty 8, negotiated primarily by the commissioner who had handled Treaty 7 in southern Alberta, followed the pattern of all the other numbered treaties. The exact terms of Treaty 8 were not translated into the aboriginal languages until 1968.

When the Carrothers Commission arrived in 1965, the NWT Indians were still trying to get Ottawa to live up to the provisions of

Treaty 8. They did win one concession: no reserves were set aside in the treaty, and the first and only reserve in the entire NWT came in 1974 at the request of the Dehcho band at Hay River.

Treaty 8 was repeated on a bigger scale in 1921 with Treaty 11, which involved the rest of the Mackenzie Basin Indians. Here, too, missionaries, tribal leaders, and even Indian agents pleaded unavailingly for years with Ottawa to negotiate a treaty. In 1907 H.A. Conroy, inspector for Treaty 8, visited the various bands along the Mackenzie and found them "distressed ... by widespread disease and hardship. The situation from Fort Simpson to Fort McPherson seems to demand federal action." (The Indian Affairs accountant said blandly that no funds were available.)

The causes of the sad economic plight of the NWT Indians have never been adequately explained by historians, though Father René Fumoloe has revealed a great deal in his milestone study of Treaties 8 and 11, *As Long as This Land Shall Last*. In northern Saskatchewan, Alberta, and B.C., game and fur supplies were reduced as early as the 1890s by intruding whites and half-breeds. Ironically, high prices for furs, which had seemed to promise economic security, brought devastation because they encouraged whites and half-breeds to compete with the aboriginals.

According to *Denendeh*, the history of NWT Indians published by the Dene Nation, the bush Indians lived in single family groups and stayed in well-defined territorial limits. The family lived on the land, moving now and then as the catch and the seasons dictated. The men and their dogs hunted for meat – caribou, moose, hare, ptarmigan. Only a few devices were used, such as snares, deadfalls, box traps, and, after their invention by white men, steel leg-hold traps. A certain balance of nature was struck.

But the intruders moved into the land with grim efficiency. They usually travelled alone or in pairs, and they wasted no time. They would set out 300 to 500 leg-hold traps in two or three lines, and they would relentlessly empty and rebait them as quickly as they could snowshoe down the line. When the catch got scanty, they moved elsewhere and stripped new territories. Trapline rights meant nothing to them. Those who worked with poison brought in another dimension of horror: the kind of thing that Farley Mowat described as happening in the Barrens during the 1920s, when whites poisoned hundreds of caribou carcasses and left them to be eaten by white fox, wolverine, and other tundra animals. The other major factor involving the

Mackenzie Indians was disease. For nearly a century, they had peri-odically been reduced by epidemics that destroyed entire bands.

In 1913 Thomas Fawcett, chief surveyor of the department, toured the Mackenzie to "protect native and non-native inhabitants from the incursions of later settlers." Until then, there had been little intrusion, apart from the whalers and trappers in the Delta after 1900. Some set-tlements were well established. At Simpson, French Canadian voyageurs and the HBC's Orkney boatmen retired with their Indian families. In the Delta, Aklavik was becoming a trading centre for muskrat hunters and trappers, while McPherson was a jumping-off place for white officials, Mounties, and missionaries. Fawcett, like others at the time, recommended that the Mackenzie Indians be brought into Treaty 8, but he was refused. As a result of his report, however, some land was allocated under Treaty 8 to non-treaty Indian bands. The grants amounted to tiny, informal Indian reserves.

It wasn't until Imperial Oil began its petroleum development and others began serious exploration of the Athabaska tar sands that Ottawa decided on a new treaty. It was rushed through in 1921 but didn't have much immediate impact on either the Indians or the bureaucracy. Ottawa installed Indian agents at Smith and Simpson and carried out some normal treaty provisions. The NWT Indians continued to live traditionally.

All That Rises Must Converge

The 1950s and 1960s were not a particularly good time to be an Indian, even in the NWT. Not having reserves, however, saved them from the worst restrictions of living under the Indian Act, which even today seems almost unbearably oppressive to anyone brought up in the traditions of British citizenship. The Indian Act has to be read to be believed: it asserts total authority over registered Indians. For example, occupants of reserves don't own them: reserves are defined as "tracts of land, the legal title of which is vested in Her Majesty."

It is no wonder that Indian leaders have felt that their ancestors were cheated in the various treaties they signed with the white man. The white negotiators talked about how the Indians and their descen-dants would possess and be protected on the reserve lands "as long as the rivers flow and the land lasts." But it appears from the Indian Act of 1951 (as amended in 1970) that the Indians were not owners but tenants.

It was not only in the question of land title that Canadian Indians had a grievance. The Indian Act gives the superintendent almost god-like authority on the reserves: over housing, schooling, personal property, the right of succession, property ownership, behaviour, and amusements. Each item is detailed and described. Under clauses 93 and 94 dealing with the illegality of liquor, the superintendent has the power to seize property or search premises without a warrant. One of the basic provisions of the act for generations was that status Indians were denied the right to use or possess alcohol on or off the reserves. In later years, several provinces allowed them to drink in licensed beer parlours or lounges.

Perhaps the most bewildering maze built into Indian policy over 140 years involved that treasured right of free citizens in a democracy: the franchise, or the right to vote. From the middle of the 19th century on, Canadian Indians were offered "enfranchisement" as part of a policy more and more committed to the assimilation of the entire Indian population. (Until the 1940s, the Inuit escaped assimilation pressure through being totally ignored by the government.)

Enfranchisement, as set forth in the Indian Act of 1876 and earlier legislation going back twenty-five years before that, was part of a program to make Indians on reserves conform to white standards of behaviour. If he stayed out of debt, learned to read and write, and behaved in a manner that conformed to white moral standards, the male Indian would be permitted to possess a lot in the reserve's community and to build a house on it – thus learning another white value: property ownership. After a three-year probation period, the Indian would be given permanent ("usufructuary") possession of his lot and could sell it to another band member. But the government still held title to the land under the "usufructuary" provision.

The Indian would also be "enfranchised," which involved the right to vote in band elections on the reserve and sometimes in federal and provincial elections. Enfranchisement was much advocated by the federal government and several times was made compulsory for Indians. Of all the bizarre Catch 22s of Indian policy, it was the most paradoxical. The 1970 amendments to the 1951 Indian Act said that any Indian who accepted the right to vote in a federal or provincial election (as opposed to band elections on the reserve) immediately lost his or her status as an Indian and was required to leave the reserve within ten years. While this clause was on the books, Indian men and women were guaranteed the right to vote along with all other adult citizens under the Elections Act.

Indian policy is rife with such contradictions, but generally they fit, in a perverse way, into the historical policy of assimilation. John Leonard Taylor, in a 1984 paper on Canadian Indian policy published by DIAND, says: "An ultimate governmental goal for every Indian was enfranchisement. This involved relinquishing Indian status, the legal condition that placed an individual under the Indian Act, and taking on the privileges and responsibilities of full citizenship."

Duncan Campbell Scott, the poet who was deputy superintendent of Indian affairs from 1913 to 1932, told a parliamentary committee in 1920: "Our object is to continue until there is not a single Indian in Canada that has not been absorbed into the body politic and there is no Indian question, and no Indian Department – that is the whole object of this Bill." The bill he referred to aimed at forcing enfranchisement on every male Indian, whether he wanted it or not. Scott and Arthur Meighen, minister of the interior in Sir Robert Borden's Unionist cabinet, had been pressing the campaign for compulsory enfranchisement since 1918. It was written into law in 1920, then repealed by Mackenzie King's Liberals two years later.

R.B. Bennett's Conservative government reinstated the law in 1933, and it officially stayed on the books until 1951, when the whole Indian Act was substantially revised. In fact, the law had almost no effect on the Indian population. Bennett didn't get around to enforcing it before he was defeated in 1935, and the Liberals ignored it until they revoked it once again.

Lest anyone misunderstand the Conservative intent, Scott told Meighen in 1920 that compulsory enfranchisement would "check the intrigues of smart Indians on the reserves who are forming organizations to foster these aboriginal feelings and to thwart the efforts and policy of the Department." When Mackenzie King protested the restrictive clauses in the Indian Act in the 1920s, Meighen told him that if the government treated wards in the same way it treated citizens "it would not be dealing with wards at all." The Indians boycotted enfranchisement, forced or voluntary, from the time it was first advocated in the 1850s.

Taylor says the most recent attempt to abolish special rights for Indians was the Liberal white paper of 1969, which proposed the abolition of the entire Department of Indian Affairs and the absorption of Indians into the citizenry at large. By the time the white paper came out, the native political organizations were so powerful that they quickly forced Prime Minister Trudeau and DIAND Minister Jean Chrétien to abandon it.

But the question of Indian status has not gone away. The Inuit, who never came under the Indian Act, were given the federal franchise by Parliament in 1950, while status Indians received it in 1960. In 1949 B.C. gave the provincial vote to non-status Indians, and other provinces followed, ending with Quebec in 1969.

In practice, status or treaty Indians have been allowed to vote in federal elections since 1960, but the 1970 version of the Indian Act said in Section 110: "A person with respect to whom an order for enfranchisement is made under this Act shall, from the date thereof, or from the date of enfranchisement provided for therein, be deemed not to be an Indian within the meaning of this Act or any other statute or law."

This is a clear contradiction of the right granted by Parliament in 1960. Such an anomaly lends credence to the observation made by Sally Weaver, historian of Indian policy:

> In my experience I have found both ministers and civil servants unaware of past policies and the implications of these policies for both the client and the government. When ministers and civil servants leave the portfolio they often take with them their individual experiences. As a result, the collective experience is not synthesized and lessons from even the recent past remain unlearned.*

This may well have been the case in the NWT, where for many years the Indian Act was administered by the Department of Citizenship and Immigration (1950–65), though NWT Indians were looked after by Northern Affairs and National Resources. For a long time, the Inuit had no official status with any department and were looked after rather absent-mindedly by whatever department happened to be in charge of the NWT as a whole. The loose ends were consolidated with the creation of the Department of Indian Affairs and Northern Development in 1966, but as in the confusion over voting rights, many difficulties remain.

∼

The preceding are examples of some of the political pressures on traditional Indian leaders in the NWT, but there were even more immediate concerns.

---

*Sally Weaver, "A Commentary on the Penner Report" (1984), DIAND, Treaties Division, Research Centre.

In the early 1920s, Ottawa introduced game regulations that interfered with the free right of Indians to hunt on Crown land. From the 1930s on, the white population of the NWT had been increasing steadily. Yellowknife had become a city of whites, demanding rights that were bound to affect Indians. More whites were coming into Hay River, Simpson, Smith. A whole new mining community – Pine Point – was rising between Resolution and Hay River. Seismic crews were stitching tundra and *taiga* with their petroleum exploration trails.

Finally, there was transportation. As early as 1931, white trappers started using planes to fly in and out, and the Mounties found it necessary to rule that they could use planes only to reach their headquarters camps. As long as there were no roads or railways coming into the Territories, the worst of the white riffraff could be discouraged, but by the 1960s, even that kind of isolation was a thing of the past.

In 1959 the highway from Edmonton reached Hay River, and by 1961 it was into Yellowknife. A different class began to arrive in the summers: hippies. One year, hippies occupied the retired Boston water bomber anchored in cement at the Yellowknife airport. They camped in the fuselage for weeks until booted out by the cops. After that, the bomb-bay doors were welded shut. Other hippies hitched rides along the Mackenzie as far as Aklavik, rode in 18-wheelers, drove rickety jalopies. They liked the Indians just fine and tended to camp on Indian land and, if invited, to eat whatever their hosts offered them.

There were even a few farmers squatting on Crown land outside Yellowknife, trying to establish truck gardens and a herd of cattle. Unfortunately for them, the feds would neither sell nor lease them Crown land while a land settlement with the indigenes was being considered.

Indian economic problems did not improve, though Ottawa encouraged co-ops and cottage industries for handicrafts. Ottawa set up annual meetings in Smith between the chiefs and the regional superintendent of Indian affairs. When the chiefs found that their advice was ignored and their demands were unmet, they boycotted the meetings. For instance, the sixteen chiefs were enraged on learning that Ottawa had been planning a national park around Snowdrift at the eastern end of Great Slave Lake. The plans had been under way for ten years, without a word to the Chipewyans who lived there; the park would be on land used for hunting, trapping, and fishing.

Considering all these elements, the chiefs came to the conclusion that the federal administrators were offering no serious solutions to immediate problems and were hiding Ottawa's real agenda. The only value they saw in the Smith meetings was a chance to get together and gossip informally among themselves. In the long run, this communication proved extremely important: it lit several beacons, one of them the Thebacha Association to promote leadership and economic opportunity. As the word spread among the tribal groups, co-ops and associations were founded elsewhere.

Meanwhile, a flood of civil servants, all ignorant of the North and its peoples, was drastically changing Yellowknife and moving into other communities. The chiefs saw with foreboding that the GNWT Department of Local Government was devoting energy to white concerns totally foreign to the NWT: the director, Sid Hancock, reported that recreation officers were offering grants to promote activities like water safety, square dancing, figure skating, and drama. No Indian served on the NWT Council until 1969 when Chief John Tetlichi of McPherson was appointed. The first Indian to be elected was Louis Rabesca of Rae the following year. The first elected Inuk was Simonie Michael of Frobisher Bay in 1967.

One event, a triumph for individual and Indian rights, proved to be a two-edged sword. Joe Drybones, a Dog Rib, was arrested in the lobby of the Yellowknife Inn in 1967 and charged under the Indian Act with "being drunk off a reserve." He was fined $10 and sentenced to three days in jail. Judge William Morrow, successor to the legendary Judge Sissons and himself a great innovator, reversed the verdict on the basis of the 1960 Diefenbaker Bill of Rights. Morrow found that application of the Indian Act was a violation of civil rights. The case went to the Supreme Court of Canada in 1970 and gave Indians everywhere in Canada the right to drink in public. It was a great triumph for the legal rights of Indians but proved a mixed blessing as the alcohol problem among aboriginals worsened at an ever increasing rate everywhere.

Good or bad, the 1960s developments were slowly changing the NWT's traditional patterns. It was not surprising that the chiefs didn't give constitutional reform much attention when the Carrothers Commission came to town in 1965–66. How were the chiefs to know that the balance was about to be tipped in their direction?

The Company of Young Canadians

While social and political revolution was sweeping the NWT from end to end, quite different upheavals were shaking the rest of the world. White and black youngsters joined in a campaign of civil disobedience in the U.S. South. Colonial subjects threw out the British, French, Dutch, and Portuguese in Asia and Africa. Anti-war protests forced President Lyndon Johnson into retirement while the Vietnam War raged. Religious intolerance, political oppression, economic bondage, race prejudice became the targets of well-organized, well-off idealists around the world.

In the United States, the most visible arenas involved black civil rights and opposition to Washington's military adventures in Southeast Asia. In Canada, poverty, Quebec separatism, regional inequality, and the problems of the indigenous peoples became central issues. Everything was visible and audible every day on television and radio, and the conscience of the middle class was awakened.

In earlier eras, idealistic young people would become Christian missionaries to the downtrodden heathen, but this was a secular and ecumenical age. Church leaders supplied moral support and some financing, but the field work was done by the young, usually radical and idealistic. These lay missionaries served in Canadian University Students Overseas (CUSO) or the American Peace Corps. For problems at home, the United States had Volunteers in Service to America (VISTA) and in Canada Lester Pearson set up the Company of Young Canadians (CYC) in 1966.

These organizations had a dual purpose: to harness the idealistic zeal of young people and to make sure that they were safely involved in causes other than revolution and radical reform. CYC members were paid by Ottawa but were outside the main bureaucracy and had a good deal of freedom as they worked in rural and urban slums. They had to be invited by the residents of the areas they served, but there was always a local clergyman, citizens' group, or native organization to request their services.

This was what happened in the NWT. The Roman Catholics and Anglicans were aware of Indian problems, and other major Christian churches were showing interest, along with international relief organizations such as OXFAM, which worked for the alleviation of starvation, disease, and oppression in the Third World. The CYC was asked to send workers into the NWT. The first was Steve Iveson in

1967, followed by Peter Puxley and Caroline Pickles. They began working in Indian communities south of Great Slave Lake and in Rae among the Dog Ribs. Their most important job was to recruit young Indians and Métis who would then become community workers within the various bands.

From the start, the CYC workers were greeted with suspicion and hostility by the white community. Forty-seven years earlier, Duncan Campbell Scott had spoken angrily of "smart Indians" making trouble on the reserves. Many of the most prominent white settlers in Yellowknife and Hay River looked on the white CYC workers and the native community workers in exactly the same way. It should be remembered that in the late 1960s, the bulk of Yellowknife's population consisted of people happily involved in private enterprises like mining or the bureaucratic structures of government. To such conservative elements – which included NWT Commissioner Ben Sivertz – the CYC workers were radical interlopers, stirring up the natives.

There was a famous incident at the student hostel in Yellowknife, Akaitcho Hall. During the school term, the residence was full of students; during the summer, young people from all over were permitted to stay. Steve Iveson moved in and began to make friends with Indians and Inuit of his own age. They talked a great deal about injustice and alternatives, and Iveson met a number of people who would later become community workers, either in the CYC or in the GNWT. What enraged Sivertz and other whites was an incident involving the rules posted for residents of Akaitcho Hall. Iveson found the rigid, paternalistic regulations both annoying and amusing, and he mailed a copy of them to David Lewis, leader of the New Democratic Party. Lewis read them in the House of Commons, holding up the gnwt to ridicule. This angered the GNWT and the Yellowknife city fathers, and the CYC and the native community workers were labelled subversive.

Iveson, Puxley (who arrived in 1969), and Caroline Pickles found the Mackenzie Basin ripe for organization. There was a whole generation of young Indians who spoke English well, had graduated from high school (and sometimes had further education), had travelled, and had read widely. They were aware of their own problems and were bursting to do something about them. The first six recruits were to have historic impact: James Wah Shee, Louis Rabesca, Charlie Charlo, Roy Daniels, Ed Bird, and Mona Jacobs. They were joined by a young power lineman of mixed Cree, Dog Rib, and white ancestry, Georges Erasmus.

Caroline Pickles, a dynamic blonde from Scarborough, Ontario, came to Rae in 1969 as a community organizer for the GNWT. There she met one of Steve Iveson's recruits, twenty-four-year-old James Wah Shee, a darkly handsome young man who had been caught between traditional and new Indian ways. As a small child, he had lived with his family in the bush. In those days, there was no permanent Indian settlement at Rae, although there was a Bay post, a free-trader, and a Catholic mission, which included a hospital and residential school. Around 1950 the Dog Ribs began building log cabins at Marian Lake, and by 1960 they were linked to Yellowknife by road. When James was seven, he was sent to residential school. He recalled:

> I had four elder brothers and once Dad saw that they wanted to stay in the bush, he and my Mother agreed to my going to school. I liked living in the bush as a child. We lived in a double-sided canvas tent and seldom saw anyone else. Dad and my brothers hunted and trapped – the dogs would go out and find moose or caribou and they would hunt them down. When we ran out of game, we'd move someplace else. In the spring, we'd all come in to Fort Rae for Treaty Day. It was a big celebration and we saw all the other families. It was a good life. We never went hungry.

Wah Shee discovered he had artistic talent and was sent to Wisconsin to study, afterwards returning to Rae where his family had finally settled. That was where Caroline Pickles found him and – they fell in love.

The Indian Brotherhood

Nineteen hundred and sixty-six was the year the Alaska Federation of Natives (AFN) was formed. Canadians knew and cared nothing about Alaska, but the AFN became a signpost for Canadian northern developments over the next fifteen years.

Alaska, like the Yukon, is overwhelmingly white – only 15 percent Eskimo, Indian, and Aleut (5.5 percent Eskimo). But the Inupiat Eskimos, who live on the North Slope next to the Arctic Ocean, have extraordinary leverage when it comes to the vast petroleum deposits in their territory. For generations, geologists had known that there was an enormous pool of oil and natural gas along the coasts of the Arctic Ocean and the Beaufort Sea – the area that includes both

Alaska's North Slope and the NWT's Mackenzie Delta. In the 1960s, Atlantic Richfield, British Petroleum (BP), and Esso (now Exxon) were seeking the elusive oil pool around Prudhoe Bay.

Everybody said it was only a matter of time before they made a big strike. The Alaska natives, especially the Inupiat Eskimos, thought it would be just as well to have an organization that could deal with the state and federal governments and with the oil companies. The strike came in 1968 and involved both oil and gas. For the time being, the companies decided to cap the gas deposits and concentrate on the oil. Frantic efforts began to find ways of delivering oil to American users in the south. There were three possibilities: shipment by tanker; a pipeline across Alaska to the Gulf of Alaska where crude would be shipped south by giant tankers; and a pipeline through Alaska and Canada to U.S. refineries.

The American supertanker *Manhattan* proved in 1969 and 1970 that ships could get through the ice – but also that the method was not economical. The oil men therefore decided to shove a 48-inch pipeline across Alaska and build a tanker port at Valdez. They were so sure of themselves that they bought a billion dollars worth of pipe from Japan and got speedy delivery by the end of 1969. On 12 September 1969, the State of Alaska auctioned off $900 million worth of oil leases in Anchorage. A boom was expected.

At that moment, five organizations sought an injunction against the pipeline: Friends of the Earth, the Wilderness Society, the Environment Defense Fund, the Cordova District Fisheries Union, and the Canadian Wildlife Federation. The newly fledged AFN added its voice, saying that nothing should be done until its land claims were settled. The courts granted an injunction, and U.S. Interior Secretary Stewart Udall announced a land freeze "pending settlement of native land claims."

With so much money at stake, the oil, gas, and pipeline companies put enormous pressure on Congress to make a deal with the natives. In 1971 the Native Land Claims Act was passed. It gave forty million acres to the Eskimos, Indians, and Aleuts, plus a billion dollars over twenty years, partly from oil royalties. President Nixon lifted the land freeze, and the pipeline went ahead.

In every respect, the Alaskan example was to have an impact on Canada: the land claims settlement was instantly hailed as a model for Ottawa (though it was later condemned by various parties). In addition, the idea of building an oil pipeline across Alaska drew attention to the Canadian oil and gas resources that had been discovered in the Beaufort Sea, the High Arctic, and the Mackenzie Delta. It would be very expensive to get them to market, but perhaps Canada could piggyback on the Americans. There definitely was not enough Canadian oil discovered as yet, but there was plenty of Beaufort Sea natural gas. Why not build a 48-inch gas pipeline across Alaska and down through Canada to the United States? Or, better yet, build an all-Canadian pipeline down the Mackenzie River Valley to the Beaufort, then send a branch line along the coast to Prudhoe Bay and thus tap the Prudhoe reserves until the Canadian gas wells came into production?

The concept was vast but appealed to the multinational petroleum companies, to some bankers, and to the Canadian Liberal government. If carried out, the Canadian pipeline would be an enormous undertaking and would have a profound effect on the lives of both the Mackenzie Indians and the Delta Inuvialuit. This kind of thinking ushered in a seven-year period in the NWT that was marked by preoccupation with petroleum development – and also by the development of Canadian aboriginal organizations, which would ultimately be much more effective than the AFN.

∾

It was inevitable that entrepreneurs in Calgary, Toronto, Edmonton, and Vancouver should start thinking of big development in the Canadian North: petroleum exploration had been going on since the 1950s, and often the companies involved in Canada were the same ones with crews in Alaska. Imperial Oil had been active in the NWT for over forty years and was to make the first Delta oil strike in 1971. Peter Bawden of Calgary drilled the first hole (dry) in the High Arctic in 1960–61. Intelligent petroleum men like Jack Gallagher and Bob Blair were starting to prepare for the day when they would have to make deals with the northern aboriginals as well as with the federal government.

Ottawa also was aware that it soon should sit down with the Indian chiefs, just as Sir John A. Macdonald had to deal with the Indians before he built the CPR. But Ottawa was beginning to understand that the old treaty system would not work any more. The Nelson Commission, which was set up in 1959 to activate Treaties 8 and 11, soon sputtered out. The chiefs had been burned so badly that they were looking for a new kind of deal.

This time there would have to be serious settlement of land claims, with the terms written into the agreement for all to see, including the Canadian law courts.*

Many of the mandarins (and a few corporate planners) felt that they might be able to deal more effectively with younger, better educated Indians than with the chiefs, many of whom spoke little or no English. Why not follow Alaska's example and help the natives set up political organizations? After all, some Ottawa boffins reasoned, it might be easier to control people whose salaries were being paid by the taxpayer.

There were other pressures in the south favouring native political groups. Various Christian churches had given money to indigenous blacks in Africa when they were preparing to turn the old European colonies into independent nations. The Anglicans and Roman Catholics, with long experience in the Canadian North, wanted to see independent or quasi-independent Indian organizations. There still was no talk of Inuit political structures.

∼

In July 1968, DIAND sponsored a meeting in Yellowknife to talk about consultation on the Indian Act. Leon Sambale and Joe Squirrel, both from Providence, suggested an Indian federation to resolve treaty issues. Steve Iveson helped the movement along. George Manuel, the B.C. Indian leader, led community workshops in Simpson, and Alberta's Harold Cardinal gave his support.

The timing was just right. The annual confabs of the chiefs and elders in Smith and other Mackenzie communities had shown the NWT's several Indian tribal groups that they needed to work together. Now the elders were joined by articulate, energetic young men and women who spoke and wrote English and were trained in various modern organizational techniques. And the native groups were starting to get funding from Ottawa and the churches.

So the yeast was working in several ways. One of the most touching was the impact of love: several white women who came to the

---

*In 1969 Chief Pierre Catholique of Snowdrift stomped out of a Yellowknife meeting with DIAND officials saying: "From now on, if twenty-one government people come to a meeting, twenty-one Indian leaders must come and sit across the table from them. From now on, we, the chiefs, must talk to the government only when we are all together."

native communities found lovers or husbands. Caroline Pickles was perhaps the most prominent. In Rae, she and James Wah Shee put together an unbeatable team of community organizers. Soon they were deeply involved in the founding of the Indian Brotherhood of the NWT.*

Georges Erasmus, another CYC volunteer, grew up in a broken home in Yellowknife and Rae. Unlike Wah Shee – his long-time rival – Erasmus was bitter about the residential school system which, he said, had caused him to lose his native language. He was aggressive, ambitious, and an excellent organizer and speaker. Before long, he was running the CYC community programs.

A third impressive young leader was Nick Sibbeston, a Dehcho Métis from Fort Simpson, two years older than Wah Shee. Sibbeston was yet another product of the residential school system and spent eleven years away from home as a child. He would have lost the language of his mother's people had it not been for his Dehcho grandmother. He put the language to good use in 1970 when he defeated Don Stewart for the NWT Council and became the first Métis to be elected. Sibbeston went on to become the first native lawyer in the Territories and, in the 1980s, government leader.

～

In October 1969, sixteen chiefs from seventeen bands formed the NWT Indian Brotherhood in Yellowknife. Mona Jacob was interim president until displaced by Roy Daniels four months later. Vice-presidents were Neil Colin, Joe Catholique, Charlie Charlo, and Ray Sonfrère. James Wah Shee became president in 1971. Thus a new element was introduced into the political scene: the chiefs and elders now had a way to work in tandem with the hard-driving young community workers. Expansion was made possible by financial support from DIAND's vigorous new minister, Jean Chrétien, and the Brotherhood opened an office in Yellowknife, hired staff and community workers, and started a newspaper. Wah Shee travelled up and down the Mackenzie, taking the gospel to the communities.

In the summer of 1971, the Brotherhood held a general assembly in Rae, and modern technology was introduced, which made com-

---

*Later, Caroline was to be an influence on Peter Ernerk, the Keewatin-Inuit politician and civil servant. Still later she married Jack Anawak, who was elected Liberal MP for Arctic East in 1988. She herself finally became a justice of the peace and a vital force in Rankin Inlet.

munication among the elders, chiefs, and community workers easy. The technology allowed simultaneous translation into several dialects and languages. At the same time, the CBC began broadcasting the proceedings to the communities in several native languages.* The main business of the Fort Rae assembly was land: it was agreed that no more development should occur in tribal territories until there was a settlement taking into account Treaties 8 and 11.

The Brotherhood was now in business, with the full endorsement of the chiefs from all over the Mackenzie Valley. Wah Shee hired lawyers and other experts as advisers, and negotiating teams were picked. Several CYC community workers joined the teams. There was plenty to do. Already, the petroleum companies were sending in public relations people to sell the idea of a 48-inch natural gas pipeline from Alberta to the Beaufort Sea.

There was also the question of the Métis. Traditionally, status and non-status Indians had lived tranquilly with their blood relatives, but

---

*One incident at the Fort Rae Assembly illustrated the advantages of having technical aids to communication. For centuries Indian leaders had been accustomed to having white men tell them one thing in set speeches and then say something quite different in the written treaty.

Two representatives of Parks Canada, dressed in three-piece suits and ties, visited Rae to outline Ottawa's plans for a National Park near Snowdrift and Fort Reliance at the eastern corner of Great Slave Lake.

The chiefs feared interference with game, and as part of their argument in favour of a park, one official promised permanent jobs.

The spokesperson for the chiefs relentlessly questioned the officials: "What kind of jobs?"

"Permanent jobs!"

"You mean like park rangers?" she asked. "The Indians would be good at that. They know all about the land, the animals, and the plants. They could tell the tourists many wonderful stories."

"Well ... not exactly"

"Why not?"

"Park rangers have to have university degrees and know the scientific names of plants and animals. So they would naturally come from southern Canada."

"What kinds of jobs then?"

"There would be custodial jobs ... brush cutting ... cleaning up ..."

"You mean JANITORIAL jobs?"

"Well ..."

"Tell us how many jobs are held by Indians in the National Parks across the country!"

"Oh ... lots!"

"But just how many?"

The Ottawa men were flustered and conferred while the old men waited patiently, faces impassive. Finally, they said: "It's ... six ..."

The old men smiled, then cackled, then roared with laughter.

The white men left.

there was a political gap between them that had been fostered by Ottawa. Mixed-bloods had no rights under the Indian Act, and the chiefs often made sure that only registered Indians benefited from the act's inadequate rights and privileges. It didn't take a political genius to see that the support of several thousand mixed-bloods would strengthen the Indian hand in dealing with Ottawa. The mixed-bloods – or Métis, as they began to call themselves in tribute to the true Métis of the Red River Valley – were starting to go through much the same process as the Indians.

The Métis Association

When it came down to actually negotiating a deal, the Métis Association was the joker in the political pack. For a hundred years or so, Ottawa didn't recognize even the existence of the mixed-bloods: the census listed Eskimos, Indians, and "others" (i.e., whites, blacks, yellows, browns, and perhaps "bois brûlé"). Tom Berger estimated the number of non-status Indians and Métis in the NWT at 4,500, adding that the number who thought of themselves as "distinctly Métis" was "somewhere between 1,000 and 1,500. Rick Hardy, the first effective president of the Métis Association, estimated the association's membership at 6,000 and the total Indian-Métis population at 12,000. The GNWT estimated in 1985 that there were 18,024 Inuit (including the Inuvialuit); 7,416 status Indians; 2,862 Métis, and 21,410 non-native.

This showed the political importance of the Métis in such a fragmented territory. Whites formed 41 percent of the population, Inuit 35 percent, status Indians 14 percent, non-status 2.5 percent, and Métis 5.6 percent. The Indians needed the support of every Métis and non-status they could get to show that they made up nearly a quarter of the NWT population. Even with that support, the whites outnumbered them. That was why the Indian Brotherhood made an intense effort to absorb the Métis Association politically.

The history of mixed-bloods in the NWT is complex, and their status cannot be outlined simply. Terrence Lusty of the University of Calgary said in a 1973 paper ("The Métis Social-Political Movement"): "The blending of French and Indian gave birth to a new race of people called 'Métis' while the inter-breeding of Scots, English and Irish with Indians resulted in the 'half-breed.'" Rick Hardy, a scholar as well as a politician and successful lawyer, accepts

Lusty's distinction between Métis and half-breed, but he refines the situation:

> There are what may be described as the "old" Métis families. These people are generally third- and fourth-generation Métis who are descendants of persons who took scrip payments in either 1899 or 1921 [i.e., under Treaties 8 and 11]. Further, there are those Métis families who have immigrated into the region beginning approximately in the 1900s, with the major influx in the late 1950s and early 1960s. Finally, there are those people commonly known as non-status Indians.*

Hardy leaves out the background. The original half-breeds in Rupert's Land were the offspring of Scottish and French employees of the HBC or the North West Company. They intermarried with Sah'tu and Dehcho girls and settled in Fort Simpson when they retired as Mackenzie rivermen, building a well-established community. Simpson has always been a key distribution point, at the junction of the Mackenzie and the Liard. The Nor'Westers first, then the HBC, built posts on an island at the mouth of the turbulent Liard, which links the NWT with the mountains and what is now British Columbia. The Bay established a large farm to supply vegetables, later a federal government experimental farm.

In the Delta, two mixed-blood communities developed. At McPherson, Bay men married Gwich'in girls, while at Aklavik white whalers from Herschel Island married Inupiat Eskimo girls. In both cases, the white settlers often became trappers and adopted native lifestyles. At the other end of the Mackenzie Valley, Fort Smith and nearby Fort Fitzgerald were links between the Mackenzie and the Athabaska fur-trading systems. The posts were in the heart of Chipewyan country, but another element began coming in from the south.

After the Red River Rebellion of 1869, many prairie Métis moved northwest to the Saskatchewan River. After the 1885 Riel Rebellion, some of them moved into Athabaska country and came into contact (and contention) with the Chipewyans. There was some tension as Métis-Plains Cree, Woodland Cree, and Chipewyans jostled for the

---

*Richard I. Hardy, "Metis Rights in the Mackenzie District," *Canadian Native Law Reporter*, 1980.

rich fur harvest. Very soon, more tensions built up when white trappers and prospectors moved into the country and gradually drifted
into the NWT via Smith. As noted earlier, the threat of half-breed and
white trappers was an issue in the negotiation of Treaty 8.

More recently, the suspicions and jealousies of the NWT Indians
and their non-status and Métis relatives toward the Cree Métis
became apparent in Hay River. From time immemorial, there had
been a Dehcho encampment on the Hay. The white settlement, largely involved in the shipment of supplies from Alberta to Yellowknife,
was built on the opposite bank of the river, and there was comparatively little communication between the races. After the Second
World War, a commercial fishery was developed on the south shore
of Great Slave Lake, and most of the fishermen were Cree Métis from
Saskatchewan and Manitoba. They built a completely new community, West Channel, which had little to do with either whites or Dehcho.

At one stage, Hay River had five distinct communities. There was
the original Dehcho settlement, with small log cabins scattered
around the Catholic mission. There was the original white community directly across the river, with wharfs, tugs, warehouses, and a bat-
tered hotel known universally as "the Zoo." Whites and half-breed
rivermen lived in flimsy shacks. Then in 1963 severe floods forced
partial evacuation, and a new town was built a few kilometres upriver. It had a shopping plaza built in a hollow square like a frontier fort
to give protection from blizzards. Across the river from the new town,
dubbed "Disneyland" by its residents, was a new Indian town, with
electricity, sanitation services, fresh water, and modern, prefab houses. For a long time, the older people in the original Dehcho settlement
refused to move to the new Indian village; they said it was too crowded
and regimented.

～

Hay River, Simpson, and Smith provided many examples of complex
racial relationships. First, there were the families of the white men
who married Indians. As Rick Hardy said of his Nova Scotia-born
father: "Jack Hardy's more Indian than the Indians!" But many an
Indian girl had a passing relationship with a white visitor and took the
resulting baby home to her parents. Such babies grew up with no
input from their white father's culture and naturally developed the
closest of ties with their Indian relatives.

But there were, and are, other Métis. They started coming into the

Territories before the Klondike gold rush and multiplied during the Yellowknife rush of the 1930s. Some lived on the land and took half-breed or Indian wives. Others worked in the mines, or as airplane pilots, rivermen, schoolteachers, social workers, carpenters, members of Parliament. Many married white girls in the towns and lived totally in a white culture. Some worked in the Alberta and Arctic oil patches and came home occasionally to see families in Simpson or Arctic Red River.

From the start, there were obvious reasons for non-status Indians and Métis dropping into white society if they could. By suppressing the Indian side of their ancestry, they sometimes were able to escape discrimination. Some felt that mine bosses were ready to hire anyone they could depend on to work long hours and show up regularly. There was a grim joke that mine bosses abused muckers without discrimination as to race, creed, or colour. "If he'll only act like a white man, he can have anything he wants," was the litany of the mine bosses. Indians replied that they had no desire to act or live like white men, and some Métis said that even when they did, they were discriminated against.

~

No easy explanations fit all the varieties of mixed-bloods in the NWT. Status Indians were unwilling to share the provisions of treaties with them, as Fred Carrothers found when he talked to the Indians at Fort Resolution in 1965. Ottawa swung wildly from one extreme to another. When the Indian Brotherhood offered to merge with the Métis Association to negotiate land claims, Ottawa refused, demanding that each group talk separately. Later, the feds demanded that they make one joint claim.

In 1973 Ottawa was seriously talking deal, and the Métis got around to establishing a stable association. The Indian organizations had developed effectively from the Thebacha Association to the Indian Brotherhood, but the Métis had difficulty getting off the ground. The first Métis president was Dave McNabb of Hay River, but a year after he was elected the association had collapsed. In 1974 Rick Hardy, then twenty-five, got help from Ottawa and the Brotherhood and attended a general assembly of aboriginal peoples in Fort Good Hope. It planned to merge Indians and Métis. The general situation was improving: Nick Sibbeston was on the NWT Council, and Wally Firth, a Métis from Fort McPherson, was an NDP member of Parliament. He won in 1972 and 1974.

But this was a time of turmoil for all the natives of the NWT: the Indian Brotherhood was beginning to split into factions. The petroleum companies were moving in, and a business-oriented federal government was putting pressure on the indigenes for a land settlement. The outside world would soon start seeing the NWT vividly and dramatically through the experience of the Berger Commission. But first there was the organization of the mixed peoples who inhabited the Mackenzie Delta and the rim of the Beaufort Sea.

COPE

The Inuit of the eastern Arctic and the Inuvialuit of the Beaufort Sea moved along different paths and at different paces from the Indian Brotherhood and the Métis Association. In 1969 a group of Delta people organized the Committee for the Original People's Entitlement (COPE) on the assumption that all people with aboriginal blood in the area should have a single body to negotiate for them. COPE's founders were two extraordinary women, Agnes Semmler and Nellie Cournoyea.

Agnes Semmler was a Gwich'in Métis who had grown up trapping muskrats along the Peel River. She was married to a famous free- trader, Slim Semmler. Nellie Cournoyea was the daughter of a Norwegian trapper and an Inuvialuit mother and grew up, as they say in that part of the world, "on the ice." She was CBC's first native woman radio station manager. As a young woman, she married a white man, had two children, and lived for several years in Ottawa. One of the original COPE group was Wally Firth, who also worked at CBC in Inuvik as an announcer/operator. He was also a commercial pilot.

COPE, with Agnes Semmler as its first president, sought to build an organization that would include all aboriginal groups. Rick Hardy and Charlie Overold, both to become presidents of the Métis Association, were early members, and COPE lent $5,000 to the fledgling Métis group. It was also in on the founding of the national Inuit organization, Inuit Tapirisat of Canada (ITC). In 1970 COPE sent a delegation to a meeting of Indian chiefs in Yellowknife, but it was asked to leave because the chiefs said that Ottawa would not approve a single organization. As late as 1975, when James Wah Shee was forced out by Georges Erasmus, COPE sent a team to the Indian Brotherhood assembly at Rae. Caroline Pickles Wah Shee described it this way:

> The meeting had been going on a long time and ... things were very
> tense when the delegation from the Delta arrived. You could tell
> them by their Mother Hubbard parkas and sun-burst hoods. They
> looked quite different from the Dene. They didn't have anything to
> say in argument; they were just there to give moral support. As a
> matter of fact, they didn't even have enough money to buy food.
> That was typical of the Delta people – they decided the important
> thing was to pass the hat and get enough money to pay for the air
> charter. In the end they were billeted in Dog Rib homes.

This was the spirit of the first successful native political organization in the NWT. In no small way it was inspired by its founders,
Nellie Cournoyea and Agnes Semmler. They have a reputation
throughout the length and breadth of the Territories for generosity
and far-sightedness. Agnes Semmler ultimately became the first
native deputy commissioner, a symbolic position by the time she
occupied it. Nellie Cournoyea served for many years as an MLA in
several cabinet posts and in 1991 became government leader. During
the 1980s, both women were important figures in the negotiations
that led to the first land claims settlement, the Inuvialuit agreement of
the western Arctic.

The Dene Nation

In 1975 the NWT Indian Brotherhood stated its position on land
claims and political rights in the Dene Declaration, which spoke of
"The Dene" rather than of "Indian" tribes. The word "Dene" is com-
mon to several NWT Indian groups and means "The People" or "The
Human Beings." After the declaration was adopted, it was inevitable
that the Indian Brotherhood would be reorganized into the Dene
Nation in 1978. This occurred two years before the National Indian
Brotherhood became the Assembly of First Nations, and it was not
very surprising when the aggressive and attractive creator of the Dene
Nation, Georges Erasmus, became grand chief of the assembly.
Erasmus stated the new position clearly in 1978: "People are using
the word 'claim' ... That's something the government would really
like us to believe that we have a claim. Our problem has been the
Government of Canada has a claim on our land. We have no claim.
The land belongs to the Dene. We have no claim."

Erasmus was the chief rival of James Wah Shee in the Indian

Brotherhood. Both men were surrounded by sympathetic white advisers whose salaries depended on the largesse of the Liberal government. Those advising Erasmus may have been a little more radical, but that was an academic issue. Erasmus was tougher and more radical than anyone else in the western Arctic.

Take the Dene Declaration of 1975, with all its ringing phrases about freedom, independence, and aboriginal rights. Most of the white establishment believed it was simply an adaptation of Julius Nyerere's Tanzanian Declaration of Independence in Africa. Caroline Wah Shee claimed she knew for a fact that the Dene Declaration was written by Peter Puxley and some of the other white advisers. Puxley didn't quite deny writing at least one draft. But the point was that Erasmus himself knew all about Tanzania, along with the writings of Saul Alinsky and Herbert Marcuse and the leaders of the American Indian Movement (AIM). He was determined that the Indian Brotherhood should win some kind of self-government without giving up any aboriginal rights in the NWT.

James Wah Shee, who had created the Brotherhood with his linguistic and diplomatic skills, was much more inclined to work out a deal that might be acceptable to both the Indians and the whites. He hired lawyers and researchers to help him make his case; Erasmus was surrounded by political theorists like Mel Watkins and firebrands from the CYC.

Technology played an important role both inside the Indian Brotherhood and in its relations with the public. The highly successful general assemblies were made possible by air transportation and sophisticated communication equipment. It would have taken weeks for traditional elders to paddle from far-flung corners; now a charter flight could whisk half a community to a council hall in hours. No longer was there difficulty in getting ideas across to delegates speaking different languages or dialects: simultaneous translation brought the message through instantly.

The Brotherhood adapted in other ways. For all of these toys of the 20th century it needed money – for charter flights, translation equipment, salaries for interpreters, typists, copyists, researchers, treaty experts, lawyers, speechwriters, public relations advisers. The Secretary of State came up with part of the funding. Much more was borrowed against the ultimate land claims settlement. And there were grants or loans from churches and charitable foundations.

Ottawa played the negotiations game expertly. The annual reports of the Brotherhood and the Dene Nation show that when Ottawa was displeased with the way things were going, it simply cut off funds. In 1990, when Dene President Billy Erasmus tried to rally the chiefs for a stand against Ottawa's decision to deal with the regions instead of the Dene Nation, he found that he had no money to fight with. Even the chiefs' allowances were cut as a punishment. By 1977 the Brotherhood had received $760,000 from the feds, mostly from the Secretary of State, though some money came from DIAND and the GNWT. Within a few years, the Brotherhood owed almost $3 million and the Métis more than $1 million. This would have to come out of the ultimate land claims settlements.

By 1975, when the Brotherhood was about to explode internally, operations had become most sophisticated. A campaign to win white support in the south was gaining momentum. In August 1974 the "Southern Support Group" was set up at the suggestion of Don Simpson of London, Ontario, and Peter Russell, a Toronto law professor. A year later it opened an office in Ottawa, funded by a special grant from the United Church, the Canadian Catholic Conference, and Plura, an inter-church funding agency. The Brotherhood also got financial support from OXFAM, the Canadian Association in Support of the Native Peoples, and several Christian churches. The Anglicans, Roman Catholics, and United Church established "Project North" in 1975, later joined by the Mennonites and Lutherans. Other supporters were the Ontario Federation of Labour, the United Auto Workers, the World Universal Service of Canada, and various provincial native groups. The Brotherhood's 1975 annual report said:

> Day-to-day activities of the Ottawa office include sending out a newsletter and information packages on the Dene Land Claim, answering letters providing short articles or information resources to various publications and people doing research, and meeting with various groups across Canada to discuss their involvement and how they can work with us.

The report noted that eleven Indian representatives travelled to twenty-six cities across Canada, appearing on radio and TV shows, speaking at public meetings, and meeting with "small groups of people to tell southerners about the Dene Land Claims and to ask for support." The NWT Indians met church groups, high school and university students, labour unions, business clubs, civil liberties and human rights groups, environmental protection groups, and local native people. In short, they engaged in all the activities of any high-powered, well-funded lobby group.

As the Brotherhood grew more skilled and effective in selling its message, the attractive young people, white and native, who were running it began to fall out among themselves. New factors were entering the equation. More and more issues were being brought home to the middle-aged and older indigenes in their native languages, largely through the CBC's radio service. Such issues began to be discussed more frequently by ordinary people. Young chiefs were being elected – Jim Antoine was only twenty-five – and they were, like the young men and women running the Brotherhood, well educated, sophisticated, and travelled. They were familiar with the Black Panthers, Students for a Democratic Society (SDS), the Weathermen, and, above all, AIM (or Red Power).

At first old northern hands like Don Stewart in Hay River and David Searle in Yellowknife thought these people were jokes, not to be taken seriously. Whites were as patronizing as ever in their comments about natives, which infuriated the young Indian leaders even more than their fathers had been annoyed by the tricks of the treaty makers. From 1971 on, Wah Shee was the target of both the rednecks and his rivals in the Brotherhood. He was an attractive figure, a full-blooded Dog Rib, handsome, soft-spoken and intelligent. He had a gift for dialects and showed respect for the elders. Some observers thought him a bit lazy; others believed he was in the pocket of his radical white advisers, or of his radical wife, Caroline. Still others said he wasn't tough enough for Ottawa.

As they did with all the other native leaders of the period, including Erasmus, white politicians spread stories that his "Communist" white advisers wrote his speeches and handed him policies that had more to do with the left-wing politics of the south than with the claims of the NWT Indians. In conversation with me, Wah Shee smiled patiently and explained:

> Of course people write my speeches! I'm a busy man. But I tell them what I want to say. This is what every white politician and business executive does. As for policy, the chiefs and the elders work it out and I make suggestions. When we've decided what's best for the people, I ask my white advisers to put it into the most effective language needed to get through to the white officials I'm

dealing with. It would be foolish to state policy to Ottawa in Dog
Rib or Dehcho. But the policy is ours.

It was true that Wah Shee was a busy executive. Natives had
become fashionable in the south and were in demand as speakers at
banquets and panelists at conferences. Addy Tobac, a Sah'tu from
Good Hope, explained why she dropped out of McGill University:
"They like to have Indian girls they can show off at southern univer-
sities. What they want is somebody who can wear an evening gown
and use the right fork at a formal banquet." Tobac went home and
became a community worker. Wah Shee and several other native leaders, male and female, were eminently acceptable to white society.
They were constantly on the go: to negotiations with treaty commissioners in Ottawa, to conferences across the world with other aboriginal spokesmen, to banquets in Edmonton or Vancouver, to
Brotherhood assemblies in the Mackenzie Valley.

Wah Shee also had to supervise the swarm of researchers and
community workers who were digging out facts about land claims or
exploring cultural relations. He could be astonishingly frank at times
– as when he confessed to me that he was having trouble getting an
accurate fix on trapping territories: "We asked all the hunters and
trappers to draw maps of their personal territories. When we put all
the maps together, we found they were claiming about 125 percent of
the Mackenzie Valley; you see, each one estimated his land a little
bigger than it really was."

On the question of the influence of white advisers like Steve
Iveson, Peter Puxley, and Gerald Sutton, Wah Shee had this to say ten
years later:

> Any native organization requires specialized assistants. We had no
> prior experience in many areas. What we found was that university
> intellectuals were using the Dene movement as an experiment in
> theories they had promoted at their universities. Some were so
> indoctrinated by their own views that they thought the only way to
> achieve aboriginal rights was to practise their political ideologies.
> So they advised us against participating in the NWT legislature.

The legislature was the reef that sank Wah Shee's administration
in 1975. Should members of the Brotherhood run for election with the
hope of ultimately controlling the legislature and the GNWT? Or

should they boycott it in the hope of winning a totally independent political government of their own? Everything – land claims, autonomy, cash settlements, extinguishment of aboriginal rights – was involved in that single issue. It brought into conflict two exceptionally able young men, Wah Shee and Georges Erasmus, two years his junior. When that happened early in the 1970s, various countervailing forces were in full swing:

- In the Arctic, the Inuit rescue had succeeded and the high-tech towns were being completed. The indigenes were starting to participate in their own local government through community councils, and they were electing natives to the legislature.
- In the Mackenzie area, the GNWT was quickly taking over administration (though not authority) from DIAND. The old, appointed NWT Council, operating from Ottawa, was being replaced by a democratically elected legislative assembly.
- White residents had their own representatives and were learning how to work out political problems with the Dene, Métis, and Inuit. Natives were being offered a place at the legislative table commensurate with their numbers.
- Most Dene energies were being taken up with creating a political structure on racial lines in the communities and in preparing land claims. Brotherhood researchers were painstakingly finding where traplines went and how migrating caribou moved.
- Independent of these elements but affecting all of them, the petroleum and pipeline companies were preparing major programs.
- Environmentalists were studying what would happen if 5,000 outside workers suddenly arrived in the NWT and built a thousand kilometres of pipeline in two years.

Pat Carney, later a Conservative cabinet minister, visited the settlements to sell the Indians and Métis on the idea that natural gas and pipelines would be good for them. Hired guns from the Brotherhood and industry roamed the Mackenzie, and they were soon to meet at a wordy high-noon shoot-out presided over by Mr. Justice Tom Berger.

The best-known hired gun for the Indians was Mel Watkins, professor of political science at the University of Toronto and one of the leaders of the radical wing of the NDP. He came to Yellowknife on sabbatical when his wife took a job with the CBC, and he was hired by Wah Shee as an adviser. Watkins had strong feelings that colonialism was still rampant in the NWT and could only be eradicated by native self-government. In this view, Watkins was supported by other white advisers, such as Puxley and Iveson, and by Erasmus, Herb Norwegian, Richard Nerysoo, Chief Jim Antoine, and some other young Indian staff members and chiefs. This group believed that the Brotherhood should hold out for guarantees of aboriginal rights even over land claims: there should be no extinguishment of native rights, and the Indians should have their own government and sovereign territory, with "Denendeh" ("The People's Land") dealing on a government-to-government basis with Ottawa.

In 1976 the Indian negotiators offered Ottawa an "agreement" that called for "a Dene Government with jurisdiction over a geographical area and over subject matters within the jurisdiction of either the Government of Canada or the GNWT." Concessions were offered to non-native residents, and the draft agreement did not specify whether Métis and non-status Indians should be included (the status Indians were now starting to call themselves "Dene"). Ottawa rejected the proposal and continued its offer of cash and land in exchange for the extinguishment of aboriginal rights.

In September 1977, the Métis Association, negotiating on its own, presented a claim that was much more moderate than that of the Brotherhood. It was still not clear how far the Brotherhood wanted to go in the direction of absolute independence from Canada. At this stage, the feds demanded that the Indians and Métis settle their differences and present a single claim. To underline the point, DIAND Minister Hugh Faulkner abruptly cut off funding to both native organizations, a ban that continued until April 1980.

∿

Wah Shee was in the thick of the fight with Ottawa, but even before the difficulties with the Métis he found himself in major disagreement with his white advisers and some of his Indian staff. The issue was local government. Traditionally, under Treaties 8 and 11, Indian settlements were administered by DIAND (and its preceding ministries) under the Indian Act. DIAND dealt directly with the chiefs and band councils. If there were whites in a community, they were ignored by the Indians.

Under the new GNWT established in Yellowknife in 1967, community councils were set up to solve local problems. They were elected by all residents, Indian, Métis, and white, and sometimes bypassed the chiefs and band councils. Community councils worked well in the eastern Arctic where the Inuit were being given their first political input of any kind, but the Mackenzie Indians strongly opposed them. However, as time went on, younger natives felt that the community councils could help them more than the chiefs or the Indian agent.

Wah Shee believed the Indians might lose control of their own communities through the local and regional structure of the GNWT. He began to feel that it would be a good idea to start working within the GNWT system and, eventually, control it. This was anathema to some of the chiefs and elders and to many of the young organizers determined to establish an Indian government totally separate from the GNWT. They wanted nothing to do with the Yellowknife administration, even if they controlled it.

Wah Shee, however, felt he had to compromise with political realities. He knew that Ottawa was about to make the NWT Council fully elected, with fifteen members. He saw a chance to take over the whole government – if only the Indians, Inuit, and Métis could work together. So he ran for council in 1975 and was elected. He found that the strongly entrenched whites were ready for a new boy. When he wore a fringed moosehide jacket and beaded moccasins to council, Speaker David Searle said he was improperly dressed. Wah Shee blandly replied that he was wearing traditional ceremonial dress suitable to a chief in conference. The others laughed and accepted his explanation.

But it wasn't easy for the various natives on the council – now starting to call itself a legislative assembly – to find a common policy or even common interests. The only other Indian elected was George Barnaby from Good Hope, and there was only one Métis, Bill Lafferty from Simpson, who had spent much of his working life with whites in Alberta and who was not sympathetic either to the Brotherhood or to the Métis Association. There were six whites and six Inuit.

The Erasmus faction strongly opposed any Indian representation. Barnaby resigned, saying: "The Territorial Council is one place where Dene law is not respected at all. There is little involvement by the people. Whenever only a few people decide for the rest of the population, it oppresses people." This left Wah Shee isolated, and he soon realized his policies were in for a rough ride. Under pressure, he resigned from council, but it was too late.

In July 1975 there was a joint assembly of the Brotherhood and the Métis Association in Simpson, and the Dene Declaration was adopted unanimously by more than 300 delegates. It was a historic milestone because it put the Brotherhood on record as supporting the radicals. The declaration started off ringingly: "We the Dene of the NWT insist on the right to be regarded by ourselves and the world as a nation."

There were other stirring paragraphs: "Colonialism and imperialism are now dead or dying. Recent years have witnessed the birth of new nations or rebirth of old nations out of the ashes of colonialism." The declaration stopped short of declaring a sovereign nation, independent of Canada, but it insisted on "the right to self-determination as a distinct people and the recognition of the Dene Nation ... What we seek then is independence and self-determination within the country of Canada."

Wah Shee supported the declaration, although it marked a change in the Brotherhood's approach to land claims negotiations. He said in 1987: "The declaration was an expression of the Dene being a unique society. It was to declare we didn't want to participate in Canadian institutions. It took a long time for the government to recognize there were aboriginal rights."

Erasmus, who was close to the white advisers in 1975 but fired them in 1977 after he had succeeded Wah Shee, said they had influence years earlier when they began comparing the Canadian aboriginal population with the experience of indigenes in other parts of the world. He said in 1987: "The first thing that happened was a violent reaction against everything white when we looked at everyone's liberation experience. The relationship between the white advisers and the Indian field workers was on a basis of equality. The white advisers had an influence but no one was in awe of them."

DIAND Minister Judd Buchanan denounced the declaration as a separatist document. William R. Morrison wrote in 1985 in a DIAND paper: "Notwithstanding the reference to self-determination within Canada, the Declaration is written in a tone designed, probably deliberately, to give nightmares to a federal government engaged in endless delicate manoeuvrings with the province of Quebec."*

Quoting a Brotherhood document entitled "Recognition of the

---

*William A. Morrison, "A Survey of the History and Claims of the Native Peoples of Northern Canada," DIAND Research Centre (1985).

Dene Nation through Dene Government," Morrison listed the demands for provincial-like jurisdiction claimed exclusively by the natives: education; institutions of government (including "a provincial equivalent which would be the replacement of the existing Territorial Government"); administration of justice (with a system of Dene law in non-criminal matters); health and welfare; local trade and commerce; labour relations; natural resources; human rights; family relations; transportation; local community development; agriculture; environment; culture; direct and indirect taxation; fisheries; divorce law; land and water resources; parks; immigration; employment; communications; banks; and regional economic development.

Under "special aboriginal powers," the declaration demanded limits on federal power and "external jurisdiction" (i.e., the right to deal directly with foreign governments). Morrison added drily: "The only significant powers the Dene would see remaining with the Federal Government would be the power to run the army and the postal service. Despite Dene assurances to the contrary, there is little to distinguish the proposal from separation."

In 1978, when he was undisputed president of the Dene Nation, the political party that succeeded the Brotherhood that year, Erasmus said in his annual report to the Norman assembly:

> We have the full right, if we desire, of establishing a separate country of our own with a completely independent government – independent of the Canadian Federal Government.
>
> We have the right to completely and radically restructure government services, government systems, etc., etc.
>
> We are negotiating for a division of the powers which would be ours if we were seeking total sovereignty, between a government of our own and the federal government. This is what we are seeking and we have no intention of giving up our rights to total independence for less.
>
> We have achieved international recognition as an aboriginal nation with rights to self-determination.

~

With the Dene Declaration proclaimed, the stage was set for the "gunfight at the OK Corral" – which would coincide with the high-noon shoot-out between the hired guns at the Berger inquiry. James Wah Shee would have no more luck than the Clantons in his duel with

Georges Erasmus. There were grounds for rivalry. Whereas Wah Shee was a full-blooded status Dog Rib from Fort Rae with a knack for native languages, Erasmus's mother was Dog Rib, his father Cree Métis from outside the NWT, and he spoke no native language. Both men were handsome and articulate.

The Brotherhood's board of directors consisted of Wah Shee; Richard Nerysoo, a young Gwich'in from McPherson, vice-president; Chief Jim Antoine, Simpson; Eddy Koyina, North Slave region; François Paulette, South Slave; Chief Paul Andrew, North Mackenzie; and John Blake, Delta.

In the summer of 1975, Wah Shee attended meetings in Ottawa and, according to Caroline, his wife at the time, he fell ill. While he was out of the Territories, the Brotherhood staff, led by Erasmus, who was head of community organization, led a revolt against him. They presented an ultimatum to the directors, saying they would refuse to work under Wah Shee and claiming he was derelict in his duties. Wah Shee, arriving in Yellowknife, found himself locked out of his own office. He appealed to the board and there was a showdown. Wah Shee submitted a letter of resignation, then appealed over the board's head to a general assembly of chiefs and elders at Rae, his home territory. He was confident that the chiefs, with whom he had always had good relations, would support him.

The assembly met for five days in December, and the minutes, though skeletal, tell a dramatic story. Vice-president Richard Nerysoo opened the meeting and explained the charges. Paul Andrew from Fort Norman said the board had "lost faith and truth" in Wah Shee. Chief Alexis Arrowsmith of the Dog Ribs "accused the Board of running the Brotherhood and not consulting the people of the communities." The chiefs were seriously divided.

After three days, Nerysoo was asked to leave the chair and was replaced by Peter Liske, a compromise chair. As anger rose, there was a mounting demand that the rebellious staff be made to state its complaints. Erasmus arrived after a long delay and said that the staff was "not satisfied with James's performance as a leader. The Brotherhood are fighting for control of the land and believe it belongs to the Dene. The Dene need a strong leader they can have faith in."

On the fifth day, Wah Shee withdrew his resignation. After further strong attacks and counterattacks by the exhausted delegates, Chief Jim Antoine asked that Wah Shee's resignation be accepted without a vote, but in the end the assembly voted twenty-six to seventeen against Wah Shee. George Manuel, president of the National Indian Brotherhood, was a guest. He said he was sorry "to see there is so much individualism amongst the native peoples in the Territories – that's why the white man is stealing the land from under our noses."

With Wah Shee deposed, Nerysoo became acting president but it was generally agreed that he was, at twenty-two, too inexperienced for the job. An election was called in seven months, and Erasmus became president, with George Barnaby his vice-president.* Erasmus had triumphed but his troubles were just starting. The first one was that the Métis Association rejected a proposal to form one association. The Berger Inquiry was going on, and on its last day of hearings, in November 1976, the Métis split totally with the Brotherhood and supported the building of a gas pipeline as soon as possible.

Now the cracks in the Brotherhood were becoming even more apparent. Late in 1977, Erasmus abruptly fired all the white advisers and consultants who had supported his rise to power (Mel Watkins had long since gone back to the University of Toronto, his northern work completed). "We couldn't agree on priorities," Erasmus told me in 1987. "In 1976 the white advisers didn't believe that land claims were the number one priority – they thought the most important thing was to educate communities and individuals. We thought this was secondary. We wanted land claims and political rights established."

It was more complicated than that. Erasmus was discovering the hard political pressures that had pushed Wah Shee in the direction of compromise. The radical advisers, white and native, were pushing for an independent state within Canada (at the very least). But the people needed jobs, local schools, and health services – some of the things being offered by the GNWT. The federal government was dangling a carrot in front of their noses: sign a land claims agreement and get a big cash settlement. And the petroleum companies, along with the white business community in Yellowknife, had been promising jobs and prosperity all along the Mackenzie in return for a gas pipeline.

The ordinary Dene in the communities wanted things settled. The

---

Denendeh, the 1884 book published by the Dene Nation to celebrate the culture and traditions of the Indian peoples of the NWT, contains a chronology of events affecting the Dene from 1967 to 1984. There is no mention of the confrontation between Wah Shee and Erasmus. *Denendeh* was published when Stephen Kakfwi was president of the Dene Nation. A Dene from Good Hope, he disagreed with most of Erasmus's policies.

feds were hanging tough especially after they found that the Berger Commission had apparently stopped the pipeline in its tracks – funds were cut off and the bureaucrats were stonewalling. The cornerstone of the Erasmus position was federal acceptance of inextinguishable aboriginal rights before any land claims were even discussed.

The weakening aboriginal position was well illustrated by the movement away from Erasmus and the Dene Declaration. In 1977 the feds had threatened to approach the regional native leaders individually, and they were as good as their word. As early as September 1977, the Métis made a separate land claim that suggested "reconstituting the GNWT to have greater authority and jurisdictions to respond to the real needs of the aboriginal peoples." The Métis also suggested "the ownership and use and enjoyment of the lands needed by the aboriginal peoples for preserving, protecting and enhancing the native traditional lifestyle and land economy, such lands to be known as 'aboriginal lands.'" When the Métis Declaration came out in 1980, it declared the Métis to be "loyal citizens of Canada."

᷉

The flashiest event of 1978 was anti-climactic. The Dene Declaration was made in 1975, but the Brotherhood didn't become the Dene Nation until 1978, and then it was not a new or expectant free state but "a corporation under the laws of the NWT." Leaving out the rhetoric and the cultural importance of the word Dene, "The Dene Nation" was and remains a political party, though Erasmus and his successors saw it as much more. Its constitution was somewhat tamer than the Dene Declaration:

> The objectives of The Dene Nation are to uphold the rights and interests of the Dene Peoples in reference to their treaties and otherwise; to develop, discuss and promote policies for the Dene Peoples; to conduct, foster and support programs and policies for the economic, social, educational, health and cultural benefits of the Dene Peoples; to give voice to the opinions of the Dene Peoples; to cooperate with other organizations of similar or friendly purpose.

"The Dene Nation" has a fine ring to it and was useful in drawing southern attention to the aspirations of the NWT Indians, but there were practical reasons for changing the name of the Indian

Brotherhood. For years, Erasmus and others had been trying to draw the non-status Indians and Métis under their banner, with very limited success. For one thing, the Brotherhood was responsible to the assembly of chiefs and band councillors, and under the Indian Act, no Métis or non-status Indian could vote for a chief or band councillor. The president, vice-president, and five-person board were elected every two years by the general assembly.

In these circumstances could a Métis or non-status Indian be president, vice-president, or member of the board? In 1976 the Brotherhood met this problem by passing a resolution in Simpson to admit non-status Dene. It was not until 1979, after the Dene Nation had replaced the Brotherhood, that a non-status Dene, Herb Norwegian, was elected to office. When Erasmus retired, Norwegian served as acting president until he was defeated by Stephen Kakfwi.*

At the 1977 Fitzgerald assembly, the delegates spent a great deal of time debating the question of exactly who was a true native of the Mackenzie Valley and as such deserving of aboriginal rights. In changing the name of the Brotherhood to the Dene Nation, the new constitution provided that "The Dene Nation" (the corporation, that is) should be open to "all treaty people" and "all those who have formally declared themselves under Dene Registry since 23 June 1977."

Such status Indians and "declared Dene" would be "full members," with the right to vote or run for regional vice-president (and thus become a member of the board). Any active member was eligible for the executive (i.e., president, vice-president, secretary, or treasurer). As with the Brotherhood, the Dene Nation's constitution provided for the election every two years of the president and vice-president at the general assembly.

The definition of a "declared Dene" was: "Descendants of the aboriginal people of the NWT, the Dene, who have formally declared themselves in support of the 'Dene Position' submitted to the Government of Canada in October, 1976, subject to the conditions

---

*Erasmus himself was in a somewhat embarrassing position. The Brotherhood's chiefs and elders had, from the first, been jealous of the Cree who had been pushing into the Territories for nearly a century. Membership in the Brotherhood at first was limited to those springing from the indigenous Chipewyan, Dehcho, Sah'tu, Dog Rib, and Gwich'in. Erasmus's paternal ancestry was Cree Métis and it was important for his ambitions to have his NWT native rights clarified beyond question. The Brotherhood, and the Dene Nation, solved the difficulty by admitting the Cree had NWT territorial rights.

laid down at Dene Assemblies." Thus, any Métis who declared himself or herself a member of the Dene Nation was automatically subject to Dene policy, regardless of whether it conflicted with the policies of the Métis Association.

At the Fitzgerald meeting, a number of Métis and non-status Indians attended and spoke, most of them agreeing with the positions expressed by Erasmus. Bob Overvold, a Métis vice-president, said he quit because he disagreed with Rick Hardy, who had proposed that the petroleum companies set up a native development corporation. Nick Sibbeston, the first Métis elected to the NWT Assembly, supported the Indians and opposed the Métis Association.

The Fitzgerald minutes reveal a good deal about both Dene and Métis attitudes. Erasmus was chairman and he kept proceedings moving, encouraging young and old to participate. Alex Beggaire, an older delegate, said: "Look, you people, you're talking about leaving treaty! Do you know what's going to happen if you're not taking treaty? Look at hospital bills! If you've got a kid, who the hell is going to pay hospital bills? Not welfare! Nobody is going to pay hospital bills if you're not working!" Beggaire was answered by Billy Erasmus of Yellowknife, Georges's younger brother and a youth delegate:

> I don't know what this fellow's been drinking but he's not thinking like an Indian anyway. I'm a young man; I'm not a chief, and I'm not a head man or anything, but it gets me mad to listen to people talk like that! We're Dene people and we're supposed to think that way. We're thinking that everything is going to go wrong. We're thinking of sickness, of people dying – we're not supposed to think like that.

George Barnaby then spoke:

> I think this whole myth that a person's kids are going to die because he is not treaty is full of BS! There's a lot of treaty people who pay their own hospital bills. That's the law. Territorial council makes the law and they don't respect the treaty. For people who have no money, their hospital bills are paid so there is really no difference whether you are treaty or non-treaty.

Georges Erasmus intervened smoothly, explaining that no one was being asked to leave treaty: "For all the people who want to receive treaty and want things the way they've always been, there's no problem. That's the way it's going to be. Nobody is telling you or even asking you to do anything different." He made it very clear, however, that the speaker might change his mind about the benefits of treaties when he learned more about their provisions. He emphasized his political position: "We must have a Dene territory, a Dene land, and on that land a Dene government! There must be no territorial council on top of us! We must have a direct relationship with the federal government!"

An exchange with Billy Erasmus shed new light on the Dene attitude toward white residents of the NWT. It happened on the last day, when delegates were discussing subsurface mining rights and territorial rights for non-Dene. In 1976 the Brotherhood had promised to respect the political rights and land ownership of non-Dene in a society where there was a Dene government and territory. Georges Erasmus said: "To get what we want – to get control – we're going to have to give up a bit of land so that we would be able to control the rest of it."

Billy Erasmus brought up environmental issues and mentioned "the arsenic and that kind of thing" coming from Yellowknife gold mines. Georges Erasmus replied: "When we have control, we decide what we want to do the way we're going right here. It's up to the people. No one person is going to tell the rest what we're going to be doing. We all decide together what we want done on our land."

Billy Erasmus said some people understood that in towns like Yellowknife, "the town council would still operate the mines around the Indian families." Georges Erasmus said: "As for Yellowknife, we'd give it up! We would let it go the way it's going right now, and it would not be in Dene land. That small community would be left out and would be run just the way it is right now." Billy Erasmus shot back: "But that small, little community is affecting all of Great Slave Lake because of the arsenic and there's other towns like that – we would be able to control that!"

Georges Erasmus then made a statement that was certain to give federal negotiators and white residents a good deal to think about: "If what they're doing in Yellowknife in that mine is like right now, it's affecting land all over the place, then it would be a concern of our people because it's affecting a lot of land and polluting things. It would be a common concern so we would definitely deal with it!"

Compare this with the Brotherhood promise in 1976 to "recognize and respect the rights of the non-Dene," who would have "the right to self-determination and the use and development of their own institutions."

～

The flowering of the Dene Nation occurred at a time when southern whites were prosperous and concerned about both the welfare of the environment and the plight of the aboriginal peoples of Canada. The popularity of the Berger Commission, in the south as well as the North, was part of this benign atmosphere. Chief Frank T'Seleie warned oil tycoon Bob Blair at the Berger hearings that the Dene would give their lives to stop a pipeline.

But the times were changing rapidly. The financial market was becoming unfavourable for megaprojects. Money for native projects was getting tighter. The federal government was not buckling under Dene pressure for self-government and was still demanding extinguishment of aboriginal land rights in return for a land claims settlement. As early as 1978, COPE agreed in principle to the separate land deal that led to the Inuvialuit settlement in 1984.

Erasmus, losing support in the Dene communities, decided to retire, leaving the Dene Nation to his non-status vice-president, Herb Norwegian. Norwegian warned the NWT Legislative Assembly that there would be blood in the streets if a pipeline came, but it was a hollow threat. He himself was beaten by Stephen Kakfwi for the presidency of the Dene Nation. Erasmus moved into national Indian politics with great success and became the grand chief of the Assembly of First Nations and in 1990 co-chairman of a royal commission on the future of the aboriginal peoples.

Kakfwi, more moderate and more diplomatic than either Erasmus or Norwegian, faced an almost impossible task as leader of the overall Dene effort to establish some kind of Indian government representing all the linguistic and cultural Dene groups in the Mackenzie Valley. Gradually at first, then more quickly, the Dene regions began making separate deals, following the example of the Inuvialuit, who had agreed in principle to a settlement as early as 1978. The Dene Nation soon was not the sole voice for the Gwich'in, Dehcho, Sah'tu, Dog Rib, Chipewyan, and Northern Cree.

By the 1990s, the Dene Nation was a hollow shell, led now by Billy Erasmus. As he plaintively said at the end of his 1991–92 report: "As our elders tell us, we must never lose sight of the spiritual guidance necessary to carry the Dene through these difficult times. If we ask for help we will receive it."

The rise and fall of the Indian Brotherhood and the Dene Nation coincided with the determined efforts of the oil, gas, and pipeline interests to "develop" the Mackenzie Valley. In the 1970s, there was a three-way struggle for the hearts and souls of Canadian voters. It involved the NWT natives, the petroleum industry, and the forces of national, liberal goodwill as exemplified in the Berger Commission's hearings. The three forces came together along the Mackenzie River. The story of the pipeline had all the elements of high drama as well as high finance.

Part Three

REVOLUTION CULMINATES

Chapter 8

Pipeliners

We were all quite a few years ahead of our time.
– Bob Blair

The grandiose schemes in the 1970s to build a natural gas pipeline down the Mackenzie Valley failed, but they had a considerable impact on the NWT and on Canada in general. For instance, environmentalists found it was possible to challenge the world's biggest corporations – and win. Not far behind this achievement was the fact that the native peoples learned how to play the white man's politics and manipulate the levers of power; this lesson was learned by not just a few Indian and Inuit leaders but their peoples as a whole.

The financial struggle over the pipeline involved Canada's last great surge of nationalism before Brian Mulroney's Tories adopted continentalism as a national policy. For a while, the centre of financial gravity shifted from Toronto to Calgary. There were heroes, villains, and victims, hired guns and political doctrinaires; the political and social development of the NWT speeded up immensely.

The idea of developing the Mackenzie and Beaufort Sea arose from events happening far away and totally unrelated to the NWT. By the 1950s, the United States and Canada had placed the automobile at the centre of the universe, and millions of big, expensive, fuel-guzzling cars spewed out of Detroit's factories every year. This was made possible by cheap, abundant gasoline: from Texas and Oklahoma; from Venezuela and Mexico; from Saudi Arabia and Iran; and from Alberta.

At the same time, however, it was getting much harder to find new fields that would keep cheap gasoline flowing for generations to come. The geologists and their seismic crews began going farther afield. The Arctic had long been known to have enormous deposits of oil and natural gas, but until the second half of the 20th century, there was no way either to get at them or to ship the product to civilization even if it could be brought to the surface. The U.S. Navy made Alaska's North Slope an oil reserve as early as 1911, but it wasn't until the 1960s that the international oil giants began drilling.

The economics of the oil business have always been peculiar, and this affected exploration of the Canadian and American Arctic. In the case of Saudi Arabia, where the oil is close both to the surface and to ocean transport, vast profits can be made even when the product is sold very cheaply. But in the North Sea or the Arctic, the product is expensive and dangerous to reach and deliver. And, everywhere, finding the oil is a crap shoot, as difficult and problematical as the gold prospector's search for the mother lode. Thus, for generations, few but the wildcatters gave any serious thought to developing the frontier fields.

Then, in the 1960s, politics intervened: the succession of Arab-Israeli wars made it all too possible that Middle Eastern oil might be cut off from North American consumers. Suddenly it appeared that automobile drivers might have to pay much higher prices for gasoline. So frontier gas became an economic possibility.

It was with this speculative glint in their corporate eyes that oil men sent out seismic crews across the NWT and Alaska's North Slope. They were looking for an "elephant" – a field containing at least ten billion barrels – and they found it at Prudhoe Bay. The explorers were Atlantic Richfield (ARCO) from California, British Petroleum (BP), and SOHIO (Standard Oil [Ohio]), one of the several spin-offs of Standard Oil. ARCO's strike was typical of the oil business, coming after many unsuccessful efforts in the same area. Exxon (Standard Oil, N.J.) had spent $100 million searching for oil and building an airport. The results were so discouraging that when Exxon abandoned its efforts, it called its airport "Deadhorse."

Yet Deadhorse airport itself was a first-rate example of the trial and error methods used in the Arctic. Exxon needed to move heavy equipment by four-engined Hercules air freighter. After many failed experiments, Exxon laid down a thick gravel and binder pancake atop the tundra, and this diffused heat and spread shock and pressure. The biggest transports could land and take off without difficulty. Soon there were roads built on the same principle, linking Deadhorse with the shallow-water wharf at Prudhoe Bay. The local service roads were prototypes for the trans-Alaska road, which served the pipeline carrying oil from the Beaufort to Prince William Sound off the Gulf of Alaska.

This Alaskan experience was of great importance to companies thinking of developing frontier oil and gas resources in the Canadian Arctic, and there were direct links from the start. For instance, although the U.S. supertanker *Manhattan* was able to get through the Northwest Passage in 1969, the permanent ice-fields in the Arctic Ocean and the few ice-filled passageways made shipment of oil prohibitively expensive, no matter where it originated. In the western Arctic, especially, the sea shelf was so shallow that it was hard to find ports even for small vessels. Supply freighters going into Prudhoe Bay had to be lightered off from a considerable distance.

Under the circumstances, an oil pipeline across Alaska and then shipment by tanker to Washington and California seemed to be the simplest and cheapest solution. Petroleum and shipping men anticipated no delays: they were accustomed to having billion-dollar projects rubber-stamped by Congress or by individual states (in the case of a foreign country, they might have to buy the whole government). Environmental questions were not expected: why should they be? It had never happened before.

So sure were ARCO, BP, and SOHIO, the partners in the Prudhoe Bay field, that they ordered their pipe from Japan and when it was delivered in a jiffy, stored it on the shores of the North Slope and Prince William Sound, waiting for the start of pipeline construction. It was to sit there rusting for several years.

∼

The multinational oil companies – known to the corporate world as "The Seven Sisters" – were discomfited when the Alaska pipeline was delayed by environmental concerns and the claims of the Eskimos, Indians, and Aleuts. But as usual, they had alternative plans, and these involved Canada. As soon as it was discovered that there was a big pool of oil and gas beneath the North Slope (and even before the Prudhoe Bay strike), some petroleum men thought of building an Arctic oil pipeline, or a natural gas pipeline, or both, across Canada. Consequently, for some time the United States had been exerting heavy pressure on Ottawa to permit the construction of a pipeline from Alaska to Montana, which would cross Canadian territory.

California, Washington, and Oregon were strongly opposed to having heavy tanker traffic along their Pacific shores. British Columbia made similar objections to the Liberal government in

Ottawa. On the other hand, Ottawa and many Canadians prominent in private enterprise wanted no part of an American financial and physical intrusion into Canada; at the very least, Ottawa felt, there should be financial partnership between American and Canadian firms.

In 1967 the first steps were taken to find out whether a Canadian gas pipeline would be feasible. TransCanada PipeLines,* based in Calgary and Toronto, joined forces with Michigan-Wisconsin Pipe Line (Detroit) and Natural Gas Pipelines (Chicago) and began exploring costs, possible routes, and environmental hazards. When TransCanada launched its Arctic inquiry, Vern Horte was group vice-president, and he soon became president. He was an Albertan and a veteran of the petroleum business who saw enormous potential in a northern pipeline. In 1970 he brought ARCO, Humble Oil, and SOHIO into a consortium and called it the Northwest Project Study Group, with headquarters in Calgary.

The Alberta Gas Trunk Line Company (AGTL, now NOVA Corporation) tried to join the project in its early stages but was snubbed. That was a fatal mistake and proved to be the opening skirmish of an epic war between two of the highest rollers in the business. The driving force in AGTL was Bob Blair, who was literally born into the oil business: his father, Sid Blair, an engineer, ran a refinery when Bob was born in Trinidad. When the oil wars started, Bob Blair was forty, a soft-spoken, thoughtful man with a mystical sense of Canadian nationalism. He was a third-generation Albertan, and his father was a distinguished executive who ultimately became chairman of Bechtel Canada, a branch of Bechtel San Francisco, the same construction firm that helped build the CANOL Project in 1943–44.**

After the snub to AGTL, Blair set up the Gas Arctic Systems Study Group and began rounding up partners for a battle with Vern Horte. Alberta Gas Trunk was an odd firm, but it suited Bob Blair down to the ground. He had spent many years as a rising but frustrated executive in American-owned companies. AGTL was completely

---

*TransCanada was already a famous Canadian institution but a highly controversial one: in 1956 it was at the centre of the infamous pipeline debate in Parliament, when C.D. Howe rammed through a proposal for a Canadian-route pipeline linking Alberta with central Canada. The dispute ultimately led to John Diefenbaker's 1957 victory.

**Bechtel specialized in building megaprojects all over the world, particularly in the petroleum industry. It built oil installations in the Arabian Desert, much of the James Bay hydroelectric project in Quebec, the Churchill Falls power project in Labrador, and the Syncrude tar sands development at Fort McMurray, Alberta.

Albertan, established in 1954 by the Social Credit government to operate Alberta's pipelines as a common carrier. The company was privately owned, but two of its seven directors represented the provincial government and it really was an arm of that government.

Blair had two objectives as the recently appointed president of AGTL: first responsible for many pipelines in Alberta, he wanted them to get a piece of any action from Arctic wells, Canadian or American; second, he wanted to make sure that Canadian companies controlled all pipelines anywhere in Canada. This was anathema to the multinationals and to the American pipeline and gas distribution companies, all of which were accustomed to owning and controlling the means of distribution.

Blair and Horte

When Bob Blair and Vern Horte began their Byzantine manoeuvres in 1970, the Prudhoe Bay field was dormant, waiting for settlement of native land claims. In the NWT, the new GNWT was taking over some functions from DIAND and was setting up several levels of democratic (and bureaucratic) government. The Indian Brotherhood, COPE, and Inuit Tapirisat of Canada (ITC) were being born, and the Métis Association wasn't even that far along. Stuart Hodgson was the "Umingmuk commissioner," charming every settlement from Resolute to Fort Liard.

In those days, it meant very little to northerners that Calgary was emerging as a world principality in the oil business. Jack Gallagher sank his first dry hole on Melville Island in the High Arctic in 1969–70, and Panarctic Oil was methodically exploring the Arctic archipelagos. Some oil and more gas was found on the shores of the Beaufort Sea, and very large amounts of gas were discovered in the Arctic islands. As northern petroleum ventures gained in popularity, Calgary was becoming a world centre of Arctic technology. Ron Southern's Alberta Trailer Company (ATCO) was building a large proportion of the portable buildings used by oil and mining crews in Alaska as well as in the Territories. FOREMOST was designing innovative equipment for use on the delicate tundra – vehicles with enormous tires, which used lubricants that wouldn't freeze. Such equipment could work in -70°F. Fred Mannix, Inc., with 132 companies by 1983, was into everything.

The resources of such highly sophisticated companies were available to both Horte and Blair, and both used them intensively. The Northwest Project Study Group, with headquarters in Calgary, kept its staff small but hired many consultants. Blair, with a built-in Canadian bias, tended to hire Canadians; Horte, with dominant American partners, hired American companies or their Canadian subsidiaries.

Blair's intense activity in the early stages was extraordinary and tended to even up the odds favouring the Northwest Project Study Group. His group included Canadian National Railways; Columbia Gas System Inc. of Wilmington, Delaware; Northern Natural Gas of Omaha, Nebraska; Texas Eastern Transmission of Houston; and Pacific Lighting Gas Development of Los Angeles. He also talked to Panarctic and Dome Petroleum about the chances of bringing Arctic islands gas to a pipehead in the Delta.

Blair learned that West Coast Transmission, the giant B.C. supplier dominated by Frank McMahon and Kelly Gibson, had gone into partnership with Bechtel Canada and El Paso (Texas) Gas to form Mountain Pacific Pipeline. The idea was to run a gas pipeline through the B.C. and U.S. Rockies to California. While the scheme never got off the ground, Blair knew that if its participants were involved in a major project, they would not be joining Horte's Northwest Project Study Group. Don Peacock, who wrote *People, Peregrines and Arctic Pipelines* in 1977 with financial assistance from the Blair consortium, believes that Blair was trying to get Canadian financing for the whole pipeline development; it is certainly true that he had a long-range vision of Canadian Arctic oil and gas developments far beyond exploitation of the Prudhoe Bay field.

From the first, both Horte and Blair emphasized environmental studies, Blair perhaps a little more than Horte. One of his most remarkable decisions was to set up the independent Environmental Protection Board. The board, headed by Carson H. Templeton, a Winnipeg consulting engineer, was funded by Gas Arctic but could initiate its own studies and release its reports directly to the press or to the government. Environmental responsibility was a new departure for most corporations, especially in the petroleum industry. During the CANOL Project and the DEW Line building, much of the North was littered with abandoned debris – uncounted thousands of empty oil drums, tanks full of PCBs, worn-out tires, abandoned vehicles, scraps of insulation, even kitchen garbage.

By the late 1950s, there was the beginning of a public outcry against pollution, and Ottawa began ordering companies with oil or mining leases to clean up after themselves. They were even required to pay attention to any poisons they might release into the ground, air, and streams. Both Horte and Blair were keenly aware of events in Alaska, where environmental groups such as the Sierra Club and the Canadian Wildlife Federation were showing remarkable political clout. So both consortiums began an education program aimed at the residents of the Mackenzie Valley, showing pipeline models and flying in experts to talk to the indigenes. Pat Carney, then a respected *Vancouver Sun* business writer, was hired as a communications consultant and set up a public relations firm, Gemini North, in Yellowknife. She gave Blair sensible advice in a report she prepared for him in 1970 (quoted in Peacock's book):

> The size and environmental regime pose special engineering and construction problems. Similarly, the economic, sociological and ecological features will be given unprecedented weight in determining the success of any license application. These unique problems demand unique solutions.

Carney struck at the heart of the matter when she said either pipeline consortium would have to get the blessing of the Canadian government before laying a single metre of pipe, even though the Liberal cabinet was clearly in favour of a gas pipeline – and the sooner the better. On 13 August 1970, Energy Minister Joe Greene and DIAND Minister Jean Chrétien issued a set of guidelines that described Arctic pipelines as "a potential major economic contribution to the country." Both oil and gas pipelines received cautious approval in principle, although there were warnings that thick hedges of social and environmental regulations could be expected.

Greene hinted that the government wanted only one pipeline proposal, strongly implying that the Northwest Project Study Group and Gas Arctic should settle their differences and combine resources. But by this time, Blair's consortium was a serious challenger. In 1971 AGTL and CNR hired Pemcan Services of Calgary to do a feasibility study for development of something called the "corridor concept." This was a grandiose scheme involving oil and gas pipelines, roads, railways, and water transport in the Mackenzie Valley. Pemcan was a formidable engineering consortium which had completed sixty-five major projects in mid-Canada and the North. It included the Mannix

Company, Techman Ltd., Shawinigan Engineering, Templeton Engineering, and Montreal Engineering.

What Blair had going for him was his concept of financing. Northwest, dominated by Americans, proposed a 48-inch pipeline from Prudhoe to Montana, where it would connect with existing (or newly built) American pipeline networks. Blair, as president of AGTL, planned his "big-inch" pipeline only as far as the Alberta border, where it would feed into existing Alberta and interprovincial lines that would carry the product east, west, or south as the market demanded. This routing cut $1.2 billion off the estimated $4 billion projected by Northwest.

~

Petroleum economics have always been wacky, but they get infinitely worse when the entrepreneurs reach frontiers in remote and difficult regions. In the 1960s, the Saudis could sell crude to Esso/Exxon for $1.25 a barrel and still make enough profit to pay for government and social welfare in a feudal desert state with a small population. Meanwhile, Alberta and Texas wells were producing crude for anywhere from $1.50 to $2.00 a barrel. The world price averaged out at around $3.00.

But on the northern frontier, costs were out of sight. The Sun Oil (Sunco) mine at McMurray, Alberta, which extracted oil from the Athabaska tar sands, found costs running from $6 to $7 a barrel. In the Arctic, costs were astronomically above that, and there was a big question as to whether northern petroleum would ever be available at an affordable price. In the 1970s, one question was asked more and more frequently: If it costs $5 to produce $3 worth of oil or gas, can anyone afford it? The petroleum companies never bothered to answer the question: they found ingenious ways around it.

The principal one was to persuade governments to give them tax rebates in return for exploration programs. Under Trudeau's National Energy Program (NEP), companies exploring in the High Arctic, like Dome Petroleum and Panarctic, received as much as 120 percent of their costs in tax rebates, which could be credited against losses in other enterprises. Theoretically, the companies could go on drilling dry holes forever, with Ottawa paying the shot and a good bit left over. In the short term, it didn't matter to the companies whether they found oil or gas, and the question of the cost of extracting it didn't seriously enter their calculations.

In the long term, however, the companies would have to make a big strike and get it to market if they were to obtain the huge profits for which their stockholders longed. Besides, company executives realized the government probably wouldn't go on paying exploration costs in full (or more than in full) forever. On top of all this, there was galloping inflation in the 1970s. The cost of the Alyeska oil pipeline in Alaska was first projected at $1 billion but actually reached $8 billion six years later. This meant that estimates on the viability of frontier gas and oil were drastically altered every year. Blair and Horte found themselves playing a wild Monopoly game of paper figures. Blair's economics looked much better than Horte's estimates, but only in the mad world of oil/gas financing.

As inflation changed the whole economic scene, the basic question changed a little too: the formula involving $5 worth of energy for $3 worth of energy finally forced the entrepreneurs to face the real cost of producing and bringing to market frontier crude oil and natural gas.

Once again the petroleum men answered the question by not answering it. They went on making billion-dollar deals.

Squaring Off

By the middle of 1971, Northwest had lined up the major gas companies in the eastern United States, while Arctic Gas had arrangements with most of the western ones. Northwest had already spent nearly $50 million and AGTL alone $12 million. The Alaskan native land claims settlement was moving through Congress, and it looked as if the Alyeska pipeline would be able to get going in 1972. Plans for the gas pipeline involving Canada were falling far behind, and the Canadian government was getting impatient. Joe Greene let Horte and Blair know that Ottawa felt the rivals should merge now and make a single application.

Earle Gray, public relations chief of Gas Arctic, says in his book, *Super Pipe:* "Participants in each of the competing proposals were under no illusions that ultimately they would nearly all have to join forces if a pipeline was to be built. It was not the type of competition where a single company could win the franchise and do the job by itself."

The marriage of Northwest and Gas Arctic may have been inevitable, but the mating dance was long and exhausting. In the spring and summer of 1971, Horte and Blair held confidential meetings in Toronto, Houston, Seattle, Denver, Omaha, Calgary, and Chicago. Considering that both their offices were in Calgary, there was reason to ask whether these trips were really necessary. Horte, with Exxon now a part of Northwest and with strong financial ties in the East, felt that his group should be dominant. But Blair demanded major concessions. He wanted the Canadian pipeline installations to be owned and controlled by Canadian companies; the Americans could finance and own the pipelines in Alaska and the Lower 48. Second, he wanted the Environmental Protection Board to continue its independent research in the merged company. Third, he wanted a major role in choosing a chairperson and chief executive officer.

As the furtive negotiations proceeded in airport hotels and gas company boardrooms, Blair won some but never enough concessions. Under heavy pressure from Ottawa and an ultimatum from his American partners, Blair reluctantly agreed to join Northwest. At a meeting in Omaha, three co-chairs were picked: Horte, Blair, and W.N. (Deke) Mack, president of Michigan-Wisconsin Gas, one of the original Northwest partners. Mack was an easterner and an Ivy-Leaguer, and Blair admitted often butting heads with him. On 8 June 1972 the official marriage took place in Houston with Horte in the chair.

The new consortium was called Arctic Gas and there were twelve original partners, soon joined by several more: notably CP Investments, Imperial Oil, Shell Canada, and Gulf Canada. One of the most significant was the Canadian Development Corporation (CDC), a Crown company set up by the Liberal government to buy up or buy into foreign-controlled companies and thus increase Canadian industrial ownership. Sitting on the board of directors of Arctic Gas was the head of the CDC, Marshall A. Crowe. Soon he was to become chairman of the National Energy Board and would have a dramatic role in the pipeline projects. The very presence of CDC indicated the Canadian government's favourable involvement in these mega-projects.

∽

The first big job of the new partners was to pick a chairman. Here again Horte and Blair were in strong disagreement. Blair favoured a strong figure from the oil or gas business, almost certainly a Canadian. An impartial observer might have felt that Blair himself was the only person who could fill the bill, but in a Houston taxi ride he and Horte had agreed that neither of them wanted the job.

Horte and the Standard Oil group had their own favourite: Bill Wilder, president of Wood Gundy Inc. of Toronto, Canada's biggest investment dealer. Jack Armstrong, president of Imperial Oil (owned by Exxon), thought Wilder was the only man in Canada fit for the job because Wood Gundy had close ties with Morgan Stanley, the Wall Street financial firm. Exxon believed Morgan Stanley essential in any bond-floating venture. So Wilder was chosen over Blair's misgivings, and he quickly nominated Horte president and chief executive officer.

The battle went on. Wilder clipped the wings of the Environmental Protection Board by reserving Arctic Gas's authority over the kind of research done and the form, content, and timing of the board's reports to the public.*

Blair found it as difficult to implement his views on financing from inside Arctic Gas as he had from outside. The gas pipeline in Alaska, like the oil pipeline, would be financed and controlled by American money: but what about the Canadian sections? Blair still wanted these – in the Yukon, B.C., and Alberta – financed and controlled from within Canada. The American partners, particularly the Exxon group, favoured one company, which inevitably would be dominated by the Americans. Only grudgingly did Wilder and Horte accept the idea of "substantial" Canadian participation in the financing.

~

In some areas, Arctic Gas plunged ahead with enormous force. An engineering consortium – Northern Engineering Service – was set up in Calgary to handle the multitude of studies, surveys, and analyses needed before an application could be made to the Canadian and American governments. This supplemented the work Blair had instituted with Pemcan and the Environmental Protection Board.

Everything seemed clear sailing to the Canadian government. Prime Minister Trudeau made a major speech in Edmonton in which he envisioned a tremendous development in the North, including railways and highways to the Arctic and a super-port capable of operating all year round. The 1970 government guidelines were widened and strengthened in 1972 by DIAND's Jean Chrétien, who told Parliament that any pipeline proposals would have to have "substan-

---

*It's a tribute to the integrity of the board and its members that even Mr. Justice Berger was satisfied with its research.

tial opportunity for Canadian participation in financing, engineering, construction, ownership and management."

Northern Engineering sent teams to study climate, the effects of extreme cold on people and machines, and impact on the tundra. The problems were difficult. For instance, in Alaska it was found that crude would move through a pipeline at 170°F (94°C), which meant that if a pipeline was laid on the tundra, it would melt through the permafrost until the pipe bent enough from its own weight to break and spill. This challenge was met by placing the pipeline on a thick berm of asphalt and gravel that dispersed the heat, or by raising it on stilts, which allowed the heat to dissipate in the atmosphere. The Alaska system worked so well that up to 1989 there were no major spills or breaks, and the environment had not been seriously damaged.

Gas pipelines had a reverse problem: the gas would be chilled before entering the pipeline, but it would be under tremendous pressure – Arctic Gas proposed 1,680 pounds per square inch (PSI) in a 48-inch pipe, compared with 800 to 1,000 PSI in southern lines. There was always the danger of a pipeline flaw, crystallization of metal due to cold, or failure of a joint. This might result in fire or even explosion, and cut-off valves had to be planned at regular intervals. Both types of pipeline were susceptible to damage from earth tremors and, in Alaska, the oil pipeline ran through an earthquake zone. At Prudhoe Bay, there was no danger from the Arctic Ocean or the ice-pack because the wells were drilled on the tundra. But the new Canadian fields in the Arctic archipelago and off the Delta coast were constantly threatened by the expanding and contracting ice-field. In open waters, there was always the danger of icebergs.

Imperial Oil built artificial islands on the shallow continental shelf of the Beaufort. The first island, Immerk, was created in 1972. During the next nine years, nineteen more were built. The islands were ingenious: huge, concrete caissons were built in Vancouver and other southern ports and towed through the Bering Sea around Alaska to the Beaufort, where they were sunk, usually in an octagonal shape. The formerly water-tight boxes of concrete were filled with sea water so that they sank to the ocean floor. Then they were pumped full of sand by dredging ships, and the hole in the middle was filled with sand, creating an actual island.

Drilling derricks, storage tanks, and pipeline facilities were built, along with a helicopter landing pad and some kind of landing stage for barges, tugs, and small boats. Between 1965 and 1981, 130 exploratory wells were drilled from such islands, from drilling platforms or from drill ships anchored in the Beaufort. Even a man-made island might be wrecked by shifts of the ice-pack or by a roving iceberg, so most islands were built near the coast where the water is not more than twenty-five metres deep. Up to that point, the ice is "land fast" and permanent.

The second big Beaufort operator in the 1960s and 1970s was Dome, and it had its own drill ship, the *Canmar Explorer III*, a 158-metre vessel with a 37-metre drilling platform. The ship carried 106 people, including a marine crew of 20. While it could drill hundreds of metres beneath the ocean floor, it was subject to currents, ice-field pressure, and scouring. Dome engineers found that the ice-pack tended to scour the ocean floor to a water depth of 120 metres, and there was serious scouring up to 40 metres.

For decades, the petroleum companies have gone to great lengths to find ways of setting up stable drilling platforms and ocean-floor pipelines. The pioneer work in this field was done in the subtropical Gulf of Mexico and off the California coast. But it was of no use in the Arctic. Imperial, Dome, and Gulf Canada, the biggest Beaufort players, found they would have to sink pipelines below the ocean floor to avoid being scoured by the ice-pack every year. (This was the same lesson learned by CANOL engineers in 1943 when they were running their four-inch pipe across the Mackenzie.)

One experimental ship built for Dome in Texas was almost unbelievably ingenious. Working on the principle that drilling ships had to float wherever the ice-pack took them, the designers developed a flexible drilling string, which in effect became an umbilical cord tied to the ocean bottom. It was so flexible that it could move in a great circle eight kilometres across. Of course, there would always be the danger that an Arctic storm might drive the ice-pack farther than predicted, snapping the umbilical cord. If such an accident occurred after the drillers had struck oil or gas, the disaster would be unimaginable, with petroleum pouring out of a hole in the bottom of the sea and no possible way to cap it. The exotic concept of the umbilical cord disappeared in the 1980s as the big operators built more and more islands. Although they discovered very large deposits of oil and gas, no major Arctic Ocean spills had occurred up to 1989.

Petroleum geologists estimate that there are 36 billion barrels of crude locked up in the Beaufort and 339 trillion cubic feet of natural gas. This compared with 9.6 billion barrels of crude and 26 trillion cubic feet of gas at Prudhoe Bay. The Beaufort players envisaged their crude being carried in specially designed icebreakers/tankers or by an under-the-sea pipeline from Richards Island to pumps mounted on artificial islands. Richards Island is across Kugmallit Bay from Tuktoyaktuk at the mouth of the Mackenzie. A 48-inch pipeline would link Richards Island with Edmonton via the Mackenzie.

The Beaufort operations were unrelated to the High Arctic exploration, which involved another, even bigger, gas field. One plan there was to build a liquefied natural gas (LNG) plant on Melville Island and move the gas south in ice-breaking LNG ships travelling the eastern route around Baffin Island.

Both High Arctic and Beaufort exploration were going on during Arctic Gas's efforts to launch a gas pipeline down the Mackenzie, but most of the partners were concerned only with Prudhoe Bay. In the case of the Beaufort gas field, Arctic Gas had rather vague plans to hook a spur line into the main Prudhoe Bay gas pipeline. (Bob Blair's final proposal of a "Maple Leaf Pipeline" was the first to consider the Beaufort gas field as an end in itself.)

The Prudhoe pipeline route would bring Arctic Gas into conflict with environmentalists in the hearings before Mr. Justice Berger and Canada's National Energy Board. The environmentalists submitted evidence purporting to show that even a solidly land-based pipeline would pose a threat to plants and animals. For instance, hundreds of thousands of caribou in the Porcupine herd migrate annually from Alaska to the Yukon and NWT and back again, some of them past Arctic Village in Alaska's Brooks Range, on to the Porcupine River valley, and past the Yukon Gwich'in settlement of Old Crow. Other caribou move along the Arctic coast past the British Mountains into the edge of the Delta.

Could these animals get over a 48-inch pipeline sitting on a two-metre berm? Would they be frightened away by the smell of oil or gas or steel, the sound of pumps and the hum of electricity? Would they be poisoned by oil spills? Shot by pipeline builders or maintenance men? Both the Alaskan and Canadian corporations paid a good deal of attention to environmental questions and, in fact, the caribou adapted surprisingly well to the barriers. Engineers created a number of gates along the Alyeska pipeline by putting it on 4.6-metre stilts, leaving extensive underpasses for the animals. Caribou learned to graze under the pipe as they drifted from one country to the other.

Another issue involved the Arctic shoreline. Arctic Gas wanted to run its pipeline along the treeless tundra from Prudhoe Bay to the Delta. There it would hook up to the pipeline running south along the Mackenzie. Almost everyone agreed that a major project in this narrow, exposed corridor might endanger the migrating Porcupine herd, and indeed, the United States had established the Arctic Wild Game Reservation on the Alaska side of the Yukon boundary.

The Mackenzie Delta was a difficult area to build in and susceptible to grave damage, with its many streams and ponds, river channels, and miles of swamps. It would be hard to anchor pipelines, pumping stations, and service roads on muskeg, which in turn sat on permafrost. Consequently, there were serious doubts about the feasibility of the short route from Prudhoe along the coastline.

The needs and safety of the indigenes in the Delta and Mackenzie Valley were also of major concern to Horte's Northwest and Blair's Gas Arctic even before their merger. Gemini North researchers visited the Mackenzie communities, trying to determine whether the Indians and Inuvialuit could be sold on a pipeline. Questionnaires were distributed to find out how many natives and Métis still hunted and trapped for a living, how important wild food was in their diet, and how many wanted training for white-style jobs.

Although anthropologists had been studying the aboriginals for generations, nobody had ever done consumer surveys. Gemini North found gaps in northern education: for instance, to the Indians "gas" meant what powered their outboard engines, and they had a hard job understanding what was meant by "natural gas." Pat Carney's people had the usual difficulties of high-pressure poll-takers employed by sophisticated firms: they knew little about the people they were surveying, and few of them spoke any of the native languages. They were also preaching a gospel that ran counter to that of the young white and native community organizers working for the Indian Brotherhood. To many of these people, the very presence of the pipeline proponents was neo-colonialism – and their radical voices had the ears of the chiefs and elders.

Perhaps the most extraordinary element in the pipeline debate was that until the Berger Inquiry began its hearings in 1975, residents of the NWT, native and white, were almost totally ignored by the planners from government and private industry. The Canadian Arctic was full of pipeline-paid engineers, anthropologists, climatologists, biologists, and economists, but they seldom talked to the people who lived in the Territories. Seemingly without consulting anyone north of the 60th parallel, Ottawa decided that a pipeline would be good for Canada. The petroleum execs worked and reworked billion-dollar deals in Houston, Toronto, Calgary, or Vancouver, and their sole concern appeared to be the corporate relationships between Shell Canada and ARCO, Bechtel and Mannix.

This was partly due to the chronic secrecy of the petroleum business and partly to the reluctance of senior civil servants to reveal their policies to anyone, including their political masters. Secrecy was a way of life in Ottawa and Houston, and secrecy had been part of the NWT since it had been Rupert's Land. In the petroleum industry, the stakes were so high and the risks so great that players tended to keep poker-faces when dealing with their partners (to say nothing of their rivals). This state of affairs was illustrated flamboyantly in Bob Blair's relationship with Arctic Gas.

In the normal course of events, the petroleum industry was a maze of interlocking companies built in a kind of financial earthquake zone. Most of them were looking for financing. Corporate structures shrank and expanded, changed out of recognition, and moved into new territory from day to day. As one Bechtel Canada veteran put it: "Whether a company is 'limited' or 'incorporated' depends entirely on the week or month." Such Byzantine manoeuvring in the boardroom carried over to the licensing hearings before regulatory bodies and to work in the field. Exploration companies spent much time and money disguising or hiding their field activities. Thus, environmental impacts were hard to assess, whether on the ecological or on the human level.

When the Berger Report was issued in 1977, the impression given by the media was that Mr. Justice Berger had initiated environmental studies to thwart the greedy aims of the petroleum industry. This was far from the truth: in fact, the oil, gas, and pipeline men had been forced to see the light by the 1969 land freeze in Alaska. Both Northwest and Arctic Gas had spent, between them, $170 million on environmental studies, and the Canadian government had made a number of independent studies. Much of Berger's report, in fact, depended on evidence he got from the pipeline consortiums.

Actually, oil and gas exploration had had very little impact on the Arctic environment and almost none on the lives of the indigenes. Exploration wells were sunk far from human habitation and, after about 1960, under fairly rigid environmental regulations. The very nature of the business protected the land and the aboriginals. Unlike gold or silver booms, where miners flocked into the nearest towns to register claims or deposit swag (and then get drunk and socialize with frontier belles), the drilling crews were flown out after three weeks of intense, isolated work; they were deposited in Edmonton or Vancouver for a week's leave, then picked up and brought back to the rig.

Roughnecks on Arctic rigs have among the worst jobs in the world – hard, dangerous, dirty, and badly paid. A typical rigger is a Saskatchewan or North Dakota farm boy trying to pick up a stake in the off-season. If he worked for a company like Peter Bawden Drilling of Calgary in the 1970s, he was not unionized and got about the same wages as a construction worker – plus free travel in and out and plenty of overtime. Drilling rigs work twenty-four hours a day, so several work crews were needed. On the drilling platform, men handled nine-metre lengths of pipe while soaked to the skin with drilling mud, whether the temperature was minus 40°F or plus 80°F (with swarms of black flies and mosquitoes). If they had any spare time after working seventy or eighty hours a week, there was little to do: certainly not hunting or fishing or even walking on the tundra. Crew planes or helicopters took departing men to the nearest point where they could catch a PWA or NWTA scheduled flight. What they did after they got to Edmonton was their own affair: some went home to wives and children; others blew their $2,000 paycheques in Las Vegas or Honolulu. Few of them spent much, if any, time in NWT towns.

Much the same situation applied to the pipeliners who moved steadily across the landscape as soon as a project was given the go-ahead. In Alaska, the pipeline roughnecks (as contrasted with the highly skilled and jealously unionized pipe welders, most of whom came in on contract from Texas and Oklahoma) were generally hired and laid off in Anchorage or Fairbanks, so the bars and red-light districts of those towns were often full of big spenders.

In contrast, in the Canadian Arctic, men were hired in Edmonton or Calgary, except for the relatively few natives who ended up working on a rig or pipeline crew. Natives were hired by company agents in local communities and probably shipped out to Alberta for training. It seemed clear after a little reflection that the NWT aboriginals who lived in the area the pipeline would go through would have little to fear from gas rigger/pipelayer contamination.

The impact on the land itself was something else, and lessons had to be learned over and over again. In 1969, when the Prudhoe Bay boom was in its first stages, the State of Alaska decided to build a highway linking Fairbanks with Prudhoe Bay. The Walter Hickel Highway (named for the state governor) was abandoned after 100 kilometres when it dissolved the surface and melted the permafrost, creating a ditch full of mud and water. As with the CANOL Project twenty-seven years earlier, weight and friction totally destroyed the face of the delicate land. It was hard to believe that Alaska highway engineers in the late 1960s should have so little awareness of the environment in which they lived. Yet three years later, in the Mackenzie Delta, the identical situation arose during the final stages of building the Dempster Highway.

The Dempster was one of Diefenbaker's "roads to resources," begun in 1958 to link Dawson City in the Yukon with Inuvik. It crossed the Ogilvie and Richardson mountains before reaching McPherson on the Peel. After that, there was seventy-five kilometres to Arctic Red River on the Mackenzie. A Winnipeg construction firm built a fine, high stretch of road two metres above the tundra. Unfortunately, no gravel was available for a pad under the highway, so the builders used frozen shale chips, which worked fine in winter but melted in summer. The road had to be rebuilt: on one stretch, it sat two metres above the tundra, while the old road next to it was a sunken ditch, five metres deep and nine metres wide. For the third time in little more than a generation, builders had to relearn the same Arctic lessons. No wonder the pipeline consortiums spent $170 million on environmental research!

After the Honeymoon Comes Divorce

In 1973 Israel was attacked for the fourth time by the Arabs, in the Yom Kippur War. In its aftermath, Saudi Arabia cut off oil supplies to Europe and North America and precipitated a major economic crisis. Even when the embargo was lifted, the price of crude had gone up fourfold. With long line-ups at the gasoline pumps and American schools closing because they had no heating oil, the need for Alaskan oil and gas (and perhaps Canadian Arctic gas) seemed urgent. Native land claims settlement had cleared the way for the Alaska oil pipeline, and consortiums of natural gas companies were gathering information to place before Canada's National Energy Board (NEB) and the U.S. Federal Power Commission (FPC).

On the face of it, Arctic Gas seemed to be in the catbird seat. The consortium had in its membership three of the "seven sisters," including the biggest corporation in the world, Exxon. It also contained most of the major North American gas and pipeline companies, CN and CP, and, finally, the Canadian government. Just to put the icing on the cake, Canadian cabinet ministers were telling the partners to hurry up and make their pitch so that the pipeline could be started.

But one man, Bob Blair, was not satisfied. He found that all of Arctic Gas's key committees were chaired by Americans and that they were determined to run what he called an "express line" right through Alberta. His company, Alberta Gas Trunk, would get no benefit from the trillions of cubic feet of natural gas pouring out of the Alaska deposits. At the same time, inflation was pushing up the cost of everything: frontier gas and crude were desperately needed, but they would cost more to obtain. The financial advisers of Arctic Gas were starting to hint that the Canadian and American governments should guarantee the financing of the pipeline.

In 1974 there were rumours in the oil patch that Gas Trunk was – totally on its own – planning a different pipeline. At the end of July, Blair said it was true: Gas Trunk had "completed the basic studies for a conventional link of Mackenzie Delta gas supply to Canadian markets." A totally Canadian pipeline! No mention was made of a gas pipeline linking the Prudhoe Bay field with the lower forty-eight states by way of Canada. Blair said he was staying in Arctic Gas, but the handwriting was on the wall, and six weeks later he formally withdrew from the troubled grand consortium.

His effrontery was breathtaking, and few people believed he could pull off what came to be known as the Maple Leaf Pipeline. It was just at this time, however, that Blair received a telephone call from Kelly H. Gibson, chairman of West Coast Transmission in Vancouver. West Coast was the offspring of Pacific Petroleum, a Calgary firm founded by Frank McMahon, who had punched through a pipeline to the Pacific coast and founded a petroleum empire. His successor in both Pacific Pete and West Coast was Kelly Gibson, an Oklahoma-born high-roller who had made the Canadian oil patch his home.

Now Gibson wanted to become Blair's partner – on condition that Gas Trunk sever its connection with Arctic Gas. West Coast had refused several offers to join the consortium and for a time had flirted with the idea of building a mountain pipeline from Alaska to California. As early as 1969, West Coast and Bechtel Canada had set up Mountain Pacific Pipeline. This scheme would be melded into a pipeline carrying Alaska gas more or less along the route of the Alaska Highway through the Yukon into British Columbia. Bechtel (San Francisco), the parent of Bechtel Canada, would build Alaska sections, while West Coast and Bechtel Canada would build all of the Canadian sections. This proposal came to nothing.

Blair proposed that the Maple Leaf route follow the Mackenzie Valley to the corner where the Yukon, NWT, B.C., and Alberta are close together. One pipeline would be built to tap existing fields in B.C.; another would hook up with Alberta Gas Trunk. At Empress, on the Alberta-Saskatchewan border, the gas would feed into the TransCanada pipeline. Any gas sold to U.S. markets would be hived off to Coleman, Alberta, and from there to the Montana Power pipeline. This Maple Leaf route was staggering in that Blair believed that all financing could be raised from private sources and most of it in Canada.

Playing Rough

Oil patch wars have been notoriously savage since the days of Dad Joiner in east Texas. The first victim of the Canadian pipeline war was a government official, and the hit squad was an environmental group that had learned how to play rough with the roughest. The incident occurred in 1974–75 when the NEB was preparing to study pipeline applications from Arctic Gas (the huge American-Canadian consortium of petroleum giants), and the Alaska Highway Gas Pipelines Project (the Maple Leaf route)

Sitting in judgment was the National Energy Board, of which Marshall Alexander Crowe was chairman. He was one of Ottawa's most knowlegeable and prestigious mandarins, a public servant above suspicion. Like Bob Blair, he was an ardent and outspoken Canadian nationalist.

The NEB was scheduled to begin its hearings late in October 1975, and Crowe was to preside. Before the hearings started, Arctic Gas requested that he step down because he had served on their board when he was head of the Canada Development Corporation. The implication was that Crowe, as a Canadian nationalist, might be biased against the American-dominated Arctic Gas of 1975 now that Bob Blair had become a pipeline rival.

At the hearing's first full meeting, an environmental group objected to Crowe on the same grounds but from a different perspective.

A.R. Lucas, speaking for the Canadian Arctic Resources Committee, felt that Crowe's background made him prejudiced in favour of a pipeline. Lucas was joined by Andrew J. Roman, representing the Consumers Association of Canada, and John A. Olthuis, speaking for the Committee for Justice and Liberty Foundation. Arctic Gas and its American partners voiced no objection to Crowe at this hearing.

Crowe addressed the complaint courteously and said that any serious concerns would be referred by the NEB itself to the courts for an opinion. The NEB asked the Federal Court of Appeal to consider the matter, and it ruled unanimously (five judges) in favour of Crowe. The matter was then appealed to the Supreme Court of Canada, which ruled five to three against Crowe. Chief Justice Bora Laskin wrote the opinion. Crowe removed himself from the pipeline panel in favour of Jack Stabback, an associate vice-chairman of the NEB. He remained chairman of the board, later becoming a central figure in an incident that brought him much unwelcome publicity and may have had an influence on his early retirement from the NEB chairmanship.*

Nothing could have encouraged the environmentalists more than Crowe's problems. Even before they were able to start the juggernaut rolling toward a mandarin above suspicion, they had tasted blood in the hearings of the Berger Inquiry. The Berger drama was taking place while Arctic Gas and Foothills were locked in bloody combat before the NEB. It was a much more spectacular show and focused on one remarkable man, Mr. Justice Tom Berger of the British Columbia Supreme Court.

---

*In September 1976, the Toronto *Globe and Mail* reported that Crowe had been the guest of Charles Hetherington, president of Panarctic, on a trip through the High Arctic. Other guests included Alastair Gillespie, Liberal minister of industry and trade in the mid-1970s and later minister of energy, and Charles Drury, minister of public works and science and technology. Crowe's judgment (though not his honour) was questioned. More than a year later, he resigned from the NEB chairmanship, two and a half years before the end of his seven-year term. Crow told the author in 1993 that he had intended to resign early, long before the Panarctic incident.

Chapter 9

Tom Berger's Magic Circus

The greatest ongoing mystery of the NWT is why Pierre Trudeau and Jean Chrétien chose Mr. Justice Thomas R. Berger to head the Mackenzie Valley Pipeline Inquiry in 1974. From 1969 on, the Liberal government had expressed stronger and stronger support for the idea of a pipeline and had encouraged Arctic Gas to make an application to the National Energy Board, with the implication that it would be quickly approved.

Yet the Berger Inquiry killed the project politically and recommended that no other pipeline up the Mackenzie should even be contemplated for ten years. "His mandate was to build a pipeline – not to stop a pipeline," Jean Chrétien said as he looked back at the ruins of Trudeau's National Energy Program.

It was not surprising that Berger acted the way he did: his record was plain for all to see, and he never hid his sympathies. He had been, briefly, an NDP member of Parliament and leader of the party in B.C. He was famous as a long-time champion of native causes and had scored a notable victory for the Nishga before the Supreme Court of Canada. He was a lawyer and judge noted for his personal integrity and his radical opinions.

So why was he picked? Asked that question today, Chrétien just shakes his head angrily and admits he made a very bad mistake. Cynics might say that governments of all political persuasions like to appoint figureheads who look good and do nothing, limited with low budgets and crippling terms of reference. Many another commission of inquiry has provided an excuse for governments to shelve a troublesome issue indefinitely.

In this case, the times were ripe for an especially liberal approach to the environment and to the rights of indigenous peoples. In the 1960s, both the U.S. and Canadian governments had considerable sympathy with radical reform: the Americans had their Peace Corps and VISTA; the Canadians had CUSO and the Company of Young

Canadians. The Liberals were forced to move left to counter the growing popularity of the NDP. In 1972, indeed, the Liberals only squeaked in with a minority government that saw the NDP holding the balance of power and exerting direct pressure on Liberal policies.

Some canny observers believe Tom Berger was made pipeline commissioner because the leader of the NDP, David Lewis, insisted. This is denied by Chrétien and Lewis is dead, so the answer may never be known. However, it should be remembered that during this period both the Liberals and the Conservatives had plenty of liberal-minded reformers: on the Liberal side, Pierre Trudeau himself, Jean Marchand, Monique Bégin, and Eric Kierans; on the Tory side, Flora Macdonald, David Crombie, and Gordon Fairweather.

In addition, there were many influential liberal or radical intellectuals and academics across the country, ranging from Mel Watkins of the NDP's "waffle group" to Professor Donald Chant of Pollution Probe. Portions of the Christian churches, too, were adopting advanced social programs and challenging the free enterprise system. Anti-war, social reform, and native rights groups were clamouring at the doors of Parliament and showing politicians of all stripes that they commanded a good many votes.

It was this public environment that Berger entered when he was chosen pipeline commissioner. His instructions were surprisingly vague and general, but it was his extraordinary character that made the difference. The most surprising thing about him was his ability to shuck off all restrictions and find ways to expand his commission until it became a national political force and a media event. The boardroom wars of Bob Blair and Vern Horte were uncomplicated and friendly compared to the manoeuvring of Tom Berger. His commission became a wonderful flying circus, travelling to Canada's three oceans and focusing national attention for the first time on environmental issues and native rights.

⁓

There have been hundreds of royal commissions and inquiries since Canada became a nation, and Berger's was neither the longest nor the most expensive. But it was the first one in the age of Marshall McLuhan, the first to be planned and executed with the media in mind. Among other things, Tom Berger is one of the greatest communicators of his era.

Apart from the weirdness of picking Berger as commissioner, it's very hard to understand just what the Liberal government had in mind in 1974. The NEB was already scheduled to examine the merits and disadvantages of a pipeline, while the FPC in Washington would cover almost the same ground. However, it may simply have been that Ottawa's mandarins and pols had been slightly infected by the rosy age of Aquarius. Chrétien says Berger was his personal choice, approved by Trudeau and by Energy Minister Donald Macdonald. Others say Trudeau was impressed with Berger's arguments on behalf of the Nishga. Whatever the reason, Berger was plucked off a B.C. provincial royal commission on family and children's law and given his northern orders.

The order-in-council setting up the Berger Commission was dated 21 March 1974 and ordered the commissioner to

> inquire into and report upon the terms and conditions that should be imposed in respect of any right-of-way that might be granted across Crown lands for the purposes of the proposed Mackenzie Valley Pipeline having regard to (a) the social, environmental and economic impact regionally, of the construction, operation and subsequent abandonment of the proposed pipeline in the Yukon and the NWT, and (b) any proposals to meet the specific environmental and social concerns set out in the Expanded Guidelines for Northern Pipelines as tabled in the House of Commons on June 28, 1972, by the Minister.

Berger was authorized to hold hearings "in Territorial centres and in such other places and at such times as he may decide from time to time" and to hire "such accountants, engineers, technical advisers, or other experts, clerks, reporters and assistants as he deems necessary or advisable." The document is only three pages long, and perhaps Berger was the only person who realized the full potential of his mandate. It seems clear now that the federal cabinet thought Berger would examine the financial and technical problems facing pipeline builders, look into the economic impact for Canada, and make some kind of motherhood statement on the environment and the impact on native peoples. Then he would meekly recommend a pipeline.

Berger chose to take the instructions about "social and environmental concerns" seriously. He found the guidelines referred to in paragraph (b) were useful because they were well-meaning but also vague and gave him a virtually open-ended mandate to move into territory undreamed of by the commission's framers. The chairman also took full advantage of his authority to spend money ($5 million altogether), hold hearings in various places in and out of the NWT, hire a large and varied staff, and subsidize public interest, environmental, and native organizations as a counter to the big bucks being spent by the pipeline consortiums. These subsidies cost the commission $1.2 million.

Berger's grasp of the national political mood was profound and his timing flawless. He was also extremely lucky: the fight to the death between Blair and Horte slowed and crippled Arctic Gas, and the successful assault on Marshall Crowe by the environmentalists delayed the NEB hearings long enough to permit Berger to get his report in first. These events, in turn, affected the FPC decisions in Washington, and by the time the various hurdles had been cleared, the economic climate had changed, Canada and the United States were in the throes of a recession, and megaprojects were impossible to sell on the financial market.

Perhaps more than any other single factor, Berger had an instinct for using the various media to promote a cause, and this involved another aspect of his amazing timing. At first, he moved very slowly, building a strong staff and planning for a blitz later on. He decided at the start that public interest groups and the aboriginals should be given a voice that could compete with the pipeliners. These organizations were given a year to catch up with the pipeliners. The radical church groups and the environmentalists hired their own experts and began developing a credible case against any pipeline.

But it was in the realm of natives residing in the NWT and the Yukon that Berger showed his true ingenuity. His experience with the Nishga had taught him the value of easy communication with ordinary native people in their own languages. Now, he took full advantage of modern communication technology, especially the network being developed by the CBC's Northern Service.

CBC Radio had moved into the North at the end of the 1950s, inheriting a number of English-language community stations. From the first, the CBC's Northern Service had tried to hire and train indigenes as announcers, reporters, and technicians. By the late 1960s, the CBC was broadcasting from Yellowknife in Chipewyan, Dog Rib, and Slavey; from Inuvik in Gwich'in; from Montreal to the eastern Arctic in Inuktitut. It was hard to find natives fluent in English and one of the indigenous languages who also had the necessary broadcasting skills. By the early 1970s, the CBC had a shallow pool of competent broadcasters.

When the Berger Commission reached the Mackenzie Valley in 1975, the Indians, Métis, and Inuvialuit of all ages were receiving extensive radio services in their own languages. In addition, a good many young natives had broadcast training. This was absolutely essential to Berger. He intended to take the commission to the people in the way judges Sissons and Morrow had taken justice to the NWT's far-flung settlements.

Berger's plan was simple but unwieldy. Instead of holding hearings in a few central communities like Yellowknife, Whitehorse, and Inuvik, thus forcing the various language groups to send delegations, he arranged for the whole operation to be taken to the settlements. Anybody was welcome to speak, and everybody from the oldest to the youngest could meet the commissioner and his staff. Representatives of the petroleum industry, environmental experts, and government officials could be challenged or supported as the indigenes chose. In keeping with the circus-like atmosphere, the hearings were informal, almost casual. If the people wanted it, Berger was willing to sit until after midnight, mingling with the villagers during the coffee breaks.

Setting up such a travelling circus and making it work was a horrendous job, but Berger's dedicated staff were wonderful organizers. Charter flights were laid on. Loose schedules were worked out. The commissioner and everybody else slept where they could – on mattresses on schoolroom floors, billeted in native homes, in tents when the weather permitted. Berger moved genially and imperturbably through it all, charming everyone with his mukluks and casual good manners: he had the knack of putting everyone at ease.

The hearings themselves were a remarkable achievement. Interpreters and translators were hired so that the proceedings could be simultaneously translated into local languages, using techniques developed at the United Nations. For the first time in history, the aboriginals as a whole were being brought into the decision-making process. Testimony was recorded electronically and transcribed into a daily transcript to provide raw material for Berger's final report. Berger asked the CBC to broadcast the hearings daily, either in full or in summary. The CBC did even better: it spent $500,000 to send a travelling staff of translators along and made sure every settlement got comprehensive coverage. This marked a huge step forward in the Northern Service.

∾

Whatever people may think of the political convictions of Tom Berger, he is one of the most appealing individuals alive today. The son of a Mountie and the grandson of a Swedish judge, he was born in Victoria in 1933. He became a lawyer in Vancouver in 1957 and soon was an advocate for the dispossessed. He went to great lengths to find precedents for his arguments. In one case involving a union (according to his biographer, Carolyn Swayze), the young barrister cited Magna Carta. Mr. Justice A.M. Manson of the B.C. Supreme Court asked him to "start with something current." Berger replied that nothing could be more current than Magna Carta which was "as much in force in B.C. today as it was in England in 1215."

In 1968, when he took on the cause of the Nishgas, he cited King George III's proclamation of 1763 on native rights to ownership of the lands they occupied. The Nishgas, residing in central British Columbia, never signed a treaty with Ottawa and had been fighting in the courts since 1913 for clear title to tribal lands. They said these rights had never been extinguished. The lower courts and the B.C. Supreme Court ruled against the Nishga, and the case was appealed in 1971 to the Supreme Court of Canada, which in 1973 split three to three, while a seventh judge threw out the Nishga case on a technicality. This was the furthest any native tribe had ever managed to get in land claims. The case was regarded as a great victory for the Nishga and for Berger.

Long before the Nishga case reached the Supreme Court, Berger was active in B.C.'s volatile politics. On his second try, he was elected to the House of Commons for the NDP. This was in the dying stages of John Diefenbaker's Conservative government, and in less than a year Berger was defeated by Liberal Ron Basford. He immediately plunged into turbulent provincial politics and in the same year (1963) was defeated for a seat in the B.C. legislature. In 1966 he was elected and for a brief time in 1969 was NDP leader, losing his seat and the leadership the same year. Social Credit Premier W.A.C. Bennett called him "a godless socialist."

Somewhat chastened, Berger returned to law and developed a reputation for good research and effective arguments. The Nishga case gave him a national reputation, and a Liberal colleague and friend in Vancouver began to negotiate his appointment to the B.C. Supreme Court, which was made by federal Justice Minister John Turner. Carolyn Swayze calls it "the most political non-political appointment ever made." Berger was an immediate success, and Mr. Justice Emmett Hall admired him so much that he wanted to see him as his successor on the Supreme Court of Canada.

In 1972 Dave Barrett led the NDP to political victory in British Columbia, and the following year he named Berger to head a royal commission into family and children's law. The commission lasted nineteen months, but Berger was long gone at the conclusion – he had been called to the Mackenzie Inquiry. Berger became commissioner the same day, 21 March 1974, that Arctic Gas made its application to the NEB and the FPC. The following year, Berger built his staff, planned his strategy, visited the Arctic, and held preliminary hearings in Yellowknife and Ottawa with engineering experts, company lawyers, native leaders, and scientists. The formal opening was in Yellowknife, 3 March 1975.

In Washington, the Federal Power Commission heard the El Paso Natural Gas application for an Alaska pipeline and the Arctic Gas application concurrently, starting 5 May 1975. The NEB opened Ottawa hearings on the Arctic Gas and Foothills applications 27 October 1975, but they were promptly interrupted by the challenge to Chairman Crowe. The real start wasn't until 12 April 1976. Adding to the excitement, Northwest Pipeline of Salt Lake City applied to the FPC 9 July 1976 to build the Alaska portion of the gas pipeline proposed by Foothills. On 31 August 1976, Foothills applied to the NEB for the Canadian portion of what came to be known as the Alaska Highway pipeline project.

~

When the Berger Commission opened in Yellowknife, it heard platoons of executives, lawyers, experts, and consultants for weeks on end. They revealed the dimensions of the project: 1,771 kilometres of pipeline; cost, $8 billion; workers, 7,200; water crossings, 600; new airstrips, 21; more than a million tonnes of steel for the 48-inch pipeline; trucks, 1,850; tractors and earth-movers, 1,100. There would also be swarms of helicopters, light planes, air freighters, and passenger liners, and scores of new tugs and barges.

Arctic Gas, well advanced over Foothills in research, promised to protect environment and indigenes. Both companies insisted that northerners and Canadians as a whole would benefit economically: not only was there the Prudhoe Bay gas but there was also the prospect of huge new supplies from the Beaufort.

As the hearings went on, Foothills consultants began revealing weaknesses in the Arctic Gas case, as damaging as the facts produced by Berger's own independent scientists and by the environmentalists. It turned out that there was one glaring error in Arctic Gas calculations. Crude oil, in order to flow freely through a 48-inch pipeline, must be kept at a temperature of 76.6°C, whereas natural gas need not be heated at all and, indeed, should be refrigerated. In theory, the transporter can move gas at any temperature. If the weather outside is too cold, there is a danger of metal crystallization causing pipe fracture, which can be compensated for by the manufacturer.

Both Arctic Gas and Foothills planned to refrigerate their gas so there would be no danger to the permafrost. Unlike Alyeska, which had to keep its hot oil pipeline above the surface on a berm or stilts, Arctic Gas decided to bury its gas pipeline because that was much cheaper. But even a relatively cool pipeline would melt the permafrost, so refrigeration was necessary. This system worked fine above the Arctic Circle, but once one got south of Norman Wells, there was the difficulty of discontinuous permafrost. Here, the refrigerated pipe caused the soil to freeze, creating a "frost bulb" that forced the earth up and tended to bend and sometimes break the pipeline. Arctic Gas proposed to deal with this by weighing down the sunken pipe with tons of earth and gravel.

However, Berger's scientists showed that the consortium's calculations were ludicrously inaccurate, underestimating the weight needed by a vast margin. Arctic Gas had to go back and re-examine its own data and then sheepishly admit that its instruments were not calibrated properly. The consortium never solved the problem to the satisfaction of Berger.

~

Up to this point, the commission resembled hundreds of previous ones: a calm judge presiding impassively over sober witnesses in three-piece suits, most of them lawyers or "experts," talking an incomprehensible jargon and answering arcane questions. This was about to change. Berger was ready to go to the people and let them have their own say in their own languages, words, and style. This technique was absolutely unheard of in the history of government commissions.

Quite suddenly, it seemed, the commissioner was entrepreneur, playwright, and director. He assured native leaders that they would get a fair hearing. At a very early stage, Chief George Kodakin of Fort Franklin on Great Bear Lake told him: "If you want to understand what the pipeline will do to our people, you need to come and live with us for six months." Berger told the chief he couldn't do it personally but he would send Michael Jackson in his place.

Jackson was a special counsel who had come to the commission from the UBC Law School. It's hard to credit, but Jackson, his wife, and their baby actually lived in Franklin for three months. Then Jackson became Berger's advance man in the valley. He said his job was to tell people "not only about the pipeline but about the future shape of northern Canada, the evolution of political institutions, the evolution of native and white self-determination, and a whole range of other issues put into perspective by the pipeline." Jackson's colleagues were the fieldworkers of the native organizations, community representatives, and members of the local chambers of commerce.

John Bayly, now a Yellowknife lawyer but then counsel for COPE, says the Inuvialuit organization sent out four workers, two native and two white, to interview every Inuvialuit adult in his or her home. Since there were perhaps 1,500 of them scattered through seven Beaufort and Delta communities, it took the interviewers several months. Bayly says the Inuvialuit were much more sophisticated in their attitudes toward whites than the Indians of the lower Mackenzie. From the days of Herschel Island, they had had intimate ties with the kabloonat.

Michael Jackson's planning brought him into close touch with Nellie Cournoyea and Agnes Semmler of COPE and with Georges Erasmus, at that time director of community organization for the Indian Brotherhood. He also got to know the idealistic young Indians and Métis who had been inspired by James Wah Shee, Erasmus, and the white advisers from the CYC. The first plan was that Jackson should conduct the lower Mackenzie and Beaufort hearings, but village residents beseeched him to have the judge come himself. Berger agreed.

The advance organization in the communities was an educational process in itself, as the young workers explained pipeline issues from permafrost damage and threat to game to the impact on land claims. For the first time, the elders who spoke no English were made aware of the true implications of a megaproject.

If the village hearings were a debate to win the hearts and minds of the indigenous peoples, Arctic Gas and Foothills lost the battle at the very start. Pat Carney of Gemini North had visited these same communities, seeking evidence for the pipeliners, but she had hardly touched the local people because she did not speak their languages and had to deal with them through interpreters, themselves ill-informed. Apart from the native and white fieldworkers who were gaining the confidence of the villagers, one of the most influential white advisers was Mel Watkins of the University of Toronto, whose political views were outlined in his book *The Colony Within* and were often echoed by native leaders.

By the time Berger was ready to take his flying circus into the boondocks in 1975, a major educative process was well under way. The general indigenous population of the Mackenzie Valley – as opposed to the chiefs, government officials, experts, and political representatives – were prepared to participate in these modern, high-tech versions of the New England town hall meeting. All in all, Berger heard almost 1,000 of these community voices, and they made many eloquent statements, a lot of them opposing the pipeline. Those who favoured the pipeline believed that the opposition had been indoctrinated by white advisers and radical young native leaders.

Gary Mullins, one of the most influential of the civil servants imported from Ottawa by the GNWT said: "Berger often said he heard 1,000 persons. That was quite wrong. What Berger heard was one person speaking 1,000 times." Mullins exaggerated in the opposite direction. Berger heard some conflicting voices, especially from whites living along the Mackenzie. But many whites were bitter because they believed that the Dene were expressing radical views put in their mouths by the young white advisers from the south. Colin Alexander, publisher of *News of the North*, said: "Judge Berger has permitted his hearings to become the sounding board for radicals of all kinds while the views of elected officials are ignored." David Searle, Speaker of the NWT Legislative Council, was even angrier: "We must cast out the socialists! We must call their names loud and clear – Mr. Berger, Mr. Watkins, to mention only two – and tell them they are not liked, they are unwanted, and ask them to leave!"

Mullins was calmer but equally critical when he said: "When people talk about the aspirations of the Basques and Bretons, the Indians of the Amazon, when people talk that way, you know where the arguments are coming from because those are not the kinds of arguments a native person is going to use in talking about the problems of the community."

Georges Erasmus was amused by these comments, saying: "We didn't need white advisers to tell us about the plight of aboriginal peoples around the world. We could read for ourselves and we made up our own minds. The white advisers were hired by us to give us useful technical advice and were very helpful. When their function ended, I got rid of them."

∼

The village hearings emphasized political and social issues beyond the engineering problems that had been discussed in Ottawa and Yellowknife. There were dramatic confrontations, headed by an exchange in Good Hope between Bob Blair and Chief Frank T'Seleie. The Sah'tu chief, sitting shoulder to shoulder with Blair, told the Foothills boss:

> There will be no pipeline because we have plans for our land. There will be no pipeline because we no longer intend to allow our land and our future to be taken away from us so that we are destroyed to make someone else rich. There will be no pipeline because we, the Dene, are awakening; to see the truth of the system of genocide that has been imposed on us and we will not go back to sleep.

In a long, rhetorical, and eloquent speech, Chief T'Seleie attacked Blair and Horte personally, claiming that they wanted to see the NWT natives destroyed. "Maybe money has become so important to you that you are losing your own humanity," T'Seleie told Blair, adding "You are like the Pentagon, Mr. Blair, planning the slaughter of innocent Vietnamese. You are the 20th century General Custer. You have come to destroy the Dene nation."

Whether or not T'Seleie was influenced or directed by radical white advisers, his anger and antagonism were real and his charges were highly sophisticated. This was a long way from the aboriginal eloquence of a Chief Joseph or a Sitting Bull. Blair answered T'Seleie with moderation, restraint, and quiet wit:

> Chief T'Seleie, you connected my name with those of some people who are not my heroes either, including General Custer. I intend to finish my own working life with better success than he finished his, as he well deserved, and I trust from the good spokesmanship and

organization I have seen here that you and the leaders of your people will finish yours with much greater success than did many of the
leaders of that time too.

Blair declined to take T'Seleie's remarks personally, attributing
them to "expressing your very great concern and anxiety, and in some
cases suspicion, of the possibility of the pipeline." Blair promised that
Foothills would not "choose to install any pipeline through any local
place if the landowners are all strongly opposed or are arguing their
claims." He offered a good many more concessions than did Arctic
Gas, which appeared to feel that native problems were the responsibility of the Canadian government.

∽

If Chief T'Seleie's attack represented the most extreme attitude of an
native against the pipeliners, the intellectuals had their sharpest
exchange when Mel Watkins clashed with Professor Charles Hobart,
a University of Alberta sociologist appearing for Arctic Gas. Watkins,
accused by the pipeliners of being an outright Marxist, strongly criticized white relations with the native peoples of Canada and maintained that the pipeline project was just another phase of white economic determinism. He wanted the natives to own and control the
renewable resources of the North and to control the non-renewable
resources. "The right to alternate development must include the right
to tax the non-renewable resource sector, or to impose royalties, and
thus fund the Dene economy and the Dene institutions," he said.

Hobart was closer to the position of DIAND, the GNWT, and
many of the white residents of Yellowknife, Whitehorse, Hay River,
and Inuvik. He suggested that native cultures and native economies
had already been so damaged by events of the 20th century that the
only solution was to provide opportunities within the overall national
economy and culture. He saw the new NWT schools in an optimistic
light and felt that native graduates would adapt readily to a wage
economy. The pipeline would provide jobs and a higher standard of
living for everybody in the North, while Watkins wanted to keep the
natives in a cultural museum, he felt. The Indian Brotherhood and the
white advisers accused Hobart of being Arctic Gas's "hired gun," but
he came very close to reflecting the philosophy of senior civil servants in the GNWT.

∽

The community hearings opened in Aklavik in April 1975 and were completed at the Dog Rib village of Detah, near Yellowknife, in August 1976. There were seventy-seven volumes of testimony from the native villages alone.

When Berger had completed the main part of his inquiry, he took his flying circus south and held hearings in ten southern cities. It was not quite clear what these hearings were supposed to accomplish, but many environmental groups took them as an occasion to show the flag and make statements of support for the anti-pipeliners. No real evidence needed by the commission was produced at the southern hearings, and the groups got no attention in Berger's final report. However, they did act as a political focus for the whole pipeline project.

Several southern interventions raised interesting points of view, among them that of Mayor Rod Sykes in Calgary, headquarters of Alberta's petroleum industry and of Bob Blair himself. Sykes, even more of an economic determinist than Professor Hobart, declared that all Canadians had as much right to the NWT's Crown lands as the native residents. Attacking the Berger Commission itself, Sykes said that the CPR and the TransCanada pipeline would never have been built if they had been delayed by such an inquiry. He called opposition to the pipeline "the politics of blackmail." Sykes, as might be expected of any mayor of Calgary, placed himself four-square on the side of private enterprise. "The Berger Commission was a disastrous and costly mistake," he declared.

The hearings ended in Yellowknife 19 November 1976, and Berger went home to Vancouver. Now he was racing the calendar to get his report into the hands of the government (and the public) before the NEB finished its report. Berger frankly hoped to influence the NEB against the pipeline applications. At the end of 1976, the NEB was still sitting, and in Washington the FPC was nearly ready to choose between Arctic Gas and El Paso's LNG project.

At this point, Berger assembled his staff in Ottawa and handed them a list of eight points, asking for an informal report based on them. Berger's eight points were: (1) no pipeline across the northern Yukon from Prudhoe Bay; (2) a national wilderness park in the Yukon, which would protect the Porcupine caribou herd; (3) a whale sanctuary in the Beaufort Sea; (4) no Mackenzie Valley pipeline for ten years; (5) settlement of native land claims in the Mackenzie Valley; (6) development of the northern economy, with emphasis on renewable resources; (7) preservation of native culture; and (8) bird sanctuaries.

In her book *Hard Choices*, biographer Carolyn Swayze says Berger's staff were stunned because they never expected him to go so far. They asked him if they could give their draft report an alternative ending that would allow the government an out. He said no – firmly. Swayze says his words were: "No, damn it: no! That's not what the people said! That's not what the evidence indicates. If we betray the people that way – if we give the politicians an out – they'll take it! I don't want them to do it on my recommendation. They'll have to do it on their own." In for a penny, in for a pound. Tom Berger was not going to make any compromises.

The Report

Berger won the race to get his report out in time to influence everybody: the first volume was sent to DIAND Minister Warren Allmand 15 April 1977. The second volume came out 30 November 1977 and was addressed to Allmand's successor, Hugh Faulkner. After Jean Chrétien's long stay, the portfolio was turning over quickly.

Quite apart from its highly controversial findings, the report itself was a landmark in Canadian literature, clearly written, well organized, and often visionary. Berger called it *Northern Frontier, Northern Homeland*, and it rang with his intense feelings for the land and its indigenous peoples: "The North is a frontier, but it is a homeland, too, the homeland of the Dene, Inuit and Métis, as it is also the home of the white people who live there. And it is a heritage, a unique environment that we are called upon to preserve for all Canadians."

The fine legal distinctions that are the everyday tools of the courtroom lawyer and jurist were present in that opening paragraph of the first volume: from the very start, Berger drew a sharp distinction between the rights of the indigenous population and the privileges of the whites in the North. He drew attention to the "homeland" of the Dene, Inuit, and Métis and to the "home" of the "white people who live there." The report was to follow this argument through the mazes of 32,353 pages of testimony.

The first volume (it was the one everyone read) contained twelve chapters, moving step by step through the arguments for and against a pipeline, and then moving into the cultural and economic impact on native people, social effects, and the native claims. Volume 2 set forth terms and conditions for a pipeline and was largely technical. It accepted the principle that ultimately there would be both gas and oil pipelines (and possibly other kinds of industrial corridors) but recommended at least ten years' delay and settlement of native claims (Berger carefully specified that these went beyond "land claims") before any pipeline was built.

After totally ruling out the proposal to build a pipeline along the shore of the Arctic Ocean, Berger cautiously gave approval to a route that would follow the Alaska Highway across the Yukon to British Columbia and Alberta, where it would link up with West Coast Transmission's B.C. pipeline and Alberta Trunk's pipeline in Alberta. At some future date, Berger said, the gas wells on the edge of and in the Beaufort Sea might be exploited; at that time, there might be a pipeline link along the Dempster Highway to hook into an Alaska Highway pipeline, probably near Whitehorse.

Berger started most of his chapters with brilliantly written essays providing overviews of whatever subject he was considering. He went far beyond pipeline questions: his vision encompassed the future of Canada as a whole. Often he was analytical; sometimes he was argumentative; once in a while he was didactic. The report thus became a tour de force dealing not only with the use of natural and manufactured resources, but also with the motivation behind approaches to human and economic rights.

Part of his argument was based on the evidence produced at the inquiry and was incontrovertible even to the pipeline consortiums. Part of his argument was based on political and social views as controversial as those of Mel Watkins. And very occasionally, he made mistakes in fact.

❧

Berger's analysis of Arctic Gas's approach was low-keyed but relentless. The consortium argued that while its presence would be huge, steps would be taken to protect the environment, its flora and fauna, and the native population. Rivers would not be polluted or despoiled; ways would be found to protect the caribou herds; and aboriginal communities would not become sewers like Herschel Island and Dawson City. Arctic Gas pointed out that seismic exploration and exploratory drilling had been taking place for years without any serious impact. When the pipeline was laid, construction camps would be well away from native settlements and construction workers kept from contact with their inhabitants.

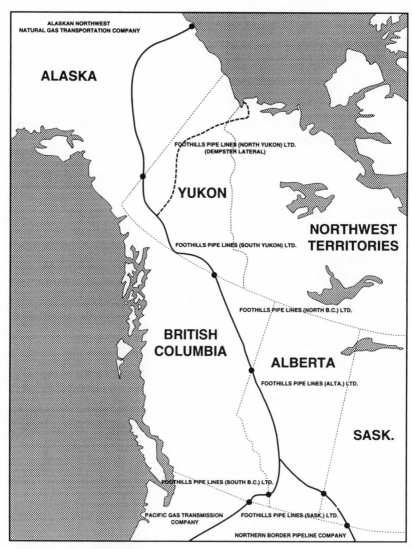

Map 5   The Alaska Highway Gas Pipeline Project

Courtesy of NOVA Corporation.

Berger showed the fallacy of this argument. He noted that 6,000 workers would be required for the pipeline and 1,200 more for building gas plants and feeder facilities. There would also be large numbers of transportation workers on the rivers and roads, others in support industries, and a good many southerners coming north to look for work. Berger talked of "action communities" – one of his incisive phrases – like Hay River, Simpson, Inuvik, Tuktoyaktuk, and Yellowknife. A million tonnes of 48-inch pipe would have to be shipped in and millions of cubic metres of gravel fill procured.

Quite apart from the pipelaying and gas plant crews, there would have to be sizable installations in many permanent communities. The numbers of barges and tugs on the Mackenzie would be doubled, jamming the river for two or three years. The Gwich'in residents of Old Crow in the Yukon had heard that the pipeliners planned an 800-man camp in their vicinity: what would happen to their daughters?

Berger doubted whether Arctic Gas (or Foothills, for that matter) could control the movements of white pipeliners and construction workers coming in from the south. He drew attention to the essential contradiction in the central economic argument of the pipeline companies: the project would bring work and prosperity to the NWT, but the work would be done by southerners quarantined from the northern communities. The commissioner said there was no way the pipeline companies could prevent southern Canadians from travelling north in the hope of finding work – just as thousands of Americans from the Lower 48 had arrived in Alaska for the oil pipeline.

Berger used the community input to great effect against the project. In his chapter on the Delta and Beaufort in the first volume, he quoted a Tuktoyaktuk Inuk as saying:

> If they drill out there (in the Beaufort Sea), if they finish off what little whales are left, what little seals are left, what little polar bears are left, with one oil spill of any size big enough to hurt these animals, we're finished. The Eskimo population and culture is finished, because you will have to live as a white man and you will have nothing left. You have no more seals to feed the foxes. You've got no more fish to feed the seals, and you've got no more seals to feed the polar bears, and the polar bears are going to go looking for some white man then because they've got nothing left to eat. Already in the eastern Arctic there are Eskimos getting seals covered with oil and there's no oil work there yet, just from ships spilling their used oil.

No ecologist with a doctorate in science could have said it better, and Berger knew it. Over and over again, he quoted cries from the heart made by individuals who came from the only races that had lived in the Arctic for millennia. However, as Berger got into consideration of the cultural impact of the pipeline and the question of aboriginal rights, he became much more contentious. At one stage, he made a sweeping statement in which he took it upon himself to explain the problems of the native residents:

> It was the long depression in the price of furs in the years of the Second World War that led to the collapse of the Northern fur economy in the 1950s. When the fur market failed, the federal government had to come to the aid of the native people. It was at this time that the welfare state made its appearance in the North. Federal policy in the North since the late 1950s has proceeded on the assumption that the traditional way of life was dying, and that native people had no alternative but the adoption of the white man's way. The short run solution to the northern crisis was the provision of health and welfare measures. The long-term solution was the education of native people to enable them to enter the wage economy.

Berger ignored the impact of defence and sovereignty policies on the Arctic and the emergency created in the Keewatin by the failure of caribou migration.

There were a few extraordinary gaps in the report: "It is now 10 years since the GNWT transferred its headquarters from Fort Smith to Yellowknife. Yet in 1976 out of 3,069 people on the GNWT payroll, only 603, or 20 percent, were native and of the 603, most worked at clerical or unskilled labor." The fact that Berger believed the NWT's government headquarters was at Smith until 1967 reveals a good deal about his thinking: he made no mention of the actual and symbolic shift of government from Ottawa to Yellowknife in 1967, and he also failed to record the speed with which natives were being recruited at all levels of government even as he wrote his report.

Berger's position was close to that of Mel Watkins: an easily defensible philosophy of history but a surprising one, coming from a judge of the B.C. Supreme Court in a supposedly impartial inquiry report.

∾

Perusal of the report reveals several anomalies. In volume 1 Berger cited the evidence of seventy-seven Indians, twenty-nine Inuit, eighteen whites, and one Métis, considered separately from the platoons of technical experts and lawyers who appeared everywhere from Inuvik to Ottawa. The report did not say what percentage of ordinary white northerners turned out to testify in predominantly white communities, nor did it indicate what percentage of whites supported the pipeline and what percentage opposed it.

Berger's entire two-volume report tended to ignore the impact on the white community, though he himself said the population of the Mackenzie and Beaufort was split about evenly into whites and natives. One obvious reason for ignoring the attitudes of whites was his contention that most would eventually return to the south. Berger rightly emphasized the impact of the hearings on the native villages and gave some remarkable figures. In McPherson, fifty-eight witnesses appeared before him; in Good Hope the number was seventy-seven, or 21 percent of the local population. On the other hand, in the predominantly white industrial community of Norman Wells, only twenty-four witnesses, 7 percent of the population, turned up.

Berger might argue, of course, that whites did not show as much interest in the hearings as the Mackenzie natives did (the Inuvialuit did not turn out in as great proportions in places like Tuktoyaktuk and Aklavik). However, the commission organizers, supported by networks of community workers, did not stage blitzes in white communities to arouse public interest. The fact remains that Berger's report was so heavily loaded toward the native position that he hardly mentioned the aspirations, fears, and opinions of white residents. His report didn't even tell its readers whether or not they were interested.

In volume 1 Berger portrayed the traditional native way of life poetically: "Long ago the native people developed an economy based on the seasonal harvesting of renewable resources which was for centuries the sole basis of their livelihood." Noting that the fur trade after 1906 brought the Delta Inuit "relative economic stability, cultural continuity and some real prosperity," the commissioner suggested that the sale of skins still might provide the base for a self-contained native society. This contrasted with conventional wisdom among GNWT officials that the indigenes would find their future in a wage economy as the natural resources of the NWT were developed.

Berger was selective in his statistics. In commenting on the rush of southern whites for jobs on the Alyeska oil pipeline in Alaska, the report made no mention of the fact that only 14 percent of the resident Alaskan population was indigenous. It properly dealt with the problems of the Gwich'in native village of Old Crow (population 216) but had nothing to say about the fact that the white population of the Yukon was somewhere between 75 and 82 percent. The report's readers were given a riveting tale of natives threatened by big government and big industry but heard almost nothing about the aspirations and problems of white southerners who had chosen to live and work in the Territories.

Native Claims

Nothing in Berger's report was so astonishing as his long sections in both volumes on native claims. Not only did the report describe them, but it appeared to be negotiating them with the federal government, with Berger acting as advocate for the natives. This was understandable in the man who took the Nishga case to the Supreme Court and who was recognized as one of the country's greatest authorities on aboriginal rights. It was not so understandable in a judge asked by the federal government to "inquire into and report upon the terms and conditions that should be imposed in respect of any right-of-way that might be granted across Crown lands" for a pipeline.

Berger took his authority to delve into native claims from his instructions "to consider the social, economic and environmental impact "of the construction of a pipeline ... The effect of these impacts cannot be disentangled from the whole question of native claims," he wrote in volume 1.

His introduction to the question of native claims ranged over the whole history of native/white relations in North America, to Treaties 8 and 11, and to Canadian policies involving the extinguishment of native land claims. Berger asked whether a settlement of other native claims to self-determination could be accommodated within the Canadian constitution. He directly challenged the extension of democratic rights to NWT residents, which had followed the recommendations of the Carrothers Commission in 1966.

Carrothers, Laing, Chrétien, and Trudeau all believed citizenship should be portable and exercised freely anywhere in the country. This would rule out special political rights for any ethnic group. Carrothers and the politicians all approved the extension of democratic rights to all residents of Canada, including those who lived in the NWT.

Trudeau specifically ruled out any kind of government founded on ethnic principles.*

Berger called the concept of native self-government "antithetical" to the vision of the future of many NWT whites "who believe the NWT should become a province like the other provinces. They see no place for native self-determination in such a future." Quoting the testimony of several native witnesses before his inquiry, he stressed native proposals for "a restructuring of political institutions" that would give them rights "to reshape their future."

"Whether native self-determination requires native hegemony over a geographical area, or whether it can be achieved through the transfer of political power over specific matters to the native people, remain questions to be resolved by negotiations," Berger wrote. He quoted Chief Paul Norman of Fort Norman as saying the settlement council system "has never worked and never will work because it is a form of tokenism to the Territorial Government."

Berger's central recommendation was that there should be no pipeline before native claims had been settled – and he stressed that these claims went far beyond the land claims in the mind of Ottawa: they embraced special political rights, control over land peripheral to acreage actually ceded to them, control over education, and control over a number of other community services. If this recommendation were accepted, the establishment of the GNWT and its devolution and development throughout the Territories would have to be suspended pending settlements with the natives resident in the pipeline areas. It was no wonder that Ottawa was seriously shaken by the Berger Report. Was it willing to accept its more radical recommendations?**

---

*Hodgson told me in Vancouver in 1986: "I've never seen anywhere in the world where ethnic government works."

**In the seven and a half months between completion of the first and second volumes of the Berger Report, the Lysyk Commission was appointed to look into the proposed pipeline through the Yukon. The chairman was an old friend of Berger's, Dean Ken Lysyk of the UBC Law School, and his colleagues were Edith Bohmer of the Council of Yukon Indians and William Phelps of the Yukon Territorial Council.

The commission visited seventeen communities, sat for twenty-two days, and brought in its report in four months. It recommended a four-year delay in the start of the Yukon part of the Alaska Highway pipeline proposed by Foothills. Dean Lysyk had nothing at all to say about native claims, but it should be noted that his terms of reference were much narrower than those governing Berger.

Impact of the Report

The first volume of the Berger Report reached the Canadian government almost a month before the National Energy Board finished its
hearings and two and a half months before the NEB announced its
choice of a pipeline route. Jean Chrétien has said that the impact of
the Berger recommendations was profound in a political sense, but
there is no evidence that they affected the NEB's rejection of Arctic
Gas and acceptance of the Foothills proposal for an Alaska Highway
pipeline. The board turned down Foothills' Maple Leaf Pipeline.

On 2 May 1977, the Federal Power Commission in Washington
threw out the El Paso application for an LNG pipeline route across
Alaska. On the other two applications before it, the FPC was split,
two commissioners recommending the Arctic Gas route across the
northern Yukon, and two the Foothills Alaska Highway route. In
August, having failed in both Canada and the United States and having spent $150 million, Arctic Gas gave up the ghost.*

By mid-1977 Bob Blair's Foothills group was the only survivor of
the pipeline battles, but West Coast, Alberta Trunk, and Northwest
Pipelines were not in a position to actually build a pipeline. The times
were increasingly against any pipeline. Petroleum prices were dropping back to manageable levels, and the energy crisis was over for the
time being: frontier gas and oil were once again unable to compete
with Middle Eastern petroleum. With inflation surging, it was estimated that the combined cost of the Foothills pipeline would be $20
billion.

Early on, Arctic Gas had asked the U.S. and Canadian governments to guarantee its investment. Both had declined and they let
Foothills know there could be no government backstop. Up to 1981,
the hopes of Bob Blair and his partners flickered bravely. In
September Senator Ted Stevens of Alaska delivered the pipeline's

---

*Marshall Crowe, chairman of the NEB at that time, told me in 1993: "Had the gov-
ernment exerted influence, it would have been for the Arctic Gas proposal for a gas
pipeline up the Mackenzie. Alastair Gillespie and Donald Macdonald, both ministers
of energy during the 1970s and important Liberal cabinet figures; DIAND Minister
Jean Chrétien; Trade Minister Jack Horner, a powerful figure in Alberta; Clerk of the
Cabinet Michael Pittfield, all made it known to me or otherwise – Chrétien by a public speech; Gillespie through a comment made to me by his wife – that the cabinet
strongly favoured 'Bill's project' [i.e., Bill Wilder, president and CEO of Gas
Arctic]. Prime Minister Trudeau kept his counsel." (Crowe had been deputy clerk of
the cabinet under Trudeau earlier.)

epitaph: "The amount to be borrowed is beyond the present capacity of the domestic financial market." The United States and Canada were already sliding into recession.*

Gotterdamerung

Thanks to the NEB's decision to accept the Alaska Highway route over that of Arctic Gas and to the changing international financial situation, the Canadian government didn't have to act on Berger's controversial recommendations. When Arctic Gas was rejected in 1977 and the whole megaproject was abandoned in 1981, Berger appeared to be a spectacular winner. Actually, he was a loser – and his defeat came from within the native organizations. The signs were becoming apparent even during Berger's highly successful community hearings.

The first voice of dissent came from Rick Hardy, president for three years of the Métis Association. He and his executive wanted the financial opportunities of a pipeline and split away from their coalition with the Indian Brotherhood. Not until Jim Bourque became head of the association did the organizations patch up their differences and begin joint land claims negotiations once more. Next, COPE began serious land and cash negotiations that were quite different from those of the Brotherhood.

The Brotherhood itself went through a bloody purge that saw the triumph of Georges Erasmus. In spite of Berger's report, the Brotherhood (now calling itself the Dene Nation) found the feds weren't ready to make concessions on self-government or rights over territorial lands not ceded to the natives in an agreement. Federal negotiators said the Dene could exercise political power in the GNWT through community councils and through members elected to the territorial assembly.

The Dene Nation found itself in a difficult position, isolated from both the Métis Association and COPE and with neither a cash settle-

---

*However, Marshall Crowe says that after both the NEB's and the American National Power Commission's rejection of the Arctic Gas proposal "the Canadian cabinet (or Alastair Gillespie) through the Canadian ambassador in Washington tried to get the U.S. to agree on the Arctic Gas line. The Canadian government would then have legislated it through the Northern Pipeline Act, overriding the NEB ... Jim Schlesinger, the U.S. secretary for energy, said 'no way!' ... So they set up the Northern Pipeline Agency to at least cut out the NEB from further mischief-making ... In fact, the new agency operated with the NEB staff."

ment, a land settlement, nor the potential benefits of industrial development. "Where are the jobs?" asked an increasing number of Dene and Métis, even in the settlements that had expressed strong opposition to the pipeline.

Dene leaders began to understand what Ottawa officials had always known: opposition to the pipeline was a wonderful tool with which to pry out a higher settlement price, but once the project was abandoned, there was no need for the government to settle at all. Thus the Dene's negotiating position was eroding rapidly by the end of the decade.

In 1980 Imperial Oil destroyed the delicate balance of the negotiators by proposing to expand its sixty-year-old Norman Wells field and build a 12-inch oil pipeline to Zama, Alberta. It was a comparatively tiny project but involved all the same principles that Berger had dealt with. At a First Nations constitutional conference in Ottawa, Erasmus told Energy Minister Marc Lalonde that if the NEB approved the Norman Wells pipeline, "it will be built over Dene bodies ... What is going to happen is that people are going to die if that pipeline is built." But this time there would be no Berger Commission. The NEB and the federal government's Environmental Assessment and Review Process (EARP) held public hearings and quickly approved the project with a one-year delay recommended.

Erasmus found little support, and he retired from the presidency of the Dene Nation to run for the leadership of the Assembly of First Nations, the premier native body in Canada. Vice-president Herb Norwegian took over leadership of the Dene Nation pending an election, and he carried on the Erasmus policy, warning that violence "as a last resort" might occur. In the election, Norwegian lost to an Erasmus opponent, Steve Kakfwi of Good Hope.

Ottawa took a firm hand with both the indigenes and the companies. John Munro, the new DIAND minister, came north to confer privately with native chiefs and Dene Nation leaders. He offered the natives a major slice of the pie: the promise of jobs and support for native contractors bidding against southern companies. The federal government took a one-third financial interest in the project, and Esso Resources, which was developing expansion of the Norman Wells field, and Interprovincial Pipelines, which was building the pipeline, were forced to give the Dene ownership of a drilling rig and a service rig.

The first native industrial venture, Shehta Drilling, was set up with

$1 million seed money from Ottawa, and a native crew was trained on the presumption that there would be further oil and gas activity in the North. When the pipeline was built, things went quickly. There were some social disruptions, but a few native contractors actually created successful businesses. Rick Hardy's brother was one of them, and Rick became a prominent lawyer in Yellowknife. Under the final agreement worked out by Munro with the chiefs, the Dene Nation, and the Métis Association, two-thirds of the 350 construction jobs were earmarked for northerners and, as a concession to the hard-liners, construction was delayed two years.

Cindy Clegg, one of the most knowledgeable CBC reporters in the NWT, covered the Norman Wells project from start to finish. She says the change in native attitudes was quite sudden. Up to 1980, Berger's recommendations were regarded as "a sacred pact," guarding the interests of the Indians. When the "little inch" pipeline was suggested at environmental hearings in the Mackenzie communities, many natives were outraged. Soon, however, the representatives of Interprovincial Pipelines were well prepared: presumably they had read and profited from the Berger Report.

"At that time, land claims were going absolutely nowhere," Clegg told me. "The political situation was at one stage, the economic situation was at another. Right after the Berger Report came out, funding was cut off for the Dene Nation and it had to lay off thirty-three people. Although at the environmental hearings the people all said we don't want it, the general economic situation began to deteriorate and the oil and gas drilling companies began to pull out. Even those people who were protesting the pipeline began to worry about having no industry. Munro was able to put across his case and sweeten it with some concessions. People began to accept the inevitability of development."

Clegg painted a picture in which, quite suddenly, all the elements had changed. Although there was no land claims settlement (nor sight of one), Erasmus hailed the token delay as "a major victory for the people that will create the kind of climate needed for successful negotiation of our land claims." The deal also brought the Métis Association back into partnership with the Dene Nation.

Pipeline and field expansion were completed and in operation by early 1985 – just eight years from the time Berger had insisted that there be no pipeline until a native claims settlement had been signed and that in any case there should be a ten-year moratorium. It was only four years after Berger's report came out that the little-inch pipeline was approved. True, the 12-inch pipeline was a pygmy compared to the 48-inch giant proposed by Arctic Gas, but it was clear that the most important part of Berger's recommendations had been ignored by Ottawa: the land settlement.

Within two years of the completion of the Norman Wells pipeline, Bob Blair, by this time head of the gigantic Nova Corporation, was planning a "big inch" oil pipeline up the Mackenzie Valley from the Beaufort Sea. No one had had broader experience with the impact of the Berger Commission. Blair expected that there would be no repetition of such an inquiry; the only problem, he thought, would be raising money to build a pipeline.

The Victims

No other commission in Canada's history has been more colourful and dramatic than the one headed by Tom Berger. At its core was the flinty integrity of its chairman, who refused to compromise on most of the issues before him. The colour and drama of the commissioner's gaudy progression through the native villages of the NWT and the cities of the south brought home the issues of environmental protection and minority rights. Perhaps the commission's greatest success was as a teaching instrument: it awakened the Dene, Métis, and Inuvialuit in remote communities to the world pressing in on them. Ironically, that very awareness may have led the indigenes to abandon the principles outlined so cogently by Berger.

Were there any victims of what turned out to be a $170-million fiasco? Certainly among the losers were Arctic Gas, the Foothills group, and El Paso Gas. All of them lost a great deal of money and time. But in the end they went back to the marketplace without much difficulty: there were no spectacular bankruptcies. Bob Blair, indeed, turned Alberta Gas Trunk into Nova Corporation and became one of the major players in the Canadian oil patch. The Liberal cabinet ministers who strongly supported a megaproject to build the Mackenzie River gas pipeline – Chrétien, Alastair Gillespie, Jack Horner, Joe Greene, Donald Macdonald, and perhaps others – were big losers in the short run, and soon the voters were rejecting Prime Minister Trudeau's whole National Energy Program. But there were also two individual victims – both of them men of great character and unblemished reputation, both of them brought down by another giant of integrity, Chief Justice Bora Laskin of the Supreme Court of Canada.

The first victim was Marshall Crowe, chairman of the National Energy Board. It was Chief Justice Laskin who wrote the opinion for the five-three Supreme Court majority that removed Crowe from the NEB panel considering the Arctic Gas pipeline proposal. Crowe's personal honour was not questioned, but he was a marked man with the anti-pipeline environmentalists later when accused of bad judgment in accepting a tour of the Arctic provided by Panarctic Oils. Ironically, the NEB's decision to throw out Arctic Gas's application for a Mackenzie Valley pipeline made Crowe almost as unpopular as Berger with several powerful cabinet ministers.

No charges or even serious allegations were made, but environmentalists and petroleum promoters alike were pleased when Crowe took early retirement from the NEB and began a new (and successful) career as a lobbyist. The lesson for the Canadian public was that a spotless record cannot protect a civil servant from ruthless adversaries. The 1977 junket had nothing to do with the pipeline dispute, but unhappily, many remembered the Supreme Court ruling against Crowe in 1975.

The other victim was Berger himself. His fall occurred five years after the pipeline inquiry and was not directly linked to it. But there is no doubt that the reputation he had acquired as a defender of native rights contributed to the dilemma he found himself in from 1981 to 1983. In the wake of the colourful Mackenzie hearings and his eloquent report, Berger became a mythic figure across the nation. In 1980 Conservative Health Minister David Crombie asked him to chair a royal commission on the health of native children, but the project fell through when the Liberals returned to power.

Back on the B.C. Supreme Court, Berger became increasingly outspoken. In 1981 he published *Fragile Freedoms: Human Rights and Dissent in Canada* and told a University of Guelph audience: "In the end, no matter what ideology they profess, our leaders share one firm conviction: that native rights should not be inviolable, the power of the state must encompass them." He spoke during the national debate on whether aboriginal rights should be enshrined in Canada's new constitution, and biographer Carolyn Swayze said he could not have chosen a harsher criticism to level against Prime Minister Trudeau. Indeed, Trudeau, on a Vancouver TV talk show, accused Berger of "getting off the Bench and entering the political arena at a very inopportune time." Even though, according to Swayze, Trudeau had misinterpreted Berger and later apologized to him, the fat was in the fire.

The Canadian Judicial Council launched an investigation of Berger, and its chairman, Justice George Addy, a federal judge, complained to Chief Justice Bora Laskin of the Supreme Court of Canada. Berger defended himself vigorously, saying: "I believe a judge has the right – a duty, in fact – to speak out on an appropriate occasion on questions of human rights and fundamental freedoms, particularly minority rights." But both the Judicial Council and the Supreme Court found against him. Chief Justice Laskin issued a scathing opinion which said, in part:

> Judges are expected to abstain from participation in political controversy. To a large degree, Judge Berger was re-activating his Mackenzie Valley Pipeline Inquiry, a matter which was years behind him and should properly be left dormant for a political decision, if any, and not for his initiative in the midst of a sensitive political controversy.

Laskin said sternly: "Judges have no freedom of speech and one who feels compelled to speak out is best advised to resign from the Bench." Berger was stunned and in early 1983 felt he had to resign. He returned to private practice, but even here, according to his biographer, he faced criticism from the legal profession, some of whose members are critical of judges who want to return to the courtroom as advocates.

The blow was all the more bitter because Berger, like Crowe, was extremely proud of his record of personal integrity. Neither man resigned voluntarily on a matter of principle: each was brought up short on fine shadings of behaviour skilfully used by impersonal adversaries. The exemplary mandarin and the principled judge would well reflect on the gloomy words from Shakespeare's *Cymbeline*: "Golden lads and girls all must, / As chimney sweepers, come to dust."

Chapter 10

Political Evolution and Devolution

A Historical Year – 1975

A lot of things happened all at once in 1975. Tom Berger took his Flying Circus to the people. The Indian Brotherhood issued the Dene Declaration and fired James Wah Shee. And full representative government came to the NWT, marking an enormous step on the road to responsible government.

The true significance of these events was not understood for a while. At first, it seemed that the flashy events around the Berger Commission and the struggle for control of the Indian Brotherhood and Métis Association were of central importance, but eventually it became evident that the changes in government structure not only were having a major impact on day-to-day life but also were a tool used by the NWT people, native and white, on an ever increasing scale.

From 1970 to 1975, the NWT Council had ten elected and four appointed members, with all executive power held by the commissioner. In 1975 the NWT Act was amended so that all council members were elected and the number was increased to fifteen; two were allowed to sit on the executive committee, which advised the commissioner (though he did not have to take its advice).

When Stuart Hodgson became commissioner in 1967, the executive committee consisted of himself, the deputy commissioner, and the assistant commissioner. Most government functions were handled by DIAND officials, either in Ottawa or in the NWT, or by civil servants in Ottawa who were attached to other departments concerned with the North, such as Defence, Health and Welfare, Energy, Mines and Resources, and Fisheries. After Yellowknife became the nominal capital, many functions were transferred from DIAND and the other federal ministries to the GNWT, thus creating an instant bureaucracy inside the Territories.

In 1976 the GNWT's annual report printed a management chart showing that the commissioner ranked directly below the DIAND minister and reported directly to him. Everyone in the GNWT was responsible to the commissioner: the Legislative Council, the deputy commissioner, the assistant commissioner, all boards and corporations, and all regional and departmental directors. In theory, the commissioner was the equal of the DIAND deputy minister and held equivalent civil service rank. In practice, the deputy minister had much more real power in terms of policy and finance and, of course, immediate and constant access to the minister and to mandarins on the same level.

In the GNWT Annual Report, 1976, Dr. Walter Kupsch of the Carrothers Commission wrote of the 1967 expansion of the executive council: "The implications are enormous, since elected members are directly involved in the formation of policy. Also implied is a shift in emphasis which may lead to an Executive Branch wholly responsible to the Legislature."

The Indian Brotherhood was directly opposed to this concept. It envisaged a NWT divided into several parts, each controlled by an aboriginal group independent of the others and largely independent of Ottawa. Instead, Ottawa decreed representative government for all of the NWT and elected by all of the ethnic and cultural groups. The ultimate aim was responsible government for the whole of the Territories, patterned on that of Canada as one nation.

The Brotherhood asked for self-determination, citing the recently independent nations of Africa and Asia. The Berger Inquiry provided a forum for anti-colonialist arguments. The Dene Declaration – issued even as Hodgson was trying vainly to get DIAND to define a native northerner and adopt a policy of hiring them for the GNWT – was full of ringing phrases like: "Colonialism and imperialism are now dead or dying. Recent years have witnessed the birth of new nations or the rebirth of old nations out of the ashes of colonialism."

The Brotherhood fired Wah Shee and boycotted the territorial council. Ottawa, and much of the white world, puzzled over just what the Indians wanted when the Dene Declaration stated: "We, the Dene, are struggling with the recognition of the Dene Nation by the governments and peoples of the world." One Dene position paper said:

When we say Dene Government we clearly mean an institution set up by the Dene, based on Dene traditions and values. Under the new institutions that will be negotiated, we will guarantee full political rights for everyone. The Dene have clearly stated they do not want independence from Canada, but inter-dependence with the rest of the country. Our position is not a separatist position. What we have very clearly set out as part of our goal is the process of de-colonialization of our people. The recognition of our rights to exist as a people, to have our own institutions, to have our own government, will only establish the framework in which we will begin to do the work of de-colonialization.

In a manifesto published by Christian church supporters in 1977, the Brotherhood said:

> We must have our own exclusive jurisdiction within Canada. We must have our own political institutions through which we both govern ourselves internally as we choose and continue to present our collective interests externally to the rest of Canada. Only with our own exclusive political jurisdiction can we meet these requirements. Unless these requirements are met, it is meaningless to talk of the Dene as a people, or of Dene Culture as being a continuing reality. Any other arrangement would be genocide.

It was hard to reduce such flaming rhetoric to understandable levels of communication. Most of the more extreme statements were made at a time of great political tension, when native leaders were bending every effort to stopping the big-inch pipeline. Rhetoric obviously was a bargaining tool. It was also a bargaining tool in the land claims negotiations, in which Ottawa repeatedly told the Indians that ethnic government was a total impossibility. When Mr. Justice Berger expressed sympathy during community hearings and in his report, Dene hopes were raised, but the decision of the Liberal government to simply ignore the Berger recommendations returned the land claims negotiations to the position they had been in before anybody had started talking about a pipeline.

∽

When Ottawa announced the new northern policy in 1953, it seemed unlikely that elaborate changes in the NWT's political structure were envisaged. There were too many urgent crises to be met: saving the Keewatin Inuits from starvation; satisfying American defence

demands; protecting Canada's Arctic sovereignty. After such problems were solved, the business community expected development of
mineral resources. As far as the indigenes went, there was no immediate pressure to change policies enshrined in the Indian Act for
seventy-seven years. The Métis could fend for themselves – as they
always had. The Inuit were a totally unknown quantity and might be
abandoned after the first humanitarian fervour had died down.

In those early days of bureaucratic revolution, there was a brisk
Ottawa debate between the Christian missionaries and the HBC men
on one side and the new breed of civil servants and social scientists
on the other. One side wanted to let the Inuit remain as noble savages;
the other had an idea that they might be brought into the 20th century through education and kindness. The mandarins who handled the
budget were appalled by the idea that the native peoples might have
to be permanently subsidized. Perhaps, their thinking went, the
Indians and Inuit could be trained to work in a wage economy and
thus relieve southern taxpayers from their moral obligations. Gary
Mullins, assistant commissioner in charge of financial planning in the
late 1970s, summed up the dilemma this way:

> In the 1950s we found the Inuit were starving and as Canadians we
> felt we could not allow fellow Canadians to starve even if they his-
> torically had relied on caribou and other animals, the migratory pat-
> terns of which had changed. Okay, we say, let's feed them – but that
> starts an irreversible chain of events. If you decide that these people
> are going to have to take care of themselves in some other way than
> relying on a migratory and not particularly reliable source of food,
> you put them in communities. But they have to have alternatives.
> They have to be educated. For a child to be educated, he not only
> has to have a place to go to school but also a place to study – a child
> cannot study in an igloo at night without electricity. So, eventually,
> you're getting into communities and housing. These are provided by
> the taxpayers for the users, the native people. Houses are not some-
> thing they provide for themselves because they don't have the
> resources to acquire homes for themselves. All of the extras – med-
> ical services, welfare, social services, the wage economy, commu-
> nity conveniences – go with a house.

Ottawa's dilemma began with starving Inuit. It soon spread to the
Mackenzie Indians, who were not starving but were almost as badly

in need of medical services, adequate schools, and some kind of supplement to inadequate incomes. By the end of the 1950s, white intervention had spread throughout the NWT. Even the greenest of the
new administrators saw major differences between Inuit and Indian
problems. So much so that Ottawa politicians, in contrast to the civil
servants who ran the program, began to consider the possibility of
creating two territories, one in the Arctic for the Inuit and one in the
west for the Indians, Métis, and white settlers.

The non-natives, almost all in the west, had to be considered
because they formed at least 40 percent of the population and embodied the only coherent political force. Many were loudly demanding
democratic rights, including control of local taxation and participation in regional and nationally elected governments. Some observers
predicted that they would create a territory or province of their own,
and there were voices from Regina and Edmonton suggesting that
parts of the NWT might become adjuncts of Saskatchewan and
Alberta. Some with long memories remembered the agitation of
1900, which had led to the formation of two new provinces and the
expansion of three others (Manitoba, Ontario, and Quebec). (It had
also led to almost total domination and suppression of the Indian and
Métis populations by the federal and provincial governments.)

Such topics were serious issues in 1963 when two bills to divide
the NWT went before the House of Commons – only to die on the
order paper because the divided and collapsing Diefenbaker government was in no shape to bring coherence to its northern policy. Lester
Pearson's Liberals saw that something had to be done, but the
Carrothers Commission recommended against division and proposed
reforms that would introduce representative, then responsible government. To the chagrin of many an old northern mandarin, Arthur
Laing agreed to move the seat of NWT administration to
Yellowknife, to establish the rudiments of a legislative assembly, and
to introduce local democratic government to the dozens of new communities of the tundra and *taiga*. Democracy was to apply to native
and white alike.

To some extent, Ottawa was only following the international
winds of change, which had been noted in Africa by Britain's prime
minister, Harold MacMillan. His milestone speech in the 1960s
underscored the fact that old-style colonialism was rapidly being
replaced. The complaint of the young Canadian native leaders was
that Ottawa's reforms didn't go far enough and were headed in the

wrong direction. They and the farther-sighted planners of the GNWT warned Ottawa that the traditional white system of electing representatives and letting them decide on the fate of the country was in sharp variance with the native tradition of having the whole community participate in decision-making.

This cultural difference was to prevent a settlement of native claims for many years, and those in charge of establishing the new democracy found that their product was hard to sell in the Mackenzie communities. Nevertheless, Arthur Laing was committed to the process, and his chosen instrument was Stuart Hodgson. The two of them soon found that the recommendations of the Carrothers Report were easier to enunciate than to put into effect.

~

The early part of this book dealt with the vast physical problems of feeding, housing, and building schools and hospitals for the Inuit and, to a lesser extent, for the status and non-status Indians. Commissioner/Deputy Minister Gordon Robertson found it hard to recruit suitable people who could adapt to a difficult environment and to aboriginal cultures. In the early days, there were instances of incompetence, design failure, and shady deals, but such problems could be routinely remedied within a few years.

The situation was completely different when it came to democratization. Even though the Inuit had been ignored for three centuries, they rapidly grasped the issues at stake and learned how to use the tools of government. In 1977 Ray Creery, vice-chairman of the GNWT committee on devolution, travelled to twenty-four communities. He reported the views of Simonie Attungalla, a resident of Frobisher Bay (now Iqualuit) at a meeting in the South Baffin community:

> He said if the village council was given responsibility for local social development, he would like to see the council get the necessary resources. Additional responsibilities should be given at a slow pace, not too much at one time. The giving of responsibility in social development, education and other departments all at once would be the downfall of council because they couldn't handle that ... He said it is not productive to use southern models, examples drawn from northern experience were useful but not those from the south.

In the west, the central problem was different. Indian bands had been living for some time in semi-permanent settlements clustered around the missions and HBC posts, and they were used to government agents enforcing the Indian Act. Ottawa had always encouraged them to form band councils led by chiefs who were either elected or hereditary. Indian Act conflicts were worked out between the band council and the Indian agent.

When Ottawa announced its new devolution program, the elders and chiefs were reluctant to give their perks up to community councils that might be dominated by whites and Métis. The Indian Act administrators were just as reluctant to surrender their authority. Sometimes the policy changes made in far-off Ottawa hit the NWT with dislocating force. In 1970, for instance, DIAND's operational staff was suddenly transferred to the control of the GNWT. Many Indian elders, who believed they had no reason to trust the new GNWT, felt betrayed when the DIAND offices closed and their complaints were referred to a different set of administrators. Indians strongly believed that Ottawa had breached the terms of Treaties 8 and 11 because the GNWT was not connected to either the Indian Act or the treaties.

Hodgson found his efforts to hand over a measure of government to the local settlements frustrated at every turn both by white administrators and by Indian chiefs, elders, and native community workers who wanted nothing to do with the GNWT. Assistant Commissioner E.M.R. Cotterill headed up a task force on management and personnel. Sid Hancock was placed in charge of local government, with instructions to encourage settlement councils that would take over some of the functions of the local administrators from the GNWT.

While "evolution and devolution" was the official policy of Arthur Laing and his successor, Jean Chrétien, many DIAND civil servants believed the aboriginal peoples would not be ready to take over their own affairs for generations. There was also another factor. The Ottawa bureaucracy was becoming so vast and so complex that it didn't want to give away any power, even to the mushrooming white bureaucracy in Yellowknife. The greatest irony was that Hodgson was trying to hand over his immense personal powers, but his subordinates were reluctant to give up any of theirs.

It was no wonder that Mel Watkins and other white advisers believed that Ottawa had no intention of abandoning colonialism. Noting the European colonial record, they felt that the only way for northern natives to win a measure of autonomy was to overthrow the colonial masters, as had been done in other parts of the world. It was hard for the more radical advisers to believe that Ottawa had actually heard the messages of Nehru, Ho Chi Minh, Sukarno, Nkomo, Nyerere, and Kenyatta.

Even after the relatively liberal and far-sighted recommendations of the Carrothers Commission in 1966, the idea that Ottawa might give Indians and Inuit a measure of political autonomy and built-in guarantees for their traditional cultures did not appear to be a consideration for those who were planning the constitutional future of the NWT and its inhabitants. Nevertheless, the political leaders of Canada (both Liberal and Conservative) were dedicated to drastic reform of the colonial structure in the North. Sometimes they went too far and in the wrong direction, as in 1969 when Chrétien and Trudeau introduced their notorious white paper on Indian policy, which would have abolished DIAND and the Indian Act and encouraged aboriginals to become citizens like everyone else. In the face of a storm of Indian protest, the white paper was abandoned.

In 1972 Chrétien announced a 1971–81 northern policy mainly concerned with industrial development and the exploitation of nonrenewable resources. This was the policy that was designed to prepare the way for the Mackenzie Valley pipeline and energy corridor. It did not deal with social or political plans or with native claims, which were to be handled in separate negotiations and programs, some of them already under way. The Chrétien northern policy was scuppered by the Berger Inquiry. And this, in turn, had an impact on land claims negotiations and the development of responsible government – what in the NWT was called "devolution."

∾

In view of the confusion of the country's political masters, it was not surprising that Hodgson had trouble persuading two levels of civil servants and four fairly distinct aboriginal groups to enthusiastically endorse a devolution policy that was understood by no one. The wonder was that the settlement councils worked at all, and it was a tribute to the new public school system that within a few years it produced a considerable number of young natives competent to take over running the affairs of the communities.

Hodgson went on struggling with his own and Ottawa's bureaucrats. By 1976 he had in hand Assistant Commissioner Cotterill's task force report on personnel and management. He was also looking forward to retiring and turning over the commissionership to John Parker. On the basis of Cotterill's task force findings, Hodgson issued a "final report," which made nineteen recommendations. The first was to increase the ratio of native northerners in the NWT public service. Hodgson wrote bluntly that this recommendation roused strong protest from white civil servants, who complained that they had been passed over.

The commissioner added: "The second and more universal complaint was the definition of native northerners as Indian, Inuit or Métis; this definition was felt to be discriminatory." Noting that there was no set definition for a native northerner, the commissioner said he would ask DIAND to develop one, but he warned: "Territorial government employees have to understand that over 60 percent of the population is Indian, Inuit or Métis, but this ratio is far from reflected in government employment statistics." A basic principle, Hodgson said, was "equal and meaningful participation for all of Canada's territorial citizens, regardless of station, in political, social and economic activities, and in traditional ways of life, in accordance with the ability, desires and wishes of the individual."

He listed two goals and several guidelines. The goals were: (1) controlled growth, expansion and development "in keeping with the aspirations of the people, their culture, tradition, pursuits, lifestyles and skills, while affording useful and meaningful employment opportunities at all levels of society"; (2) development of local self-government by giving the GNWT control over the provision of social services. The principal guidelines were: (1) increased employment for native people, including training for higher service; (2) preservation of northern lifestyles; (3) controlled development of municipal and community services for a growing population, consistent with good health and sanitation standards; (4) development of the design and construction of communities; (5) an increase in the participation and responsibility of native people within the institutions of the GNWT; (6) transition of government to major involvement by electoral representatives; (7) improved efficiency of the GNWT.

There was one significant thing about Hodgson's report and the recommendations of the task force. While the commissioner said he was trying to define northern natives in a different way from "Indians, Inuit and Métis," his "basic principle" did not refer to natives at all – only to "all of Canada's territorial citizens, regardless of station."

This, of course, would put white residents on the same footing as the aboriginals and was at the heart of Ottawa's policy.

At the very time Hodgson was implementing his basic policy, it was being challenged by the Dene Declaration, and Tom Berger was lending a friendly ear to aboriginal views emphasizing qualitative differences between NWT citizens. Whatever the respective merits of the two positions, Hodgson's policy was totally divorced from traditional colonialism. For instance, the task force's seventeenth recommendation said: "A major objective ... is that the public service should reflect at all levels the ratio of native northerners to the population of the NWT."

As of April 1976, Hodgson said, the GNWT employed just under 500 natives. He said in his conclusion that he was confident that the task force recommendations had become the policy of the GNWT and were being put into practice.

Hodgson's final report showed that in 1972–73 in the NWT, civil service turnover was 27 percent compared to 1,000 percent in the lower-paying jobs of private business, 250 percent for hotels and restaurants, and more than 100 percent for mines. GNWT staff terminations were 1,673 per year, not including teachers. In the same period, the turnover in the Soviet Arctic mining city of Norilsk was more than 200 percent per year, despite many incentives offered to southern workers. Norilsk is the site of the world's largest open-pit mines and at that time had a population of 80,000. It is located at 70 degrees north latitude, somewhat north of Inuvik.

By the time Hodgson received the Cotterill Report, he was fed up with the foot-dragging and the tensions between DIAND and GNWT civil servants, then flaring into the open. Ray Creery, certainly one of the most respected of NWT public servants, wrote in his 1977 report:

> Devolution at the level of the Territorial Government is the prerogative of the Government of Canada, which is under no compulsion to move and shows every indication of waiting until it is assured that the best possible arrangements have been worked out for the definition, maintenance and protection of native rights and benefits within an ordered and progressive northern society. This puts the onus on both Territorial Council as prime mover in constitutional development, and the native associations as prime movers in land claims, to make their advances while respecting the vital interests of each other.

Creery warned that the ambitions of those wanting responsible government were incompatible with those of the native groups. Hodgson was even closer to these warring ambitions, the departmental jealousies, and blindsidedness of both Ottawa and Yellowknife.*

By no means incidentally, as late as 1987, the NWT commissioner still retained all his baronial powers – but only on paper. Hodgson and Parker gradually gave up many of their powers voluntarily to the elected members of the Legislative Council, which after 1975 was popularly known as the Legislative Assembly. Within a very few years, the council/assembly took on the appearance and many of the functions of a provincial legislature.

∽

From the very start of the northern revolution, keeping track of finances was a major problem. In 1972 Gary Mullins was a senior analyst with the Treasury Board in Ottawa, with the responsibility of making sense of the NWT's annual budget. He was seconded to DIAND to sit on a task force dealing with budget planning and in 1975 succeeded Cotterill as assistant commissioner in charge of finances.

The difficulty, Mullins said after he left the Territories, was that Ottawa controlled all the dollars and there was no serious planning as to how they should be spent. A regional administrator tended to spend whatever he was given, then ask for more: he had no hand in planning program costs. The federal Treasury found itself being asked to cough up more and more money, without anyone having a clue as to real needs.

Mullins said there was no real budgeting system because inside the NWT, no one had any budgetary authority, and Ottawa was too remote to keep a close check on spending. This brought the mandarins back to a basic problem that has plagued nations since the ancient Greeks – and caused the English to cut off one king's head in 1649 and the French to cut off another king's head in 1793. That issue was taxation without the consent of taxpayers. Wiser Ottawa heads saw the need to make NWT residents fiscally responsible. The

---

*Gary Mullins says that in 1977, after ten years as commissioner, Hodgson asked Ottawa to transfer him to another job. When he left in 1979, he had received no such offer and finally settled for becoming czar of British Columbia's ferry boats, which were owned by the provincial government.

obvious first step was to teach northerners how to handle money, rather as if they were children being shown how to stay within parental allowances.

The trouble was that in the settlements the only people accustomed to dealing with community budgets were the whites – and not many of them. Most indigenes first needed a working knowledge of English and business arithmetic, some understanding of the nature of taxes, and information on how to run a town department. Berger noted that in native communities, the residents believed the white administrators and community councils were concerned with garbage disposal and fresh water when – the natives felt – they should have been spending their time on game management. Berger seemed to approve the criticism; he said nothing about the need to train aboriginals in the dangers of infectious diseases.

Confronted with elementary training necessities in fifty settlements, it was no wonder that many area and community administrators wanted to keep their experienced hands on the tillers. Some thought Walter Kupsch was dreaming when he wrote in the GNWT Annual Report, 1977:

> The growth of fully-elected, independent hamlet and settlement councils must benefit the GNWT as a whole for it implies that there will be a continuous flow of competent people to sit on the Territorial Council ... Self-government in the settlements also means that all groups, as well as all individuals, are assured of having a voice in the conduct of their own affairs through their elected representatives at every level of government – local, regional and Territorial.

∼

The Carrothers Commission's vision of an autonomous NWT moving toward provincehood depended on the participation of all the residents. The Indian Brotherhood's vision was quite different, and its leaders realized that the long-range planners in Ottawa (though not necessarily the administrators working for them) were banking a good deal on the success of an elected legislative council. This was the reason for the Brotherhood's boycott of council in 1975.

The council was at a delicate stage of development, and it didn't help when the only Indian members suddenly withdrew: for one thing, the Brotherhood could plausibly claim that the white members from Yellowknife, Hay River, Fort Smith, Pine Point, Inuvik, and Frobisher Bay were in a position to run the GNWT as they wished. The Inuit members from Baffin Island and the High Arctic were still unsure of themselves and as yet unable to form an effective political coalition. They tended to reserve their interventions in debate to discussion of local issues in their constituencies and appeared to be uneasy when asked to comment on broad territorial issues. Bill Lafferty, the Métis member from Simpson, had spent most of his working life in the Alberta oil patch and tended to vote with the whites.

Certainly, it looked to an outside observer as though the whites were fulfilling all the old colonialist predictions. David Searle, the outspoken Speaker and a Yellowknife lawyer, never lost a chance to attack the Brotherhood's white advisers as Marxists and troublemakers. Don Stewart, the grizzled mayor of Hay River, liked to tell tourists that there wouldn't be any "Indian problem" in three generations – the natives would have been assimilated. Bryan Pearson, the flamboyant storekeeper from Frobisher Bay, spoke in grandiloquent terms about looking after "my people" (by which he meant the Inuit he had been living among since he had emigrated from Britain).

After the 1975 election, the natives appeared to outnumber the whites eight to seven, but this was an illusion even before the only two Indians, James Wah Shee, representing the Dog Ribs in Rae, and George Barnaby, representing the Sah'tu in Good Hope, were forced out by the Brotherhood. Barnaby said bitterly after he resigned that the council never listened to the communities and was determined to rule by white ideas imported from the south. The resignations meant that the only cohesive force on council was white, chiefly based in Yellowknife. The south and north Baffin Inuit, the representatives of the Keewatin and the central and High Arctic, and the Inuvialuit representatives from the Delta had cultural and economic differences of their own.

Nevertheless, that 1975–79 council saw the natives learning the trade of government quickly. By the 1979 elections, some had mastered the arts of log-rolling, mugwumping, and back-scratching to a level that would have satisfied the most experienced old pol from the south. The pipeline debate came and went. The Berger hearings came and went. By 1979 the pipeline issue was no longer a bargaining weapon for the Brotherhood (now the Dene Nation) and Dene leaders agreed to lift their ban on participation in the legislature.

The Government Leader

The next development involved having a member of council become government leader – the rudimentary equivalent of a provincial premier, although, unlike the Yukon, the NWT did not propose to adopt official party politics at the territorial level. There were good reasons for this. The Yukon's population was nearly 80 percent white, while the NWT was divided into racial thirds and subdivided into tribal, regional, and cultural groups of aboriginals. Any further fragmentation of the ethnic groups might splinter the Territories beyond any hope of governing.

From the very start, therefore, it was evident that the GNWT must be built on compromise and conciliation rather than on political principle. Government by consensus, in the tradition of many North American Indian nations, seemed to be the ideal solution, and it has worked – after a fashion. By the early 1990s, however, major problems were emerging.

The transition from control by the commissioner and his masters in Ottawa to a fairly responsible legislative system was accomplished with great skill, considering the confrontation that had gone on between the Dene Nation and the federal government in the late 1970s. The Dene had been holding out for rigid ethnic control over their share of the Territories. The Inuit, on the other hand, knew that they were in no danger of losing political dominance of the eastern and central Arctic. The Inuvialuit of the Delta and Beaufort Sea were moderate and were ready to break ranks with their cousins, the Inuit, to make their own land claims deal with Ottawa.

The whites, who were concentrated in Yellowknife, Hay River, Inuvik, and Fort Smith, with a number scattered through the Dene and Inuit communities, were cohesive and had played a big part in representative government from the start. Such portfolios as finance and justice were generally held by whites like Tom Butters in Inuvik and Mike Ballantyne in Yellowknife. The whites were confident of maintaining their enclaves in the Mackenzie Valley.

There was one other political factor. Kabloona Dennis Patterson of Iqaluit and Gordon Wray of Baker Lake were powerful and effective cabinet members, but they drew their political clout from the prominent Inuit families they had married into. Wray told me that he had connections through his wife with 180 members of the most powerful Inuit family in Baker Lake.

But could an elected legislature handle all of the NWT's long- and short-range problems? Or would the NWT have to remain a colony of the federal government, directed from Ottawa? The question was a serious one, especially because the various aboriginal groups had so little experience in any kind of sophisticated government. Hodgson and Parker, almost alone among white federal leaders, were determined to give it a try through their devolution/evolution program.

The territorial assembly – now fully elected for the first time – was urged to set up its own government under the benign supervision of the commissioner. The person who was chosen government leader would, in many respects, replace the commissioner. The leader's powers would be limited and strictly controlled by Ottawa, but they would permit the first tottering steps toward responsible government. The cabinet, too, would be a new step. Instead of an executive committee, appointed by and responsible to the commissioner, it would spring from the Legislative Assembly and be responsible to it.

The method of selecting a government leader and a cabinet was unique (in Canada at least) to the NWT. The twenty-four elected members of the assembly first chose one of their own to be leader. He or she was not necessarily the strongest, most capable, or most attractive – merely the least offensive to the largest number of members. Once a government leader was chosen, the whole assembly selected a cabinet of seven to administer thirteen to fifteen departments and agencies.

The government leader had far less power than a prime minister or premier in a partisan system. He or she did not designate the members of the cabinet as prime ministers do in the south. Both leader and cabinet were picked after a process of dickering and discussion among representatives of areas with very different agendas. In 1991, for example, the two candidates for leader were Nellie Cournoyea and Stephen Kakfwi. Both were strong, experienced legislators. Cournoyea had been a founder of COPE, a negotiator for the Inuvialuit in the first land claims settlement, and a veteran cabinet minister. Kakfwi had been a strong president of the Dene Nation. But they could not be considered solely for their personal talents – each represented one of the key aboriginal groups. In the end, it may have been Nellie Cournoyea's long-time reputation as a conciliator and negotiator that won her the leadership.

From 1979 on, the government (as exemplified by the cabinet and leader) tried valiantly to work out an over-all program, but it was hard going. The federal government held the purse-strings and discouraged long-term planning in Yellowknife. Each department and agency tended to go its own way as it had in the past, dominated and controlled by senior civil servants, almost all of them white. Cabinet ministers were often more under the control of their own bureaucrats than in command of a department. The bureaucrats, in turn, tended to guard their perks and secrets jealously from rival bureaucrats in other departments. Even when the cabinet and leader managed to work out a common policy, it had to be argued through the other seventeen members of the legislature – and there was no political party discipline to keep them in line.

For more than ten years, the system rolled along very much as it had during the years under the commissioner. Most day-to-day jobs got done, and the main shadow was uncertainty about what would happen when the land claims were settled and negotiations for native self-governments began. As long as John Parker remained commissioner (until the end of 1989) the GNWT had the benefit of his counsel and problem-solving skills. Also, this was a period of prosperity, and Ottawa was solving northern difficulties with large injections of money.

But when Parker retired and was replaced by the first native commissioner, Daniel L. Norris, a Métis from the Delta, problems of government came home to roost. And the added spectre of enormous constitutional change was looming ever closer on the horizon. If the Nunavut land claims deal with the Inuit was accepted, the NWT would be split into two quite distinct territories, and it was not at all clear what kind of government would rule either territory.

Some Inuit leaders were predicting that Nunavut's government would be patterned on aboriginal traditions, though historically the Inuit had no experience with centralized institutions of any kind. On the other hand, the Mackenzie Valley had Dene, Inuvialuit, Métis, and non-aboriginals to satisfy in one government. In the early 1990s, it was predicted that the western territories would continue for a while as the NWT, but as the Dene and Métis land settlements were completed and negotiations for self-government began, almost any variation was possible.

Planning for the future was one of the things beyond the capacity of consensus government in its 1980s and 1990s form. There were complexities throughout the process. From the first, the worst problem was apathy on the part of the back-benchers, some of whom operated as they had on the old council, sticking with local issues important to their individual constituencies. Another problem was that no ruling political party could impose discipline on its members. The government leader and each member of the cabinet were individuals with no party to which they were loyal. This sometimes led to inertia and to interpersonal difficulties between individual members. Without a cohesive and integrated party policy, it was hard to get across to the communities the urgency of some long and middle-range policies and programs.

With the help of the powerful bureaucracy built up by Gordon Robertson, Stuart Hodgson, and John Parker, the council/assembly managed to keep the GNWT operational. Responsible government staggered from one challenge to the next as NWT residents learned how to govern themselves.

Who would be the first government leader? Obviously, it could not be the president of the Dene Nation, the Métis Association, COPE, or the ITC. Nor could it be one of the old northern hands like Don Stewart or David Searle. The choice was sensible enough: George Braden, a young white who had lived in Yellowknife since his high school days. He had studied northern constitutional politics at university, had worked for Pat Carney, had done a study of the pipeline, and in 1978–79 had been a researcher for the Drury Inquiry (see page 230).

Braden had one hidden asset: many of the young Inuit, Dene, and Métis leaders had gone to high school with him, and he knew them as contemporaries. He was also a born conciliator. The early 1980s were a time of organization and development, as the new GNWT began to seize new powers from the feds. Braden said later that he was in Ottawa negotiating with the feds at least once a month during his four-year term of office.

The first native government leader was Richard Nerysoo, the attractive young Gwich'in from Fort McPherson in the Delta who had temporarily succeeded James Wah Shee as head of the Indian Brotherhood in 1975. He was very young then and soon was forced out in favour of Wah Shee's great rival, Georges Erasmus. When he became government leader after George Braden, he once again failed, and after two years he was replaced by Nick Sibbeston, a Dehcho Métis from Fort Simpson who had been the first native to defeat a white man in an election for the territorial council. Sibbeston also was the first native lawyer in the NWT.

By this time, the political GNWT was beginning to take shape, although Ottawa continued to dominate through its control of the purse-strings and the white bureaucracy in Yellowknife, and the five regions still held a great deal of power. Sibbeston's job was different from that of Braden, and he was a very different kind of personality, a man with a temper who once threw a teacup at Tagak Curley, an Inuit cabinet minister, in a council meeting.

He understood his central problem well enough: to gain legislative control over the white bureaucrats who ran things for DIAND or the GNWT. These people were mainly whites, since almost no aboriginals qualified for such skilled civil service jobs – the vast majority of natives didn't even graduate from high school, let alone university. Most jobs held by natives were in unskilled labour, in some skilled occupations (heavy equipment operator, electrician, teacher, or nurse's aide), and at the lowest level of administration. There was always politics, of course: natives were proving to be just as successful as whites at the ancient art of wheeling and dealing.

In his brief two years as leader, Sibbeston was constantly ruffling feathers, but he launched one of the most important programs in NWT history – affirmative action. Sibbeston was determined to break the white stranglehold on the bureaucracy, and he began firing civil servants and replacing them with natives who had none of the academic qualifications of the incumbents from the south. His most spectacular action was firing the deputy minister of education, Brian Lewis, and replacing him with a native. In the Kitikmeot region he abruptly moved the director to Yellowknife and replaced him with Helen Adamache, the first Inuk and the first woman to become a regional director.

After the election in 1987, Dennis Patterson, a Vancouver-born lawyer who had married an Inuk from Iqaluit, was chosen leader. He was much more diplomatic than Sibbeston, and his four-year administration had no major crises. Patterson's government continued Sibbeston's affirmative action program but failed to get enough useful education to enough NWT natives. There was still a gulf between the GNWT in Yellowknife and the communities, whether Dene, Inuvialuit, or Inuit.

This was the period in which Indians, Métis, and Inuit were making determined efforts to get seats at federal-provincial constitutional conferences. At the last one, in 1989, they were given observer status and allowed to speak. Several, including Georges Erasmus, risen from leadership of the Dene Nation to the national Assembly of First Nations, made eloquent speeches. But it was to no avail. The provinces were unwilling to give either the southern Indians and Métis or the territorial aboriginals greater constitutional rights. The long and ultimately unsuccessful battle took the attention of most people off the internal problems of the NWT.

Nellie Cournoyea became government leader in 1991, narrowly edging out Stephen Kakfwi. In November 1991 Cournoyea laid the report of the Garry Beatty project before the assembly and warned her colleagues of the urgent dangers facing the NWT government.

Garry H. Beatty was a former senior civil servant in Manitoba and Saskatchewan, and his team had been asked to review the operations and structure of the GNWT. His report was highly critical, bluntly recommending greater community participation in government and a sized-down bureaucracy in Yellowknife. He said that the departments and agencies of government should be reduced in size and number and compelled to work more cooperatively. The cabinet should be reduced and made into much more of a team. "Operating departments should be consolidated," he said baldly, uttering words that terrify all civil servants who fear for their job security.

When Nellie Cournoyea addressed the assembly as new government leader in November 1991, she spoke in favour of the Beatty recommendations and even announced voluntary cuts in the salaries of the leader, ministers, and deputy ministers. As many politicians have found, it isn't that easy to reduce a bureaucracy. After eighteen months in office, some agencies had been consolidated, but the communities were still complaining that Yellowknife was leaving them out.

Furthermore, Cournoyea found that there were rising murmurs against consensus government. On 7 April 1993, she held a press conference to defend what she called "a three-day strategic planning workshop in Fort Providence." This gathering of legislators discussed a number of urgent problems, whose solution was in some conflict with the consensus system.*

Cournoyea noted at the press conference that the GNWT had to do a lot of work in connection with the impending (six years away) formation of the new territory of Nunavut. The proposed border

---

*Cournoyea spoke just as the federal government was announcing a massive land claims settlement with the Inuit in the eastern Arctic and the creation of a new Inuit territory, Nunavut, as of 1999.

between Nunavut and the continuing NWT was disputed by the Dene, and there had to be new surveys and new negotiations between the Dene and the Inuit. Then there was the question of planning a new NWT without the presence of the eastern Arctic. Costs would have to be re-estimated and constitutional difficulties solved – not to mention all kinds of practical matters.

The leader's co-spokesperson at the press conference was Fred Koe, a Métis from the Delta. He said: "One of the objectives of this workshop was to develop a comprehensive information and decision-making framework to guide the work of the current government and legislature." This, of course, was the kind of thing consensus supporters didn't believe in. A "decision-making framework" implied that there might be a timetable, and that led to the thought that the legislators might be hustled to vote en bloc. Nellie told the press that she felt it was important to get through to the legislature (and to the communities that elected the members) the need for quick and dependable action. Koe said at one point:

> An over-riding concern among members is that new models of government in the east and west would mean very little if the local population and workforce does not have the skills and experience to take advantage of public sector employment opportunities. There will be a future workshop on training, territorial division, and self-government issues.

A journalist asked Cournoyea about consensus, saying that "there has been a great deal of criticism involving efforts to make consensus government work within the parliamentary system." Koe jumped in and said that there was "much discussion" on this topic and "general agreement from all members that the existing government can work ... Business gets done, events happen, and things are happening." Cournoyea added: "There was no support to change the system to anything else. There was clear support that the consensus government should be – if there is a problem it should be made to work."

In the end, Nellie Cournoyea was saying that the GNWT faced a mountain of preparation before major constitutional and physical change in 1999 – and she warned that neither the legislators nor the public at large were aware of the magnitude of the task. Naturally, there was the question of whether the legislators would be willing and able to do the job.

Musical Chairs

While the elected members of the NWT Legislative Assembly were striving valiantly to learn their jobs and deal with a host of mushrooming problems, change was also taking place in Ottawa. In January 1976, Jean Chrétien's successor, Judd Buchanan, announced that henceforth there would be a "government to government" relationship between Ottawa and Yellowknife. This had been recommended in 1974 by the Cotterill task force, which was critical of the interminable "division to division" system of parallel government used by DIAND even after the GNWT was set up in 1967.

Buchanan had taken over from Chrétien in 1974 at a crucial point, with the pipeline debate and later the Berger hearings becoming hot political issues in the south, the Indians and Métis in turmoil, and the devolution program slowed by rivalry and confusion. (He was succeeded in 1976 by Warren Allmand, who held sway during the political flurry that followed the publication of the first volume of the Berger Report. Allmand gave way to Hugh Faulkner in 1977.)

After passing on his management task force report to Hodgson, Cotterill went to Ottawa as assistant deputy minister to Deputy Minister Arthur Kroeger. The two mandarins were looking for a much broader strategy that would replace Chrétien's resources policy of 1972. Buchanan promised that if Yellowknife would transfer some of its powers to the settlements and regions, Ottawa would give new powers to Yellowknife. This meant that settlement, hamlet, and village councils, and regional governments, would be given a much bigger hand in local affairs. The legislature would be greatly strengthened with elected representatives becoming proper cabinet ministers.

Above all, there would be more money. The GNWT was finally to have its own budget. At last, serious financial planning could be done – if only the elected representatives would take over the role promised them by Buchanan. Settlement councils would get a chance to learn how to run everything from schools to garbage collection and the hiring of dogcatchers.

While Berger's hearings moved up and down the Mackenzie, petroleum giants met furtively in Texas airport hotels, native and Métis leaders intrigued for political control of native organizations, and Hodgson fumed over civil service rivalries, the mandarins were working out a new master plan for the long-range future. At a meeting in Edmonton, Kroeger and Cotterill agreed to launch still another constitutional inquiry – Carrothers had called for one to take place ten years after his commission. This time, the veteran Liberal cabinet minister Charles (Bud) Drury would be asked to do the job. His inquiry had none of the flash of the Berger Inquiry, but it was to cause a good deal of controversy in political circles because many of its recommendations were unacceptable to Prime Minister Trudeau and DIAND Minister John Munro.

∼

Seven years after he moved to private enterprise in Vancouver, Gary Mullins reflected on the key elements of the period of 1975–79 when he was an important player. He emphasized several major factors:

1. Stuart Hodgson's remarkable personality and his ability to make strong, personal contact with the people in every part of the NWT. Hodgson also possessed enormous drive to accomplish the things he believed in.
2. Gordon Robertson's role as clerk of the Privy Council, where he had a strong influence on Pierre Trudeau and therefore on NWT policy.
3. Pierre Trudeau did not believe in "racial government" – he wanted a GNWT for all northerners and stood firm against the demands of the Brotherhood/Dene Nation, and even the more polite pressure from the Inuit Tapirisat.
4. The territorial council recognized that if its powers were to be expanded, it would have to accept the power of the native organizations. This made it an attractive proposition for the native leaders to participate in the GNWT. (David Searle, the legislature' first Speaker, says that he and the other white members of the 1975–79 council deliberately gerrymandered the electoral boundaries to guarantee majorities for natives. Searle says this did more than anything else to persuade Erasmus to lift his boycott.)
5. The character and ability of John Parker as deputy commissioner and commissioner. "He realized the commissioner's role had to change and he became the adviser and confidante of the elected members," Mullins said. "His watchwords were accommodation, compromise, consensus."
6. "In my own case, I recognized that there must be responsible government as soon as possible. I recommended when I left that there was no need for an assistant commissioner any more."
7. The Drury Inquiry.

The Drury Inquiry

Four months after the Berger Report was delivered to Warren Allmand in April 1977, Prime Minister Trudeau announced a new federal policy for the North and named Charles (Bud) Drury to a one-man commission to study constitutional development. Drury's report was completed in January 1980, and while he was low-keyed during his investigation and restrained in his language, it was clearly intended as an answer to Mr. Justice Berger. It was by no means a reflection of Trudeau's political views, and a number of its recommendations were not implemented by John Munro, who became DIAND minister in 1980 following the brief interregnum of Joe Clark's Tory government.

Drury was without question one of Canada's most distinguished public servants: a hero of the Second World War who had won the rank of brigadier; a United Nations relief official in postwar Poland; a deputy minister of defence in the 1950s; and the holder of several portfolios in the 1960s and 1970s. He also had a successful business career in Montreal.

In the introduction to his report, Drury said: "The government should be representative of and accountable to the people of the NWT." Whereas Fred Carrothers traced the development of law and responsible government from the ancient Statutes of Justinian and stressed the primacy of the British North America Act for the NWT, Drury placed his emphasis on local or community levels of government. He studied home rule in Greenland, Alaska, the Yukon, Australia, New Zealand, and Switzerland. And he paid considerable attention to the aspirations of the Dene.

Drury said: "The conditions for better government in the NWT are within the inherent constraints faced by the Territories: namely, the size of its land mass, its fiscal dependency, its strategic location and its economic and environmental circumstances." Drury noted that the federal government in 1975 and 1977 had said that functions of government were not negotiable as part of land claims, "nor would public government based on ethnicity be acceptable to the federal government, parliament, or to the Canadian people in general." He added: "Residents should enjoy to the greatest extent possible political rights and privileges equal to those enjoyed by other Canadians."

The report had none of the eloquent razzmatazz of Berger's or the historical perspective of Carrothers's. It was a dry, businesslike document that stated, as its author saw them, the unpalatable realities of the northern future. There was no touch of the flaming rhetoric of the Dene Declaration, or of the liberal-social-democrat didacticism of the Berger Report. Above all else, Drury appeared to take the position of a reasonable and practical man choosing the only possible course when all impossible dreams – on either side – are eliminated. Here is a sample of his prose:

> The objective of the settlements with the indigenous peoples should be to compensate native collectivities for the loss of their traditional ways of life, land and land use, and to provide them with the economic and cultural strength necessary to participate in territorial and Canadian public life, to maintain the traditional ways of life, or to select a mix of both alternatives.

When this flat analysis is translated into English, it appears to be a warning to the Inuit and Indians that they will have to compromise their dreams of independent homelands. At another point he said:

> The goal of native claims should be the protection and promotion of native economic and cultural interests. With regard to native political concerns, the objectives and terms of the agreements with the native peoples, while negotiated collectively, should not be incompatible with the individual interests of both native and non-native peoples in the evolution of public government.

In other words, everybody must learn to live together! Drury's analysis of the state of evolution/devolution was devastating:

> Most residents consider the current state of government unsatisfactory. For some residents ... NWT government has expanded too quickly and in the wrong direction. The critical, decision-making authority is vested in appointed officials in Yellowknife, such as the Commissioner and Deputy-Commissioner, and in the remote offices of the DIAND Minister in Ottawa.

Lest anyone think his convoluted statements were just personal opinions, Drury backed them up with a vast body of evidence. For instance, he compared the financial position of the NWT with that of the provinces and showed that the per capita expenditures of the

GNWT were almost three times as high as the national average, $5,933 against $2,054. In 1978–79 the total revenue of the hamlet of Baker Lake was $621,105. Of this, the GNWT (actually, southern taxpayers in the long run) supplied $510,067, and only $73,130 came from local revenues. In the same period, total government expenditure per capita in Newfoundland was $2,161, compared to $5,933 in the NWT and $4,742 in the Yukon.

In 1979–80, GNWT expenditures were $236.7 million, with Ottawa paying 81 percent. Revenues from taxes and fees in the NWT were $36.4 million, or 13 percent. (Drury noted that GNWT taxes and fees were comparable with those in the Atlantic provinces.) The increase in NWT government costs was staggering as the social revolution got into full steam. In 1968–69, a year after the commissioner moved to Yellowknife, total GNWT expenditure was $19.4 million. It was $115.4 million in 1973–74 and $269.8 million in 1978–79.

There was a dramatic increase in local government costs during the same period. In 1964 there were only three incorporated communities – Yellowknife, Hay River, and Smith. The remaining fifty communities either had advisory councils or lacked any kind of formal organization. By 1979 there were twenty-five incorporated municipalities, ranging from hamlets to a single city, Yellowknife, plus twenty-six settlement councils, band councils, and regional councils.

Drury found that "alien institutions based on a southern provincial model" were being imposed on the natives too rapidly. His solution was practical: "Give authority to the people through the native claims process and/or through division of the NWT." Noting the widespread anger against community government, he reminded the prime minister that in the south, municipal political processes and institutions evolved slowly, but in the North local government was centrally planned and had been largely implemented in only ten years.

Another serious weakness was the territorial council's lack of powers possessed by provincial legislatures – the ownership, management, and development of provincial Crown lands and control over non-renewable and most renewable resources. "The Council can neither appoint nor remove the Commissioner," he said tersely. And he echoed Hodgson's frustration when he said that "the existing community government legislation and procedures are unnecessarily complex; they are elaborate, cumbersome and time-consuming, and often seem to be designed to meet the requirements of the senior government rather than to facilitate local activities or accommodate traditional practices."

As one studies the report, it becomes clear that its author was developing a coherent theory of government. Like Carrothers, he went back to first principles and enunciated three: (1) the government must be made accountable to the people; (2) institutions should reflect the values and concerns of all northerners, native and white; (3) any changes should reflect the acceptance of a majority of northerners, native and non-native, and there must be constant consultation and negotiation.

Drury listed five requirements: (i) elections giving the people the right to choose and remove those who govern them; (i) clear lines of authority to establish responsibility; (iii) separation of legislature, executive, and judiciary, making sure one did not dominate the other two; (iv) easy access to information about government policies and actions; (v) government responsiveness to the needs and desires of the people.

"At the moment the key institutions are the non-elected executive and administration, in neither of which is there much representation from the native peoples," Drury said bluntly, noting that public finances, land, and resources were all controlled by the federal government. "In large measure the territorial institutions are seen to be irrelevant to those issues that really matter to Northerners."

Over and over, Drury hammered at the fact that a majority was native and therefore had special cultural, historical, and local rights that must be considered. This went far beyond the Carrothers Report and met Tom Berger on his own ground without agreeing with him. While Drury did not endorse ethnic government, he argued that the majority should have the traditional democratic right to govern itself. He followed this up by specifically recognizing that the aboriginal peoples formed the majority of the NWT population, and he accepted the idea that the NWT might be partitioned among its residents in such a way that each aboriginal group might have a majority within its own territory (or whatever regional designation might be decided upon). This was an astounding proposal to come from an impeccable member of the federal Liberal establishment.

Drury felt decision-making should be transferred to the local level and called for strong, autonomous government with plenty of citizen participation.

He thought that education should be shared, with local government given paramountcy on the elementary level and the GNWT in control of secondary and post-secondary education. Here Drury moved into one of the most controversial areas. From the start of the Arctic revolution, Indian and Inuit leaders have complained that the public school curriculum was based on those of Saskatchewan and Alberta, not on native traditions, culture, and environmental conditions. NWT educators replied that southern standards must be taught early so that students going on to secondary and post-secondary studies could qualify. The ongoing question has been whether primary school children brought up in native-oriented programs could adjust to higher educational institutions in Yellowknife or Edmonton. Drury did not go into the issue in detail, leaving the difficult intricacies to be worked out by NWT education ministers of the future.

Drury proposed that family allowances, unemployment insurance benefits, and old age pensions should be left with Ottawa; social assistance, child welfare, and correctional services would be paid for by the GNWT, but administration would be decentralized. Local councils would control services for the aged and handicapped, day care, drug and alcohol programs, community social service projects, employment projects, and adult education.

In an effort to overcome native suspicions of community councils, Drury suggested that sixteen Mackenzie Valley communities should have a local option as to whether band councils would be incorporated with community councils. "Both the federal and territorial governments should acknowledge the community council as the prime body of the community," he wrote, adding that the feds and the territorials should be prevented from dealing directly with one another, thus bypassing community councils.

Methodically, step by step, Drury showed that he had been listening to the most serious complaints against both the DIAND mandarins and the GNWT bureaucrats. "The authority and responsibility hitherto concentrated in the hands of the Commissioner should increasingly be exercised by the elected representatives of the people," he said. "This must happen as soon as the people are willing and able to accept concentrated responsibilities."

He dealt with the almost insoluble problem of recruiting government staff by saying:

Federal public servants should preferably have a long-term commitment to residing in the NWT. More should be hired locally and have more northern training. Where no Northerners are available with adequate qualifications, first consideration should be given to upgrading Northerners already on staff before trying to recruit new people in the South.

This was exactly what Hodgson's confidential task force report had said in 1974. The Drury Report only brought out into the open the long-smouldering rage of everybody, from Dene band leaders to Hodgson to the white residents of Yellowknife. The result of all this pressure began to be seen in 1985–86 when GNWT Government Leader Nick Sibbeston launched a program of affirmative action that saw the retirement of several long-service white officials and their replacement by natives upgraded arbitrarily to take over their jobs.

 ～

By the time Drury had finished his report, Joe Clark's Conservatives were in office, and he submitted it to the new DIAND minister, Jake Epp. But before Epp could do anything about it, Trudeau's Liberals were back, and John Munro was the minister. The prime minister was preoccupied with the Canadian constitution, and northern issues were not high on the Ottawa agenda. In October 1980, Munro addressed a conference of native chiefs in Saskatoon and promised native input into the new Canadian constitution and across-Canada forums at which native rights would be discussed.

A few days later, *News of the North*, the Yellowknife newspaper, revealed a sharp exchange of letters between Munro and Drury the previous April, shortly after the Liberals returned to power. The newspaper did not reveal what Munro (or perhaps Trudeau) had said to Drury, but Drury's letter was in itself a scathing criticism of how Ottawa worked. He restated his three main recommendations: that the NWT peoples rather than the federal government should resolve their own political differences; that the issue of public government in the NWT should not be negotiated by the feds within the private context of the native claims; and that federal ministerial and departmental responsibilities should be restructured to further government-to-government relationship with the NWT.

Drury said these points were fundamental to his report but were absent from Munro's draft memorandum to cabinet on native participation in constitutional negotiations. However, he said, Munro formally subscribed to his (Drury's) fifth recommendation that "the direction and process of political change in the NWT should be determined principally by residents of the NWT." He continued:

> In order to overcome the present state of political, financial and psychological dependency of the NWT, the Federal Government must encourage all Northerners to work out their political differences by themselves within Northern forums ... While formally acknowledging this principle, the Munro memorandum reflects the spirit of an entirely opposing premise: namely, the desirability of continuing a colonial-type, interventionist control by the Federal Government over the NWT.

Then Drury got down to the root of the concern that had been troubling the young Indian leaders and their radical white advisers since the start of the pipeline agitation at the end of the 1960s:

> For your department to continue to negotiate issues of public government with private corporations, and in the context of native claims, is to deny the existence of popularly elected representative government in the NWT, and to make impossible the task of developing more trustworthy, responsible and accountable public government.

Drury told Munro that constitutional matters should be transferred from the DIAND minister to a new "Minister for Native Peoples" responsible for intergovernmental relations with the provinces and acting as an advocate of the native peoples. Drury said Munro's memo to cabinet opposed this idea as producing "lack of focus." This was sensational stuff, particularly since it came from a loyal Liberal who had sat in cabinet with Munro only a few years earlier.

Drury carried his battle to the man who had appointed him – Pierre Trudeau. In a letter to the prime minister, he said he believed the most helpful role for the federal government during "this transitional phase of political evolution" would be as "a facilitator and adviser rather than as a mediator or interventionist in Territorial political affairs." In his letter to Trudeau, Drury brusquely set out several priorities for action by the DIAND minister:

1. Modification and redefinition of the role of the commissioner
    Drury felt the commissioner's executive function should be transferred to the Legislative Council, but the commissioner should have even stronger power as agent of the federal government and principal overseer of constitutional development. Other functions

of the commissioner would be federal adviser to the executive council and the community governments as well as principal northern adviser to the federal government.

2. Redefinition of the federal government's relationship to the NWT, the objective being to move the GNWT to a governmental relationship with the feds, and recognition of the territorial council as the legislative body from which the feds would expect territorial recommendations for constitutional change.

3. Progress on the government-to-government relationship in order to set up new relationships: finances through the federal Finance Department and the Treasury Board; separation of the NWT Act from DIAND; eventual establishment of a federal ministry for native peoples; separation of the responsibilities of northern development from those of the ministry for native peoples.

4. Definition of the basis, purpose, content, and process of the feds' plans for native claims settlement and communication of these definitions to the peoples of the NWT.

The Berger Commission caused a flurry of political excitement across Canada, but the Drury Report and Drury's differences with the Liberal cabinet and DIAND mandarins passed almost unnoticed, perhaps because the constitutional debate absorbed national attention and was followed by fruitless and frustrating conferences between native leaders and the federal and provincial governments. In the years following the issuing of the Drury Report, John Munro became known not as a man who might have used its recommendations to negotiate a satisfactory settlement of native land claims but merely as the minister who persuaded the Dene to let a little-inch pipeline be built.

As for Bud Drury, his contribution to constitutional reform may be greater than at first appeared. The impact of his report was not immediately apparent, but some of its recommendations seemed to seep into the constantly evolving GNWT. The report itself was not easy to absorb, but it was full of meat and somehow reflected the man who wrote it – elegant, precise, and uncompromising. After Drury disappeared from the scene, the revolution moved right along into a new phase – land claim negotiation. Meanwhile, evolution/devolution moved deeper into the communities.

Chapter 11

Native Claims

As stated earlier, the Canadian government's traditional policy in negotiating treaties with the Indians was to wait until the land in question was needed for settlement or mining development.

Unlike France, Spain, and Portugal – and the United States – Canada accepted the principle that the indigenous population "owned" the land it lived on. The Indians were paid for their land – a very small amount, it is true, but payment nonetheless. It took the form of a small cash settlement to the chiefs and to each member of the tribe, the promise of annual payment of another small amount ("treaty money"), and a guarantee that the Indians would have, in perpetuity, certain lands known as "reserves" ("reservations" in the United States).

Scholars such as John L. Tobias say that Indian policy in British North America fell into three phases: protection from white encroachment up to 1815; "civilization" from 1815 to 1857; assimilation from that time to the present. Part of the "civilizing" process involved the white treaty makers trying to persuade the indigenes to become farmers or ranchers on their reserves. With this in mind, the natives were sometimes given farm implements and seed grains.

Treaties 8 and 11, the only ones involving NWT Indians, followed these negotiating patterns but differed in the fact that no reserves were set up (until one, requested by the Hay River Slavey band, was established by diand in 1974).

Canadian treaty negotiations over the generations had one thing in common: the payments given, such as they were, extinguished all the land claims of the aboriginals except for the very limited privileges they were to enjoy within the boundaries of the reserves. The sovereignty and paramountcy of the Crown, and later the Canadian government, were recognized by the Indians signing the treaties. This meant that the treaty Indians were expected to obey the (white) law of the land and the system of government represented by the

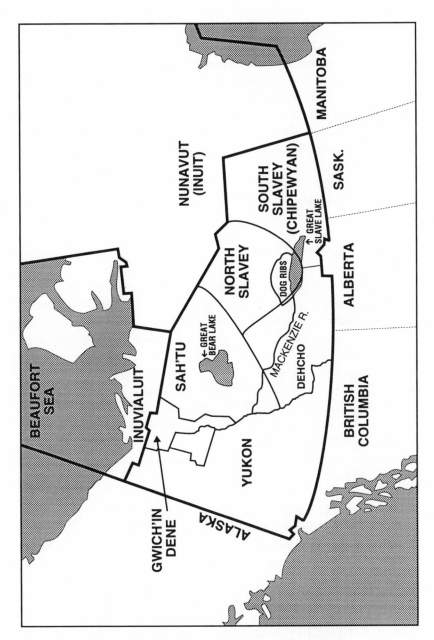

Map 6   Indian (Dene) Native Land Claims in the Northwest Territories, Negotiated or in Negotiation in 1994

Note: Gwich'in Dene and Inuvialuit share the area of the Mackenzie Delta in the Inuvik and Aklavik region.

Crown. In return, the Indians were given minor civil rights (most of them based on white models) and the protection of their treaty rights as registered Indians living on a reserve.

Recent efforts to negotiate comprehensive land claims settlements with the Inuit, Indians, and Métis of the NWT and Yukon followed the traditional pattern remarkably closely.

The 1960s saw extensive oil exploration in both the Canadian North and Alaska, and at the same time several native political groups were organized in both countries. These organizations have had major roles in negotiations with the U.S. and Canadian governments. Petroleum exploration triggered a number of criss-crossing developments:

- In Canada in 1968 the Liberal government set up a task force on northern oil development.
- The major oil companies proposed an oil pipeline across Alaska.
- Environmental groups and a fishermen's union obtained an injunction to halt the Alaska pipeline.
- The U.S. government negotiated a land settlement with Alaska's natives.
- The pipeline was built.
- In December 1969 Prime Minister Trudeau appointed Dr. Lloyd Barber Indian commissioner. His mandate covered all land claims in Canada, and it was obvious he soon would be dealing with northern claims.
- In April 1971 the Indian Brotherhood hired Toronto lawyer Gerald Sutton to do treaty research.

These events hardly amounted to more than hanging up coats before going into the meeting hall. In June 1972 DIAND announced it would offer NWT Indians reserves or cash in exchange for extinguishment of land claims and other aboriginal rights. In view of the 1971 Alaska native settlement, the Indians and Métis dismissed the offer with contempt. A year later, DIAND repeated its offer, only to be met by a legal finding by NWT Justice William Morrow that the Indians had a right to claim 700,000 square kilometres of land. The Brotherhood promptly hired eight researchers to gather evidence on how the Indians had used this land in the past.

This was all preliminary. In July 1974 DIAND opened an office for native claims in Ottawa. In August Judd Buchanan succeeded

Jean Chrétien as minister. In October Dr. Lloyd Barber spoke on aboriginal rights in Yellowknife. By this time, the Mackenzie pipeline
proposal was far advanced, and Tom Berger had been named to inves-
tigate it. As in Alaska, the stakes were enormous for everybody, and
the Inuit, Inuvialuit, Dene, and Métis leaders were not about to sell
off their ancestral lands for beads and firewater.

Both the Inuit and the Dene decided on a new approach modelled
on the tactics of aboriginal movements throwing off colonial shack-
les in Africa. They announced that they were not prepared to accept
the idea that their aboriginal rights could be extinguished through
negotiations. While willing to talk about land claims, they demanded
political negotiations first, which would establish native rights to
political self-determination.

This position was expressed in the Dene Declaration of 1975.
There was no parallel Inuit or Inuvialuit declaration, but the Inuit
made it clear that they were asking much the same things in the eastern and central Arctic. Neither the Métis Association nor COPE went
nearly as far as the Dene and Inuit.

These differences of aboriginal strategy were to create endless
confusion and would delay negotiations severely. In brief, the Indian
Brotherhood/Dene Nation wanted political, cultural, social, and economic control over most of the Mackenzie Valley. Some were calling
this area Denendeh – the people's land – and it would be virtually
independent of Ottawa.

There were two close-at-hand models for a settlement, both of
them flawed: the Alaska Native Claims Act of 1971 and the James
Bay agreement between the province of Quebec and the Woodland
Cree and Inuit, signed in November 1975.

When the Alaska accord was signed, it was praised by almost
everyone for its generosity and vision. Some 70,000 Indians, Inuits,
and Aleuts got nearly $1 billion in cash and 40 million acres of land,
11 percent of the state.

The central difference from earlier treaties was that twelve regional corporations were set up to invest the cash settlement. They were
required by law to operate as profit-seeking businesses, which meant
that settlement funds could not be earmarked for social improvements. Critics warned that the corporations, if badly run, might go
bankrupt, leaving the natives with nothing. There was also a fear that
natives might sell off their lands to white hustlers when the original
agreement ran out in 1991.

The James Bay agreement involved 6,000 Cree and 4,000 Inuit. They had to deal with the provincial rather than the federal government, and at first Quebec denied that it even needed to negotiate an agreement. The provincial government had launched the $15 billion hydroelectric project without consulting the natives, and when construction crews began to damage the environment, the natives responded angrily.

Public opinion was so strongly against the Quebec government that it reluctantly began negotiations. Ottawa, realizing that the federal government had some responsibilities to the native population living in Quebec, promised to look after several social problems. The Cree and the Quebec Inuit were at a different stage of development from the NWT indigenes. They found that they had to put their fate in the hands of white lawyers and negotiators and to accept their advice on the best deal possible from premiers Robert Bourassa and René Lévesque.

In the end, the settlement was $225 million over ten years. The Cree got ownership of 5,000 square kilometres, and the Inuit 8,300 square kilometres. Neither obtained subsurface rights. The Inuit won exclusive hunting and fishing rights over 90,000 square kilometres and the Cree similar rights over 65,000 square kilometres. Both the Quebec and federal governments were criticized for not living up to the agreement and for niggardliness. The project did a great deal of damage to the environment and promised to do more in its second and third phases, to be completed in the 1990s.

Neither the Alaska nor the James Bay settlement encouraged the hopes of the NWT indigenes.

Although the Berger Inquiry gave the Dene a platform and a national stage, the Dene Declaration was angrily rejected by DIAND Minister Judd Buchanan, who warned that if negotiations dragged on he would not hold back the pipeline. In reply, the Indians, Métis, and Inuvialuit said jointly that there would be no pipeline until there was a settlement. When Buchanan finally met the joint negotiating team of the Dene and Métis, talks broke down on the first day. That was in April 1975. In July the Métis and Indians refused to negotiate through the Office of Native Claims.

But differences were growing between the two native organizations. The Brotherhood was in a state of revolution. The white population, scared out of its wits by the tone of the Dene Declaration, kept muttering angry threats that were often openly racist.

The battle swayed back and forth as the Berger hearings moved up and down the Mackenzie. For a while, there were hopes of an early settlement when Warren Allmand succeeded Buchanan and cast a more sympathetic eye on Indian aspirations. But Ottawa clung fast to its insistence that land claims had to be settled before there could be any discussion of self-government. The Brotherhood kept demanding a political settlement first. The Métis wavered between political support for the Brotherhood and a belief that the pipeline was economically essential.

By late 1976, the Métis were receiving separate funding for their own land claim. (In 1980, they passed a Declaration of Rights that was much milder than the Dene Declaration: "We, the Métis people of the NWT, do declare that we exist as a national entity. While it is true that our nationalism does not take the form of a nation state, it is sufficient to define us as a distinctive people.")

In November 1977 the Liberals named Keith Penner the prime minister's personal representative on land claims. He pointedly bypassed the Brotherhood and told the chiefs that if the Brotherhood was too difficult, Ottawa would negotiate directly with them.

In 1975 the Supreme Court of Canada threw out the chiefs' caveat asking for the right to negotiate a land settlement. But the caveat, allowed in 1973 by Mr. Justice Morrow of the NWT Supreme Court, had served its purpose: the feds had already started negotiating seriously. It was during this period that Erasmus fired all of the Brotherhood's controversial white advisers to prove once and for all that the Dene were fully able to go it alone.

Inuit and Inuvialuit

The Inuit were also unable to present a united front favouring the establishment of what they called Nunavut – which meant, like Denendeh, the people's land. COPE, representing 2,500 Inuvialuit living in the six Beaufort Sea/Mackenzie Delta settlements of Sachs Harbour, Holman Island, Paulatuk, Tuktoyaktuk, Inuvik, and Aklavik, decided to break away from joint negotiations with the Inuit Tapirisat of Canada (ITC) and seek a settlement of its own.

They had historical, cultural, and geographical reasons. Creating any Arctic government is hard because of distances between communities, the sparseness of population, and the harshness of the environment. When Tagak Curley of Coral Harbour became the first ITC president, he was aware of the differences dividing the 17,000 Inuit in thirty communities. South Baffin had two dynamic communities, Lake Harbour and Cape Dorset, as well as important settlements like Pangnirtung and Broughton Island on the opposite coast. (Iqaluit is the regional capital, but it was founded as a white military base, Frobisher Bay, and still has a large white component.)

North Baffin has the Netsilik Inuit settlements of Arctic Bay and Pond Inlet. Foxe Basin, north of Hudson Bay, has four communities – Igloolik, Hall Beach, Repulse, and Coral Harbour. There are five settlements in the Keewatin: Baker Lake, Chesterfield Inlet, Rankin Inlet, Whale Cove, and Eskimo Point. The central Arctic, or Kitikmeot Region, has six: Cambridge Bay, Coppermine, Spence Bay, Gjoa Haven, Pelly Bay, and Bay Chimo/Bathurst Inlet. In the High Arctic, there are two settlements – Resolute and Grise Fjord, deliberately created by Ottawa as "sovereignty posts" settled with Inuit from other places.

Each of these regions has its own dialect and jealously guarded culture. Some communities, like Cambridge Bay, Baker Lake, and Coral Harbour, have been gathering places for the Inuit for centuries. Others grew up around a whaling station, an HBC post, a mission, a defence installation, or an airport. Rankin Inlet started as the site of a nickel mine. Nanisivik, near Arctic Bay in North Baffin, is also a mining community.

Tagak Curley, his successor John Amagoalik, and their colleagues worked hard to find an Inuit proposal that would fit the needs of everyone. In February 1976 the first plan for Nunavut Territory was released. It would comprise two million square kilometres, and the Inuit would be guaranteed political control through a ten-year residency requirement for voters (the same requirement was proposed by the Indian Brotherhood for Denendeh).

The Inuit asked for hunting and fishing rights in 650,000 square kilometres but no subsurface rights. Government costs would be met through a 3 percent royalty on minerals and oil, and there would be an Inuit development corporation to collect royalties and build and run communities. The rest of Nunavut would be Crown land.

A year later, the ITC withdrew this proposal on the grounds that the white advisers who had drawn it up had not asked for enough. (This was almost exactly the opposite to the problem the Indian Brotherhood had with its white advisers.) The new ITC claim demanded more political rights and subsurface mineral rights. The

ITC also demanded that the BNA Act be amended to guarantee the right of the Inuit "to exist as an independent culture within Canada." Such political proposals were unacceptable to Ottawa, as similar ones by the Dene Nation had been in the west. Negotiations broke down in 1983.

As the entire relationship between the Inuit and Ottawa increased in complexity, the ITC sensibly broke itself down to deal with specialized functions. The Nunasi Corporation was formed to look after capital investment in Inuit business and the fostering of native-owned or native-shared companies. Nunasi worked through the various Inuit regional corporations that were involved with the ITC.

The Tungavik Federation of Nunavut (TFN) was set up to negotiate a land settlement, and it took over the direct involvement of ITC, developing its own band of tough, sophisticated negotiators and giving the well-known (and politically vulnerable) leaders of the ITC a chance to fade into the background as far as the ongoing dickering was concerned.

There was a third arm to the Inuit negotiating structure. The Nunavut Constitutional Forum (NCF) was established to work out division of the Territories and the form of government Nunavut would have. Because the federal government insisted on a land claims settlement first, TFN went into the spotlight, while NCF got almost no publicity.

Although the Inuit proved remarkably tenacious, their internal problems were even more difficult than those of the Dene and the Métis. First, the Inuvialuit, led by COPE, broke away from the Nunavut negotiations and started making their own deal with Ottawa. Second, the Copper Eskimos of the central Arctic showed skittishness at the prospect of forming a new territory with the Baffin Islanders, who had been their cultural rivals for centuries. Third, the Dene and Inuit found it difficult to draw a boundary between east and west along the tree line bisecting the NWT from southeast to northwest.

When negotiations between the feds and the TFN broke down in 1983, Thomas Suluk said bitterly: "We're fed up with the government and we're fed up with talking. If it means packing up and leaving, it won't be the end of the world. After spending $6 million over the last three years and knowing it could better be used for economic development or in the communities, I'm getting impatient." Suluk was one of the toughest of the young Inuit leaders. He later became a member of Parliament.

In spite of such frustrations, the TFN persisted, well aware of its strong position as the majority racial group in the Arctic. There was no conflict over who occupied the land in question or who would politically control any new region or territory, as there was in the case of the Dene/Métis and white settlers in the Mackenzie.

One DIAND minister followed another until, in the spring of 1990, Tom Siddon was able to announce an agreement in principle that provided the Inuit with $580 million and title to 350,000 square kilometres. The historic agreement was signed 25 May 1993 by Prime Minister Brian Mulroney, went through Parliament quickly, and was proclaimed as law 9 June 1993. Within six months of proclamation, the GNWT and the Inuit were committed to working out the details of a separate Nunavut territory.

It was generally felt that the six-year process of creating two new territories – for the continuing territory which includes the Dene, Métis, Inuvialuit, and non-natives will have to be drastically changed – will be a shock to the entire nation.

Even if the Inuit have a system of government based on traditional white democratic patterns, the fact that they completely dominate Nunavut numerically and can operate in Inuktitut instead of English as they choose means that Nunavut will be a de facto native political unit. That being the case, will the federal and provincial governments be able to stop (if they want to) natives in Alberta or Labrador, or Dene in Fort Good Hope, from governing themselves? Thus the native clauses of the Charlottetown agreement may come to pass through the back door rather than the front.

The COPE Settlement

The Inuvialuit defection from the popular front of the Inuit-Métis-Dene had a significant effect on later negotiations. There were only 2,500 Inuvialuit, compared to 17,000 eastern and central Inuit, and their situation was considerably different from that of their cousins (as explained earlier).

COPE was specifically designed to represent all of the peoples of the Delta, and this point was made in the fact that the co-founders, Agnes Semmler and Nellie Cournoyea, had Indian, Inuvialuit, and white forebears. In its early stages, COPE leaders attended and supported meetings of the Indian Brotherhood. They finally stopped when Indian leaders made it clear that they intended to follow their own racial destiny. On the other hand, the Inuvialuit had few physical or cultural connections with the Inuit to the east: they felt little common cause with the negotiators from far-off Coral Harbour and Baker Lake.

As early as 1977, COPE presented an independent claim to Ottawa, stating four goals: preservation of cultural identity and values; a voice in the social and political changes going on; compensation for extinguishment of land rights; and protection of wildlife and the environment.

From the start, COPE accepted the principle of extinguishment of aboriginal rights, and an agreement in principle was reached in October 1978. The Inuvialuit suggested that their Beaufort/Delta domain might become a regional borough similar to the North Slope municipal borough in Alaska. It would have certain political rights but not on the provincial or national scale. Ottawa did not turn down this proposal but asked that it be postponed until after the land claims were settled. This was agreed to by COPE.

The Western Arctic (Inuvialuit) Claim Settlement Act was proclaimed 25 July 1984 and gave the Inuvialuit 90,000 square kilometres, about half what they had asked for originally. Each of the six communities would be surrounded by 1,800 square kilometres of land on which the residents would have surface and subsurface rights – a total of 11,000 square kilometres. The Inuvialuit land outside the communities (78,000 square kilometres) would involve surface rights but no oil and gas rights. Ownership of land would be vested in the Inuvialuit Land Corporation. Land could be leased but not sold to anyone except other Inuvialuit or the Crown. For the extinguishment of aboriginal claims, the Inuvialuit were given $45 million (1977 dollars) to be paid over a twenty-year period.

In addition, the government set up a social development fund of $7.5 million "to help the Inuvialuit solve the problems which accompany social transition." The money, available to each of the six communities, would be administered by trustees named by the Inuvialuit Regional Corporation. The social development program would "attempt to solve acknowledged social problems such as housing, health, welfare, mental health, education, elders' concerns and maintenance of traditional practices." It would "advise the Government on programs related to alcohol, dental care and nutrition," and would "also initiate and develop special education programs."

The agreement concluded with grim finality: "Canada will provide the Inuvialuit with rights, privileges and benefits in return for extinguishment of all aboriginal claims, rights, title and interests to the Inuvialuit in the NWT and Yukon, and to the adjacent islands and waters."

Hard Hammering with the Dene

The Inuvialuit settlement hit the Dene/Métis hard, serving notice that Ottawa had no intention of giving up political control of the NWT. The mandarins used several heavy-calibre weapons. Without the pressure of a petroleum or mining boom, the government could afford to wait out the natives, who were dependent on Ottawa for operating funds and were under increasing pressure from their own people to make some kind of deal. Money for staff, for investigating land claims, and for publicity was advanced against an ultimate settlement. If Ottawa didn't like the way things were going, it could (and did) withhold payment. The Brotherhood/Dene had to cut staff and close offices, and for a time the Métis Association was forced out of business completely.

The Mackenzie problems were much more complex than those of either the eastern/central Arctic or the Delta/Beaufort. It was not surprising that the Dene/Métis negotiations dragged on. Both the chiefs and the Dene/Brotherhood negotiators knew that once they had accepted a cash and land settlement in return for aboriginal rights, they were finished as a strong political force. DIAND reminded them that the Dene and Métis together only made up 40 to 45 percent of the Mackenzie population: the white majority was a ghostly spectre at the negotiations.

In September 1988 an agreement in principle was signed in Rae by the Dene/Métis and in Ottawa by Bill McKnight and Prime Minister Mulroney. Signing for the GNWT were Dennis Patterson and Stephen Kakfwi, the former Dene Nation president who had gone on to become GNWT minister for constitutional affairs. Financial compensation was $453.3 million in 1988 dollars.

Unlike COPE's settlement, the agreement did not mention extinguishment of aboriginal rights and specifically said that the lands allocated would not be designated as reserves under the Indian Act. No mention was made of a constitutional agreement to settle the political future of Denendeh, nor was division brought up.

For nineteen months the agreement in principle hung fire, until a new DIAND minister, Tom Siddon, got a "final agreement" as of 1 May 1990. The 15,000 Dene/Métis got ownership of 180,000 square kilometres (or 18 percent of their settlement area) and 10,000 square kilometres which included subsurface ownership. The federal government guaranteed that the Dene/Métis would never have less than 180,000 square kilometres.

Payment would be $500 million (1990 dollars), tax-free, to be paid over fifteen years. Several million dollars was paid as a binder. Resource royalties would be shared annually, 50 percent on the first $2 million and 10 percent of the remainder. In addition, there were the usual guarantees of game rights and a commitment that the government would "consult the Dene/Métis before opening land in the settlement area for oil and gas exploration." The agreement called for extinguishment of aboriginal rights.

Unlike the TFN settlement announced at the same time, this one contained no reference to division or to future negotiations to establish self-government. Tom Siddon said only that the deal "confirms the special status of the Dene and Métis peoples as aboriginal peoples." Significantly, he said it recognized "the rights of other northern Canadians to participating in shaping the land north of 60, the land they, too, call home." The minister said firmly: "Settlement of this claim will allow all Northerners to work together in partnership to plan and build a strong and vibrant North."

With at least eighteen months still needed for full ratification of the agreement and for working out constitutional and territorial structures, the way ahead was far from clear. The difficulty was dimly visible through the prolix verbiage of one paragraph in the DIAND announcement: "If ratified and signed, the Final Agreement will ensure legal certainty over land ownership, and confirm the application of laws and the rights of both aboriginal peoples to use the land." Once again, it appeared, a native group was being told that it could not have sovereignty over a piece of Canadian territory.

The Dene/Métis negotiators initialled the settlement – subject to future revisions – with great misgivings. When they reported to a joint assembly of chiefs and band councillors in Detah, the deal was rejected. Chief Billy Erasmus of the Dene Nation said he wanted to renegotiate a deal that would not extinguish aboriginal rights and would guarantee self-government. These were the points on which the federal government was adamant – and it had already opened the door to piecemeal negotiation by the regions. At Detah, the Métis

Association got cold feet and pulled out of the Dene/Métis front. The Gwich'in of the Delta followed them, and the leadership of the Dene Nation was left swinging in the breeze.

Federal Policies

While each agreement was tailored to the native group involved and the federal government literally gave a good deal of ground, Ottawa's position on sovereignty and the extinguishment of aboriginal rights has been remarkably consistent.

In 1981 many Dene and Métis felt that John Munro might be able to sign a deal acceptable to them. But when the Conservatives replaced the Liberals, there was considerable delay while Ottawa reassessed its policy. David Crombie became DIAND minister. As a charismatic mayor of Toronto and a progressive-minded "red Tory," Crombie was greeted hopefully by the NWT indigenes.

Nothing much happened during his regime, though it was announced that his department was drawing up plans for a much broader settlement of native claims across Canada than had ever been attempted before. Crombie was succeeded by Bill McKnight, a Saskatchewan farmer, who in 1987 released DIAND's *Comprehensive Land Claims Policy*. Its introduction said:

> There is no clear definition of the term "aboriginal title." For aboriginal peoples the term is bound up with a concept of self-identity and self-determination. For lawyers, it is one which has been referred to in case law for many years, but which has eluded judicial definition. Aboriginal groups have particularly objected to the practice of seeking to extinguish all aboriginal rights and interests in and to the settlement area in exchange for the benefits provided through the settlement agreement. The revised policy contains provisions for new approaches to the cession and surrender of title, self-government, wildlife and environmental management, the inclusion of offshore areas in negotiations, resource-revenue-sharing, and negotiating procedures.

Noting that native groups had strong reactions to the extinguishment of "all aboriginal rights," McKnight said the federal government had concluded that "alternatives to extinguishment may be considered provided that certainty in respect of lands and resources is established." He warned: "It is important to recognize that the aboriginal rights claims are only those related to the use of and title to land and resources. Other aboriginal rights, to the extent they are defined through the Constitution, are not affected by the policy."

McKnight went on to self-government, the chief bone of contention. He and his advisers said cautiously that "self-government has been referred to as the key to change for aboriginal peoples." They acknowledged "the desire expressed by communities to exercise greater control and authority over the management of their affairs." Referring specifically to community self-government, McKnight said it was DIAND's objective to increase local control and decision-making.

Going on to the the broader field of territorial government, the minister agreed there could be some increase in self-government, but "political rights would not be reserved exclusively to aboriginal people, but aboriginal interests would be incorporated and represented in institutions of public government." This would seem to say that natives would be guaranteed a share in territorial government but whites could not be denied participation. That would prevent the establishment of ethnic governments: no true Nunavuts or Denendehs would be permitted.

Here McKnight and the Conservatives were trying to cope with the thorniest of all NWT problems: the relative political powers of the white population, the Indians, and the Inuit. It was obvious that if division came, the eastern Inuit would be in a very strong position no matter what kind of territorial or quasi-provincial government was set up. In the Mackenzie, however, the political balance was delicate, and even with the support of the Métis, the Dene Nation could not quite equal the political strength of the white population.

No one, white or aboriginal, had faced the problem squarely. The Dene and Inuit proposal that white northerners must serve a ten-year residency apprenticeship before they could vote was not taken very seriously, but many whites agreed that a two- or three-year waiting period might be acceptable. No one was ready to discuss the Dene Nation suggestion that the white communities might be given extra-territorial rights, rather like the historical "free cities" of Europe. This would remove them completely from any major role in territorial policy. On the other hand, was it possible to conceive of a Mackenzie territory (or province) in which whites and aboriginals shared power? Such questions were put on the back burner while the territorial assembly learned how to deal with day-to-day political problems on an interracial level.

Significantly, McKnight said flatly at the end of his policy outline that actual negotiations of any self-government agreement would have to follow a settlement of land claims. This was a return to traditional Ottawa policy, and it was certain to weaken the position of the aboriginals.

From the viewpoint of an NWT resident, the significance of the Conservative policy was its reaffirmation that Ottawa had no intention of giving up its claim to subsurface resources. This was part of the settlements with ITC/TFN and the Dene/Métis, which DIAND completed 1 May 1990. Through three Tory ministers, DIAND had not budged an inch. The expansive dreams of industrial development that had inspired John Diefenbaker and Pierre Trudeau obviously were alive and well in the Mulroney administration.

The Gwich'in Agreement

The first Dene region to break away from the Dene Nation was in the Mackenzie Delta, next door to the Inuvialuit. This is one of the richest areas of the NWT, with an abundance of fish and muskrat, moose and caribou, along with whales in the Beaufort Sea. The ninety-mile-deep Delta comprises a swampy, muskegy tangle of land and streams, with several channels of the Mackenzie and its main tributary in the west, the Peel. The Gwich'in, who used to be called the Loucheux, share the Delta settlements of Aklavik and Inuvik with the Inuvialuit and have two towns of their own, Fort McPherson and Arctic Red River. Inuvik is the staging base for Beaufort Sea gas exploration, and the town boomed when the oil and gas men were spending money in the area.

The 2,200 Gwich'in completed their deal with the federal government 22 April 1992. It was proclaimed 22 December 1992. The Gwich'in won ownership of 22,420 square kilometres, including 6,160 square kilometres on which they have subsurface rights. They also got 1,550 square kilometres of federal land in the Yukon because their hunting, trapping, and fishing grounds have always extended into the Yukon. The Gwich'in originally migrated to Canada from what is now Alaska, and the well-known Yukon village of Old Crow is Gwich'in.

In addition to land, the Gwich'in were guaranteed $75 million

(1990 dollars) and a portion of royalties involving the whole of the Mackenzie Valley. The agreement also guaranteed negotiation of self-government at some time in the future, though it did not specify what kind of self-government.

Since Inuvik and Aklavik both have Inuvialuit as well as Gwich'in residents and the hinterlands of these towns are common hunting and fishing grounds, a board would be set up to settle rival claims and work out a system for sharing the land and the towns. There were, of course, many built-in guarantees as to wildlife and wildlife management.

As with other Canadian land claims settlements, the Gwich'in agreed to extinguishment of their aboriginal rights.

The Sah'tu Agreement

The Sah'tu tribal council initialed an agreement with Ottawa and the GNWT 4 March 1993. It provided $75 million (1990 dollars) payable over fifteen years. The 1,800 Sah'tu got 41,437 square kilometres for outright ownership, with 700 square kilometres involving subsurface rights and a further portion entailing special surface rights for such things as gravel and stone.

Like the Gwich'in, the Sah'tu will get a percentage of the royalties paid on non-renewable resources to the GNWT or the federal government. Both regions must pay back a portion of the moneys advanced to the Dene Nation against settlement and an additional amount advanced to the Sah'tu and the Gwich'in separately.

The Sah'tu (the word means "bear" and thus identifies the people around Great Bear Lake) are a mixture of North Slavey, Hareskin, and Mountain peoples. The Sah'tu boundaries overlap with their neighbours and relatives to the south and west, the Dehcho (or people of "the great river," the Mackenzie). A border commission will settle conflicting claims of Sah'tu and Dehcho trappers.

The Dehcho

The Dehcho are the South Slavey, and they live along the upper Mackenzie and to the west and south of it. Their communities are Fort Norman and Fort Simpson. Many northern Métis live among the Dehcho, especially around Simpson.

In the spring of 1993, the Dehcho made a preliminary proposal to

Ottawa that followed the lines of the Dene Nation in requesting that aboriginal rights not be extinguished after a land claims settlement. DIAND officials said there was no possibility that it would be accepted by the federal government.

The Dog Ribs

The Dog Ribs are the politically strongest Dene nation or tribe in the NWT, with a population of more than 4,000 scattered through several vigorous communities north of Great Slave Lake. They have produced many native leaders, including James Wah Shee and Georges Erasmus.

In mid-1993, the Dog Ribs were preparing a claim that was said to differ in several respects from those of the Gwich'in and Sah'tu, and also from the proposals of the Dehcho.

The Treaty 8 Tribal Council

The Chipewyans are the dominant tribal group south of Great Slave Lake and extending south to the Alberta and Saskatchewan borders. Around Fort Smith are numbers of Northern Cree, and there are South Slavey around Hay River.

These were the people who signed Treaty 8 in 1899, and they have decided to pursue their land claims through the treaty itself rather than through new land and money negotiations. This plan has been accepted by the federal government, but it was unclear in mid-1993 how the treaty negotiations would be conducted. For instance, questions were being raised as to whether land settlements would take the form of modern reserves under the Indian Act.

Chapter 12

Living Together Today

"I went to Baker Lake in 1966 as a school principal," said Bob MacQuarrie, former Speaker of the legislature. "That was the last year anybody lived in igloos: there were several just outside of town; next summer, housing was brought in."

"The Inuit moved from the Stone Age to the Space Age in seventeen years," said Gordon Wray, who got to Baker Lake in 1973, married an Inuk, and became the member of the legislature for the Keewatin and a cabinet minister.

"I don't have any romantic illusions about living in a tent in winter," said Ethel Blondin, who did live in one as a small child in the Mackenzie bush. She grew up and became the member of Parliament for Western Arctic.

∾

By the mid-1980s, the northern revolution was far from complete, but it had made an indelible mark on the peoples of the NWT. A provisional government was in place, which was changing subtly but steadily even before its members could decide on the kind of society they wanted.

Twenty years earlier, the whites had been sharply distinct from the Indians and the Indians from the Inuit. Now they were just starting to meld together, only a little yet, but searching for a new identity as true northerners.

Lots of things continued to be wrong, but the revolution was working after a fashion. It was not a total failure; there was no blood in the streets, nor the prospect of it. The new northerners were starting to work together in harmony; there was hope for the future.

Consider: A generation earlier – only one generation – the NWT (apart from some 25,000 or 30,000 semi-nomadic aboriginals) had consisted of a couple of white mining enterprises, a few military airfields, a handful of fur-trading posts with Christian missions attached.

The overwhelming majority of natives were born in tents or igloos. "Government" consisted of a godlike white man with powers of life and death over the aboriginal peoples: thank the good Lord that he came around so seldom!

In 1980 Bud Drury commented on the change. He noted that in 1964 there had been only three incorporated communities. By 1979 twenty-five communities had been incorporated and twenty-six had settlement councils.

The revolution went on. By the mid-1980s, most of the Arctic communities were incorporated hamlets; Yellowknife was a city, and there were real towns like Inuvik, Smith, Hay River, and Iqualuit.

What did all of this mean to the Inuit, Dene, and Métis?

Well, virtually all of them were living in or tied to towns – not only new communities, but planned communities. In the old days, on the prairies, say, the stages of growth were sometimes portrayed by artists like Paul Kane. He painted Fort Edmonton in 1858 – the white palisade and the red-roofed HBC buildings on a bluff high above the North Saskatchewan, the Cree camped in teepees far below on the shore of the river. This was tradition: if a Bay voyageur retired, his cabin would be outside the palisade, near a path leading to the river ford or beside a spring. His sons would build other log cabins nearby and so on and on and on, the villages spreading, sprawling, until they turned into cities like Edmonton.

ARCTIC SNAPSHOT 1

The group of Inuit apprentice film-makers are shooting a scene on the winter tundra outside Cambridge Bay. The oldest is playing the role of an Inuk hunter, wearing a traditional caribou parka. The camera turns and he walks away until he disappears into a *swale*. It looks marvellously Arctic to the kabloona supervisor. The young cameraman shakes his head.

"We gotta do it over," he says.

"Why?"

"James wasn't carrying a rifle."

"So?"

The Inuk shrugs. "If we show a hunter walking out in the tundra without a rifle, everybody in the Kitikmeot will laugh at us. Nanook's out there."

But these northern communities were different, rising suddenly on the tundra or in the bush. Engineers from far to the south came in and decided where to place the airport, where the fresh water was located, where a garbage dump could be bulldozed, how supplies should be brought in. Soon airfreighters or barges (or both) were unloading everything to build a community, all at once: prefab houses, a complete power plant, storage tanks for oil and gasoline and fuel oil, a prefab school and a prefab nursing station, prefab government and a prefab community centre. An impressive house for the administrator.

Maybe the planners thought of it as a preliminary run for building an outpost on the moon: the Arctic project, like a moon shot, was too expensive for many frills. In these new towns, there was no provision for family privacy, no building of a log cabin or a snow house where and when the spirit moved one. There was a community plan and the houses were all hooked together, one way or another, whether by utilidor (as in Inuvik) or by road links that brought in the essential water and sewage and garbage and fuel trucks (as in almost every other place).

Could little kids walk to school from home easily? Could Granny make it to the nursing station or the bingo hall? Such were the considerations as the new Camelots arose.

Southerners arriving early (like Farley Mowat in Baker Lake) were often misled by early chaos. There was a lot of clutter, confusion, inefficiency at first: the airstrip and the wharf came first, then everything was dumped in a vast pile. Prefab shacks were thrown up every which way for the construction workers. The supply dump contained fuel, plywood, bulldozers, dump trucks, tank trucks, food, clothing, furniture. Next came the power plant. Then the town.

Inuit, or Indians, or Métis, might work on the job, usually in the most menial capacities. They lived on the edge, in their tents and igloos. When the Americans put up the DEW Line stations in the 1950s, Inuit were paid $60 a month, usually in scrip. No need to spoil them!

When the white construction crews left, the natives moved into the abandoned shacks, ATCO trailers, storage sheds. They weren't much: the shacks were called "matchboxes" – not only because they looked like matchboxes but because they were packed with potential death by fire. But Bob MacQuarrie was right when he said that at least they were better than igloos in winter. Up to this point, of course, there was no "town": the place was still a transit camp.

～

Jumping forward to the mid-1980s, we focus again on the same community.

To the visitor's eye, it is well organized. Most houses seem well built for NWT conditions, though there are not enough of them for the increasing population. Considered as a mechanical entity, the town works well. The water is uncontaminated and delivered to all the houses regularly. The houses are warm enough for Arctic winter, though some of them show signs of shoddy workmanship. The school and nursing station and government facilities are impressive. The school auditorium is large and very suitable for community gatherings. There is an arena for hockey and other sports. There may well be a rec centre with video machines, pool tables, a rental library of videotapes.

There will be some kind of hotel. Air service is excellent. There may be cable television, bringing in, among other things, a private channel from Detroit. The Bay is a department store with a wide range of goods. People are well dressed. You see many skidoos or all-terrain vehicles ("three-wheelers" or "four-wheelers" in the northern parlance). Dogs are controlled. Garbage and sewage are picked up two or three times a week.

These are surface observations, to be sure. Live in such a community and you soon discover many scars, many running sores. There is always too much unemployment. Housing is always short. Too many people get drunk every weekend, and marijuana, hash, even cocaine, are easy to get. Wife-beating is widespread, and it goes with child abuse and neglect, incest, mistreatment of old people. Then there is vandalism and thievery among the young, truancy, dropping out of school, suicide and attempts at suicide.

Not a pretty picture.

But, say social planners like Will Drake of the GNWT, all these horrors exist in the south too, on about the same scale. He denies that wife-beating and incest are any more frequent among Inuit or Dene than they are among the urban poor of Toronto or Vancouver or in the rural slums of New Brunswick.

Alcoholism? A symptom of and an escape from other problems – especially poor and overcrowded housing, Drake says. Alcoholism may be a symptom of other major problems, or it may in itself be the major problem. But the whole social structure involves stress for everybody.

The evidence is everywhere. While there is not enough good housing for the indigenes, whites won't go into a community unless they have good accommodations – and that applies whether they are schoolteachers, nurses, police officers, civil servants, or construction workers. The federal Ministry of Supply and Services is kept busy building new compounds for the ever mounting numbers of people "helping the natives."

Meanwhile, a lot of Inuit and Dene can't afford to buy or build new houses, and there isn't enough rental housing, which means doubling up with in-laws: bachelor sons forced to share into middle age with Mom and Pop, Granny and Grandpa, the younger siblings.

This leads to health problems. Assistant Deputy Health Minister Mike Pontus told me in 1987 that the continuing curse of respiratory disease is caused by bad ventilation and smoking – as simple as that. Tuberculosis may have been licked, but people still suffer from colds and flu. Edna Elias, former mayor of Coppermine and a leader in women's community pressure groups, said the housing crisis is subsiding: the Inuit and Inuvialuit are having much smaller families and overcrowding was not as bad as it used to be.

ARCTIC SNAPSHOT 2

"You know why I'm called 'Whiskey Joe?'" the Inuk asked.

"No."

"I'm on a drilling rig on Melville Island. We fly out for a week's R&R in Edmonton. When it's time to go back to Rae Point, I'm drunk and miss the flight. That was the one that missed the runway and went into the Arctic. I think about thirty guys drowned. Or froze. That's why they call me 'Whiskey Joe.'"

$\sim$

But everyone has a different point of view, depending on his or her prejudices and sympathies.

Father René Fumoloe, a Catholic priest in the North for well over thirty years and one of the greatest champions of the Dene, told me that in one eighteen-month period there were sixty-five suicide attempts in Tuktoyaktuk – 15 percent of the total population.

Social planner Will Drake saw the same situation in a different light: he thought suicide attempts increased in prosperous communities like Tuktoyaktuk because "the 'have-nots' look at the possessions of the 'haves' and it makes them despair."

Edna Elias, Nick Sibbeston, Gordon Wray, and others all agreed that it has been hard to educate the aboriginals in the handling of money in a consumer society.

"The young fellows from Coppermine used to go to the Beaufort and make big money working on the oil rigs," said Elias. "We tried to get them to open bank accounts and save their money but they liked cashing their cheques at the Bay and then spending most of their money on things like rifles and skidoos and three-wheelers. When they'd come home on a week's leave they'd order a case of whiskey from Yellowknife and would party for the first half of the week, then recover in the second half. Then they'd go back to the rigs. When the jobs stopped, they wouldn't take poorer-paying ones. They'd just sit at home. It was hard educating them as to how to balance income against expenses."

Will Drake and Edna Elias made the Arctic sound just like the south and its problems with the overexpectation encouraged by television commercials. "They tried out prohibition for a few months in Cambridge Bay in the 1970s and it was disastrous," said Drake. "It created more problems than it solved and resulted in deaths and suicides." Some other communities have had better luck with prohibition, or strict rationing of booze and trying to run down the moonshiners who flourish in many settlements. Smuggling is also a problem. Drugs and booze are often brought in by kabloonat working on the rigs, on ships, or attached to the DEW Line.

Gordon Wray from Baker Lake, who has worked in local and territorial government, believes most of the trouble can be traced to unemployment, which allows too much idle time for young males. "There was no time to get into trouble when all of one's time was spent on survival," he said.

~

To understand how the North is coping, one must look at the way the residents use high technology to cope with an extreme environment.

The Arctic has always imposed its own disciplines, and today's northerners are learning how to deal with new problems with new tools. The climate rules everything. The summer is spectacular but very short. Perhaps one can relax a little then, but not much.

The storms start in September. In 1985 Broughton Island and Grise Fjord were hit by especially fierce storms. In Broughton, the gales blew down half of the home fuel tanks, and families huddled together waiting for the blizzard to let up: in a treeless world, the only available fuel is oil. In Grise Fjord, farthest north of all settlements, the wind began to blow away the houses and the entire community took refuge in the school.

In Cambridge Bay, a few fuel tanks blew down and in one house the furnace stopped. The occupants watched nervously as the temperature dropped a degree an hour for seventeen hours: what would happen if the town mechanic couldn't fix it? ... or what if he was drunk? ... or got blown out onto the tundra by the blizzard? Once in a while, one stuck one's feet in the oven of the electric stove: all the heating coils were going full blast ... Seventeen from 22°C is five degrees above freezing ... The mechanic finally came: he'd been working around the clock fixing other heating systems. He took everything in stride. "Pretty normal for this time of year," he said with a big Inuk grin. He found a broken fan belt and replaced it. After he left, it took twelve hours for the temperature to come back up to comfort level.

Traditionally, the Inuit and their dogs waited out the blizzards in snow houses – igloos – and hoped they had enough seal meat. The igloos might hold as many as sixty people in five or six families, all related to one another. Much more likely, there would be eighteen to twenty-five elders, plus children and parents of two families. As soon as the wind eased, the men would be out looking for more meat.

But today, the Inuit live in three-bedroom houses in communities ranging from 105 (Grise Fjord) to 3,000 (Iqaluit). Most of them range from 400 to 1,000. With that many people concentrated in one place, you have to have enormous quantities of supplies to wait out the blizzards. Thousands of litres of fuel oil; tonnes of flour and sugar and tea and more tonnes of frozen caribou or seal or muskox, kept in the freezer of the Hunters and Trappers Association. Roof-high stacks of warm clothing ...

The airport runway has to be kept clear even during a storm so that new supplies can be flown in if there is an emergency. The town roads have to be ploughed regularly so that the sewage tankers, the freshwater tankers, the garbage trucks can service all the houses.

Then there is the fire department. Fire is the nightmare of the Arctic, always in the back of people's minds. (There was that going for the snow house: it couldn't burn down.) The fire station's water tank has to be kept full – and unfrozen. The road to the reservoir has to be kept ploughed so that you can keep the water pipes and valves from freezing.

And you have to keep the power plant going for electric lights … appliances … furnaces … freezers … fuel and water and sewage pumps.

Yes, this is high tech. Very high tech.

Education

From the very beginning of government responsibility for the aboriginal peoples, education has been one of the most controversial issues, and it remains so. When Ottawa began building and staffing secular schools in the late 1940s, there was debate over what the indigenes should be taught, how it should be taught, and who should teach it.

Was the main purpose to help the native peoples lead more effective lives in their own environment? Or should they be taught white skills to help them survive in an industrial society, north or south?

The mission schools were primarily concerned with the souls of their pupils and paid little attention to modern skills or social responsibilities beyond those implicit in Christian belief. By the early 1960s, Ottawa was committed to public education of both the Indians and the Inuit and began hiring the best teachers it could find in the south – because there were virtually no qualified aboriginal teachers.

As noted earlier, secular teachers ignored native languages and taught only in English, but then there were no qualified teachers capable of speaking the native languages of the NWT. A few Anglican and Catholic priests learned them – but only by living among the people for many years. Even with these missionaries, the standard practice of the residential church schools was to teach in English only.

When the secular teachers – like Brian Lewis, who became director of education and deputy minister, or Bob MacQuarrie, the principal at Baker Lake – arrived, their qualifications were southern. MacQuarrie has noted that teachers were not even encouraged to learn Inuktitut, Inuvialukton, Cree, Slavey, Dog Rib, or Gwich'in.

The first necessity was to establish communication between teacher and student, and this, rightly or wrongly, was based on getting the students to learn working English. The teachers had to follow curricula based on those of Ontario or Alberta, and this involved teaching southern subjects in a southern way. Clearly not an ideal system, but the best available at the time it was introduced.

From the beginning, the lifestyle of the aboriginals clashed with the school system. Nomadic or semi-nomadic hunting and gathering peoples travel with their families, and each member had a key function. Taking children out of the family group for many months of the year seriously interfered with several aspects of native life.

For instance, children living in English-speaking boarding schools for months on end tended to forget their mother tongues and too often could not communicate with their parents when they went home. They were also prevented from learning the skills of the land from their fathers or mothers. At the same time, many children failed to gain an adequate knowledge of English or southern skills that could replace the lost native language and culture.

The seeds of tragedy were being deeply planted.

There were always a few bright children who seized any educational opportunities offered. In the west, Catholic missionaries sought out comers like Ethel Blondin and James Wah Shee and sent them to Grandin College in Fort Smith. In the east, teachers had no trouble spotting youngsters like Tagak Curley, John Amagualik, Peter Ernerk, Ann Hanson, and Edna Elias.

Bob MacQuarrie saw some of the first native graduates in Baker Lake and later taught them at Sir John Franklin High School in Yellowknife. As soon as local government was introduced, Gordon Wray says, the young graduates started to get involved in it. "We can fight the government or we can take it over," was what they said. By the mid-1970s, "an enormous amount" of political development had occurred, MacQuarrie said.

Dennis Patterson, the Iqaluit lawyer who was education minister before he was government leader, is familiar with all the problems, from truancy to affirmative action for teachers. Although he is a kabloona from Vancouver, he is married to an Inuk and has half-Inuit children. He told me the Department of Education is caught in a dilemma: on the one hand, children must be encouraged to complete at least primary education; on the other, Inuit and Dene parents long opposed the idea of having a truant officer.

"When the question of passing a compulsory education law was discussed at a meeting in Rankin Inlet, Inuit parents were so strongly opposed that they walked out," Patterson said. He managed to get a compulsory attendance act with a local opting-out provision. A school councillor would deal with absenteeism instead of a truant officer. The law increased attendance 2 percent a year for three years in a row, and by 1987 more than twenty communities had accepted it. In that year, Baffin region attendance was more than 80 percent. "There have been dramatic changes in the attitudes of parents and it's now realized that even a hunter needs a basic education," Patterson said.

From the time the federal government started building schools until 1976, educational policy, authority, curricula, and the hiring and training of staff were all in the control of Ottawa. Native parents felt that they had no input into education and, worse, that the schools were alienating children from their own land and culture. The parents pointed to the lack of teachers who spoke native languages, to the southern-oriented curricula, and to the heavy subsidization of white teachers and their families during their often brief sojourns in the North. Parents further claimed that the few high schools were tailored to the needs of the children of white northerners, preparing them to go south for university or technical training, or to fit into the broader Canadian workforce.

When Ottawa passed control of education to the GNWT, Commissioner Hodgson began making the curricula more sensitive to local and regional requirements. In 1976 local educational authorities were established. In Fort Rae/Edzo, under the prodding of one of the NWT's remarkable women, Elizabeth Mackenzie, the Dog Ribs gained control of their school and what was taught in it. The Rae/Edzo experience was so successful that it spread throughout the NWT, in both Dene and Inuit communities.

One significant development has been the establishment of regional school boards. On Baffin Island the board covers thirteen communities. Because of this and the affirmative action program, more than 10 percent of the NWT teaching force now is native.

One of the most controversial programs Patterson was involved with was education in outpost camps. For some years, a small number of Inuit families chose to live outside the communities all year round, hunting, trapping, and fishing in traditional ways. Among the 1,500 Inuit in the Iqualuit area, seventy-five live in outpost camps, and there are thirty such camps across Baffin Island.

In 1987 Patterson visited several camps and asked NWT teachers to volunteer to teach basics to the children in them. "I wouldn't recommend building schools at the camps," he told me. "Teachers will have to put up with cramped living quarters and live in the Inuit way. But I think if boys and girls got the basics, they could pick up

---

ARCTIC SNAPSHOT 3

"How much could two married teachers make?"

"Well, Betty and Bob between them get just over $100,000 a year in Pelly Bay."

"A hundred thousand! That's fantastic!"

"Not at all: they barely get by."

"How come?"

"Oh, each one has a skidoo for the winter and a three-wheeler for the summer, and you know what groceries are in Pelly. They go home for summer vacations and at Christmas. And at winter break they usually go to Hawaii, naturally. No, $100,000 isn't excessive!"

---

advanced schooling later. One seventeen-year-old boy I met wanted to learn how to read and write and calculate so that ultimately he could take over family leadership from his father." He added: "I've felt we've neglected these kids. It would be entirely politically untenable to drag them into communities to go to school."

But many experienced educators disagreed. Bob MacQuarrie didn't think the system worked, partly because native children need to be better equipped for the complex modern world than volunteer-taught classes on weekends can make them. Gordon Wray believed most Inuit young people are moving away from the land, toward northern communities first and then, possibly, toward the rest of Canada. "They want the modern way of life," he said.

Ethel Blondin, with a good deal of personal teaching experience, felt that native children should not cut themselves off from the possibilities of travel and relocation. And even Patterson, when speaking of the Dene part of his constituency, said: "This is the last generation that will speak Chip and Loucheux and Cree."

Division

"Nunavut was an ideal conception from the start. Regionalism created no problems at first. There was tremendous support right through the NWT, Northern Quebec, and Labrador."

The speaker is Tagak Curley, stormy petrel of the NWT legislature, first president of the Inuit Tapirisat of Canada, and one of the most thoughtful public figures in the Hudson Bay region. He was born at Coral Harbour on Southampton Island in 1944, the grandson of a prosperous whaler. He has lived through and experienced the whole of the Arctic revolution.

"I was a little boy living with my family in an igloo when my father told me I would have to learn to speak and to write in English," he says. "I didn't know what he meant then but later I saw that people who had been leaders of the community didn't know what was happening. That shook me up. It was a blow to the family when a good provider from a family with pride couldn't provide for his wife and children. I wanted to do something. I didn't have any major long-range vision – it was just trying to get people on their feet. In those days, the problems of building a new world to save the Inuit were almost impossible for the whites from Ottawa; to the Inuit themselves, survival seemed beyond the impossible."

When government moved north, Curley was one of the first Inuks to work for it: he was settlement manager in Repulse Bay in 1970–71. The ITC was organized in 1970, and Curley says it was almost incredibly difficult to bring the Inuit together: "Communications were terrible. There were so few of us and we were scattered over such enormous spaces. Air transport was poor and there wasn't even communication from region to region. But everyone wanted Nunavut, our own land."

There's sadness in Curley's description of those early days. He understands the series of problems that have kept Nunavut a dream on the horizon rather than a reality. First of all, the Inuvialuit broke away from the eastern Inuit to negotiate their own land deal with Ottawa. Then there were border problems between the Inuit and the Dene. Next, many central Arctic Inuit began shying away from a Nunavut that might be dominated by South Baffin.

Finally, negotiations with Ottawa met many road-blocks from federal and provincial politicians who opposed division or the possibility of provincehood. For generations, some ambitious pols from Manitoba, Saskatchewan, and Alberta have dreamed of extending their borders right to the North Pole so that the individual provinces would own the mineral and petroleum resources of the NWT.

∽

In the early stages of the Arctic revolution, the idea of division originated with whites who wanted to develop the resources of the Arctic.

It would be accomplished on longitudinal lines rather than following the tree line that separated *taiga* from tundra. This early attempt at division died when the Liberals replaced the Conservatives in 1963.

After the Inuit took up the goal of division in 1971, the idea became more popular in the eastern Arctic and among non-aboriginals. In 1980 the Legislative Assembly supported division, and in 1982, 56 percent of NWT voters favoured it. There were, however, many splits. While the Dene Nation could accept an Inuit territory, there were many differences over where the boundary should run.

The Inuit, too, were split. Those from the east and central Arctic believed that the Inuvialuit of the Beaufort Sea should be part of Nunavut. The Copper Eskimos of the central Arctic, the Caribou Inuit of the Keewatin, and the residents of South Baffin all had regional differences.

The Inuit and Dene could not settle their boundary dispute, so John Parker, who retired as NWT commissioner in 1989, was named an impartial arbitrator and chose a zigzagging line, which the Dene claimed favoured the Inuit. This line was accepted by the federal government as a basis for the western boundary of Nunavut.

On 4 May 1992, an NWT plebiscite on the boundary was held, and it was accepted by 54 percent of the voters (only 56.1 percent of those eligible voted). This narrow margin was condemned by Chief Billy Erasmus of the Dene Nation, who pointed out that while 71.6 percent of the Inuit in the east favoured the boundary, 52.7 percent of western voters of all races voted against it.

From early on in the land claims negotiations, the federal government accepted division in principle but specified that it could occur only after the claims were settled.

A constitutional alliance of the NWT was initiated by the assembly, consisting of some of its members and representatives of the various native organizations. It, in turn, was divided into the Nunavut Constitutional Forum (NCF) and the Western Constitutional Forum (WCF), the latter mainly concerned with the future of Indians, Métis, and whites.

Public hearings of both forums involved educating the general population in the various forms of government open to them on several levels. In addition, the NCF actively pressed the self-government ambitions of the Inuit of the eastern and central Arctic with the federal government.

~

Now that the Nunavut deal has been struck, how great are regional differences still and how seriously should they be taken?

Dennis Patterson, the former government leader, doesn't think they are very serious. He feels that the central Arctic and Keewatin Inuit must follow the South Baffin lead in their own interest. Only in that way can Inuit culture be preserved, he believes. But then Patterson lives in Iqualuit, and his wife's family ties are with South Baffin.

Gordon Wray, married to a Keewatin Inuk, says nobody wants to talk about the antagonisms among the various regional groups. They are particularly intense in the Keewatin, where for centuries there have been rivalries between the Caribou Inuit living inland around Garry Lake, the Baker Lake people who ate both seal and caribou, and the people from the Hudson Bay coast who subsisted solely on marine mammals.

"Nunavut was the catalyst that brought out the differences," says Wray. As a prominent politician related to a number of the most powerful Inuit families, he is cautious. But one person who wishes to remain anonymous says:

> The Copper Eskimos have no time for the South Baffin. Baker Lake people haven't much time for the coastal Inuit. The coastal people consider themselves a cut above the Caribou Eskimos. There are four groups in Baker and one group won't speak to another. The coastal/inland group is the most advanced and powerful, maybe because they have some white mix. The true inland group is shunned by the other three tribes and they're known for incest and spousal abuse. Ninety percent of the people who show up in court are from this group.

(This anonymous person has strong family ties with the powerful families, and he may show a snobbish bias.)

The most obvious symbol of the Inuit split is in the written language. In Baffin Island, syllabics are used, in the central Arctic the Roman alphabet. This means that an Inuk from Cambridge Bay cannot read an Inuktitut newspaper published in Iqualuit.

The success of Nunavut may depend on TV education. Already there are two native networks: the Inuit Broadcasting Corporation (IBC) in the eastern and central Arctic, and the Inuvialuit Communications Society (ICS) in the Delta. If the regions can agree

on a single dialect, Nunavut may become the cultural home of all
Canadian Inuit.

The Economics of Survival

The central problem of the present-day NWT is economic and it will
remain the central problem of the two new territories in the 21st
century. Where will the money come from?

Before the white man, there were only a few thousand Indians and
Inuit scattered across millions of square kilometres. There was no
agriculture in the southern sense, so everyone lived by hunting, fishing, and a little gathering. After the white man came, the chief
industries were trapping, whaling, and mining.

Today, the fur market is almost gone – prices have collapsed and
the aboriginals find hunting and trapping aren't worth the cost of bullets
and gasoline. This happened even before the animal welfare movement became a powerful political force restricting the fur market.
Whaling has been gone from the Arctic for most of this century. In
Canada's Beaufort Sea, eastern and High Arctic, only a few of the
smaller whales are taken to make muktuk and some narwhals are
hunted for their tusks.

Mines come and go, producing much wealth but few permanent
jobs. A major diamond rush occurred in the Yellowknife region in the
early 1990s and showed promise of perking up the economy. The
Dog Ribs were the only aboriginals staking claims. A petroleum
boom has been promised for nearly a century and never has material-
ized, but there certainly are great gas reserves in the Beaufort Sea and
High Arctic.

In the south, even in poor areas, the population depends in some
measure on agriculture: growing potatoes and other vegetables, raising
hogs, planting grain crops to sell. There is a fertile belt southwest of
the Mackenzie River – the HBC had a productive farm for generations at Simpson. But the season is very short and the Dene haven't
shown much interest in agriculture.

∼

NWT economic problems have been known since long before Ottawa
first decided to intervene in the lives of the indigenes. Indeed, the economic and health crisis was one of the reasons Ottawa stepped in.
From the start, the cost had to be borne by the southern taxpayer,

though the government got back a relatively small amount from the mining companies in the form of taxes.

The gold mines of Yellowknife, the uranium mine at Port Radium, and the base metals mines at Rankin Inlet, Pine Point, and Nanisivik have produced fabulous wealth and so may the new diamond mines, but ultimately all mines run out of minerals and have to close. Besides, they've never had much appeal as employers for native northerners.

Aside from such unpredictable enterprises, the NWT has always lived on government grants. From 1950 on, various planners introduced the manufacture and marketing of folk art, such as Inuit sculpture and silk-screen work, and similar enterprises. Reindeer herds were introduced from Alaska with indifferent results. A considerable freshwater fishing industry was developed on Great Slave Lake, and Arctic char fish plants have been opened at places like Cambridge Bay.

One of the most visionary of the politicians is Gordon Wray, who came from Scotland, became a community worker, and married an Inuk. He says that if the economic crisis is not solved, disaster lies ahead. He wants much better ground transportation tying the communities together, as well as better airports and upgraded air service. Better use must be made of the cottage industries using renewable resources: he thinks in terms of clothing made from animal skins, tools from caribou horns, and an Arctic catering service taking exotic foods to the south. And the tourist industry should be expanded, he says.

"Unless these things happen," Wray says, "young northerners will have to leave. They are always moving from the smaller places to Iqaluit or Yellowknife and they'll go outside if they can't get jobs." So far, few investors have shown any interest in most of Wray's schemes, although gourmet restaurants are being supplied with choice country food. Tourism is also increasing.

The trouble with all these projected or infant enterprises is that, individually, they are too small, in their initial stages at least, to support the people involved. Living in the Arctic and Mackenzie is no joke for anyone who is not heavily subsidized by the south.

Fortunately, the land itself produces a great deal of food. Few southerners realize the extent to which the North – tundra, *taiga,* or ocean – is not a barren wilderness. It teems with edible wild animals – fish and birds and sea mammals. "Country food" is not only important to both Indians and Inuit: it is still absolutely essential. The cost of imported food is so high that relatively few natives can afford much more than bare essentials. Twenty to 80 percent of the native diet comes off the land.*

While there still is plenty of game for the 35,000 to 40,000 natives, obtaining it is more expensive than anywhere else in Canada. Traditionally, native families, whether Indian or Inuit, moved with the game and fish seasons, migratory patterns, and traditions built up over centuries. Today, however, they live in settlements ranging from a hundred to several thousand people. As soon as a settlement reaches a permanent population of 500 or so, the residents quickly use up all the game within easy reach. Dog teams pulling sleds (to carry the meat back home) have a limited range, and the caribou and muskox soon learn to stay beyond it.

The aboriginals are almost totally dependent on snowmobiles, which can carry them farther and farther into the hunting territory. As the indigenous population rises, snowmobiles are an essential tool, but they are expensive: a snowmobile may cost $3,000 and last only four or five years; a good hunting rifle costs $300 to $400 and a box of magnum rifle shells $20. Then there are the costs of gasoline and spare parts.

In a town like Cambridge Bay, heads of families skidoo out on the tundra every winter weekend to hunt caribou. The Hunters and Trappers Association buys part of the hunt and keeps it in a freezer, selling at very low prices to those who cannot hunt. Apart from caribou, the hunters shoot muskox, ducks, geese, and Arctic hare, and fish for char, trout, and white fish. In the Mackenzie, the Indians have no muskox but they do have moose and several species of freshwater and lake fish.

Unemployment is still very great. Both the Dene and the Inuit have very largely taken over local political control, and there are jobs for tank truck drivers and other municipal workers, clerks at the Bay or the co-op, a few nursing and teaching aides, a few ordinary labourers in the construction trades.

---

*It's hard to accurately estimate the exact share of income that country food represents. Different agencies use different scales. For instance, northern Indians and Inuit have always eaten a higher proportion of meat and fish than southerners (even aboriginal southerners) because grains and vegetables were not available. This would account for northerners making meat and fish one-quarter to one-half of actual food consumed. On a dollar basis, country food probably accounts for at least three-quarters of the normal food budget.

At times, men work in petroleum exploration or on drilling crews, in one-time operations like building or restructuring the DEW Line, in the mines, as mechanics repairing vehicles. But there are not nearly enough such jobs. Until the early 1990s, neither the federal nor the territorial government nor private industry had come up with any real solution.

With this, there still is a housing shortage, and Nellie Cournoyea caused a good deal of discussion when she moved to stop government subsidization of civil service housing. When the instant towns were built, the federal government encouraged the indigenes to buy homes on low-interest and long-term mortgages. But few knew anything about budgeting money and, in any case, had trouble keeping up the payments. As a result, most families have been crowded into scarce rental housing owned by government corporations. Unmarried young women and men cannot obtain houses and have to stay with their parents. Sometimes even after marriage, they remain in the family home.

Imagine four generations packed into a three-bedroom prefab house! It is little wonder that there has been so much despair, especially among the young. Some sociologists believe overcrowding is the main reason for the high suicide rate.

Although the mandarins were well aware of the main economic problems from the 1940s on, Bud Drury was the first Ottawa investigator to say what must be done. The natives and their white advisers, on the other hand, have been saying that the mineral and petroleum wealth must pay for most of the costs of living. This is the reason that they've been so insistent on controlling subsurface rights. Their fallback position is that the major resource companies must pay royalties to governments controlled by the natives rather than by Ottawa.

Even if this happens under the claims settlements, mineral resources are not inexhaustible, and no one has seriously dealt with what is to be done with the generations of the future who will have no oil or mineral royalties to pay the bills.

The Canadian North is caught in an iron vise: improve the health and living conditions of the indigenous inhabitants and the population rises sharply, automatically reducing the food supply; find ways of increasing the food supply to meet the needs of a growing population and the indigenous cultures may be severely damaged. It's not an easy problem either for the mandarins, the native leaders, or the white residents, and the formation of Nunavut and perhaps a Dene Denendeh will not solve it.

Women

I'll start with a quotation from Ann Hanson, former NWT deputy commissioner and an Inuk born in a tent in an outpost camp near Lake Harbour forty-odd years ago: "It's not 'who am I?' but 'who do I want to be?'" Ann Hanson has been a wife and mother, radio broadcaster and movie star. She succeeded Agnes Semmler, a Gwich'in Métis from Aklavik, who had been the first president of COPE and one of the North's legends.

The two epitomize the enormous part women have played in the Arctic revolution. Other names are Agnes's partner in COPE, Nellie Cournoyea, Bertha Allen, Suzie Husky, Elizabeth Mackenzie, Rosemarie Kuptana, Ethel Blondin, Rhoda Inukshuk, and Edna Elias. Considering that the total native population is only about 30,000, the number of outstanding women leaders is astounding. Dennis Patterson says that "women are organizing the North at the community level," but he might have added on a territorial and national level as well. The background of many of these women is similar, whether Inuit, Dene, or Métis.

Nellie Cournoyea, born of a Norwegian father who became a trapper and an Inuvialuit mother, grew up, as they say in the Delta, "on the ice." She was a bright child who at ten was recording secretary for the Aklavik Hunters and Trappers Association. She went to school, got married, had children, lived in a white environment in Ottawa for a while with her white husband.

When she returned to the Delta, CBC hired her as an announcer/operator and then made her the first native radio station manager. That was in Inuvik, and the winds of change were blowing down the Mackenzie. Nellie and Agnes felt that the people of the Delta – all of them, native and white alike – needed some kind of organization to represent them. It became COPE: in the early days, they worked closely with young Indians organizing the Gwich'in and Sah'tu communities.

Agnes Semmler was older, a Gwich'in Métis who learned to trap and skin muskrats when she was a little girl. She married Slim Semmler, the legendary white trader of Aklavik and Inuvik. When the Indians moved in their own direction, Agnes remained on friendly terms with them. During the time COPE was seeking a land settlement, its presidency was turned over to the respected Sam Raddi, a former Inuvialuit trapper. John Parker named Agnes Semmler the first native deputy commissioner, an entirely ceremonial position when she assumed it.

～

Coming from the other end of the NWT, Ann Hanson was born in a tent and was one of those Inuit identified with a metal disk – "Annie – E.121." Like Nellie Cournoyea, she lived on the land and travelled by dog team. As a teen, she lived with an aunt in Toronto, and she also spent time in Baker Lake. She started school at thirteen and saw her first TV at fifteen.

Many southerners saw her as the star of the feature movie *White Dawn*, based on a novel by James Houston, the artist who first publicized Inuit art in the late 1940s. Ann Hanson was the beautiful Inuit girl who fell in love with the marooned white whaler (played by Timothy Bottoms). The film was based on a true incident in the 19th century when shipwrecked whalers were rescued by Inuit, then fell into a tragic culture clash. In the end, the Inuit had to kill the kabloonat in self-defence.

～

Edna Elias was born in a tent outside Coppermine, one of eleven children. When she was small, her father was away working on the DEW Line and her mother took some of the family to live on the land. Edna learned all the traditional skills except, as she says wryly, "how to make a snow house."

She married at fifteen and had two children. She had dropped out of school after grade eight but at sixteen took a job as a classroom assistant. She did this for six years. "Every year there was a new teacher I had to break in," she said. "It got boring. I decided to be a teacher myself and the government let me attend school part-time. When I got high school standing I spent two years taking teacher's training, then taught two years in South Baffin before I came back to Coppermine."

All this by the time she was twenty-five. The next stage was politics. It was no trick to take over the running of Coppermine, and at twenty-eight she became the first Inuit woman mayor. Elias said that in Coppermine and other Inuit and Inuvialuit communities men are traditionally elected to the settlement council and the executive of the Hunters and Trappers Association, while women are encouraged to run the housing association, education, and social and health programs.

In 1984–85 there were so many suicides by young Inuks in Coppermine that Elias organized a women's group, which became famous throughout the Territories as a voice for social improvement. Shortly thereafter, she went to Yellowknife as head of the GNWT's native languages program.

Asked about her own teenaged children, she said that she looked after them in Yellowknife in winter during the school year and her husband took over in Coppermine in the summer. As to languages, "my husband lost his Inuvialukton when he was sent to boarding school from the age of six to thirteen. The children learn a little Inuvialukton from their grandmother, but I think more older people are learning English from the children than the other way around."

~

Ethel Blondin is a Sah'tu from Fort Franklin on Great Slave Lake. When she was six, she started school at Fort Norman, but a year later her father took her and her mother to live in a tent on the land. Her brothers and sisters were in school. In 1959 Grolier Hall, a Catholic boarding school, opened in the new town of Inuvik. The smaller children along the Mackenzie were picked up by freight plane and rode north on sacks of potatoes to spend months away from home.

That wasn't to last for Ethel either. "Dad had started working for Imperial Esso in Norman Wells when I was eleven and he parked mother and me in a tent outside of town. I'm grateful for the experience of living on the land but I don't have any romantic illusions about living in a tent in winter. It was a real harsh environment."

At twelve, Ethel developed tuberculosis and spent the next fourteen months in almost total isolation at the Camsell Hospital in Edmonton. "I had two visitors all the time I was there," she said. She studied by correspondence, and when she finished grade nine she was invited to go to the church's leadership cadre at Grandin College in Fort Smith – the nurturing place for many of the North's native leaders.

Ethel's bumpy career was not uneventful at Grandin. "I was kicked out of the residence by one of the priests. Later he became Bishop Coteau and when I was beginning to be successful he told me that getting kicked out was the best thing that ever happened to me. I don't know what he meant."

Like many other northern women, Ethel married early and had two children. In 1970 she was in the teacher education program and in 1971 went to the University of Alberta. She taught for three years in the Inuvialuit settlement of Tuktoyaktuk, where she had the pleasure of making a presentation in Sah'tu to the Berger Commission.

Unlike many aboriginals who are satisfied to spend their lives in their own part of the NWT, Ethel Blondin says: "There's a great big world out there. People always said I was a dreamer; I have a great sense of curiosity but no romantic illusions."

When she settled down to a career, she moved ahead quickly. At Fort Providence, she was vice-principal and started an oral history program. Next, she moved to Yellowknife and Ottawa, where she was part of an affirmative action program but felt the feds didn't have their hearts in it. "The DIAND people didn't have as much commitment as the GNWT," she said.

In 1987 she was assistant deputy minister of communications in the GNWT, in charge of cultural programs. A year later, she was elected to Parliament as a Liberal from Western Arctic and reached prominence in 1990 as a member of the parliamentary committee on Meech Lake. She was the Liberal party's spokesperson on native issues. After the Liberals were elected to office in 1992, Blondin became secretary of state for youth and training programs, a junior cabinet post.

∼

Rhoda Inukshuk and Rosemarie Kuptana are names of at least equal importance to the others. I worked for Rosemarie Kuptana when I was with the Inuit Broadcasting Corporation in Cambridge Bay. She was the IBC president. Kuptana springs from a prominent family on Banks Island, identified with the Liberal party. She broke through the traditional male dominance of Eskimo institutions with a brilliant program of political manoeuvring and became a great success as head of IBC, famous for her sure-footedness in raising money among the numerous departments in Ottawa. More recently Kuptana became president of the Inuit Tapirisat of Canada (ITC) and, with Mary Simon, was a major Inuit negotiator at the Charlottetown Constitutional Conference.

Rhoda Inukshuk was the first female president of the ITC but was replaced by John Amagoalik, who in turn gave way to Rosemarie Kaptana. Rhoda reached the top because two powerful male factions were contending. Her tenure was short, and many would say that her lack of success was simply due to the refusal of many male Inuit politicians to accept the authority of a woman. After a period when Amagoalik resumed the presidency, Rosemarie Kuptana moved into the ITC presidency, where she has been much more effective than Inukshuk.

Among the women leaders, Nellie Cournoyea, Rosemarie Kuptana, and Edna Elias, all have moved cautiously, and the male-female battle north of 60 is far from over – any more than it is in the south.

The New Northerners

"The North is the federal government's last playground."
– Don Stewart

"We can fight the government ... or we can take it over."
– Ann Hanson

"What may be happening is that the white is being assimilated into the native culture.
– Dennis Patterson

In the 1970s, the rhetoric of native leaders was polluted with the slogans of anti-colonial African nationalism. Today, the rhetoric has sources closer to home. As Jack Sigvaldason, the publisher of *News of the North*, says: "If it's appropriate, you rant and rave and scream. Some of the native leaders found that out. Some of the whites are pretty good at it, too." The various residents of the NWT, of all races, found themselves in the mid-1980s trying to deal with practical political problems.

As long as the NWT was a true colony, there was no (technical) problem about its administration: the commissioner was selected by Ottawa, probably without any consultation whatsoever with the residents, and he was given a number of administrative assistants who ruled, ideally without fear or favour. The system lasted until the 1970s, when it was overtaken by elected government.

By the mid-1980s, the NWT was starting to look a little like a province – but there were major differences. Unlike the Yukon or the provinces, the NWT had not yet got around to the luxury of party politics on the territorial level, though as elsewhere in Canada, each member of Parliament represented one of the three major federal parties. Territorially, it is obvious that the NWT has so many complex geographical and racial divisions that one more might be one too many.

Candidates for the Legislative Assembly run on their own personal merits. After election, their first task is to pick an executive committee – the equivalent of a provincial cabinet – which in turn agrees on a chairperson who becomes government leader, a position somewhat equivalent to provincial premier.

While this process looks simple and straightforward, it is fraught with hazard because it reverses the party system. Over nearly 300 years, countries under the British parliamentary system have adhered to an undeviating pattern: the parties choose leaders whom they follow in general elections; the monarch (or, in Canada, the governor general as the Crown's representative) asks the leader of the largest elected party to form a government; the party leader picks the cabinet.

But in the NWT, it is not the most charismatic or powerful or principled leader who is acceptable – it is the person who is acceptable to east and west, Dene and Inuit and Métis and white. The government leader represents compromise with a capital C.

It is in this complex government structure that the NWT's constitutional future is being decided – far more than in the Parliament of Canada or at interprovincial conferences.

~

Nick Sibbeston is a Métis with a white father and a Slavey mother, but he says he has always felt part of the Dene because he grew up with his mother's people in Simpson. That fact launched him into territorial politics in 1970 when he defeated Don Stewart, the white mayor of Hay River, for the Legislative Council. Sibbeston was elected because he spoke Slavey and Stewart did not.

Later, Sibbeston became the first native lawyer in the Territories. He worked for the pipeline companies for a time during the controversial 1970s. Then he returned to the council – now an assembly – and got a reputation for being hot-tempered, impatient, sometimes difficult to work with.

He held several portfolios and became knowledgeable in local government and in relations between the Dene and Inuit. As government leader he will be remembered for launching the first major affirmative action program. Sibbeston is proud of his achievements, though he stepped on a lot of toes. In 1987 he said:

Until I took over, the Department of Personnel was handled by Commissioner Parker and this gave him control over the GNWT's top civil servants. I took over Personnel and fired the deputy, then brought in a Métis, Jake Heron. We then launched a program of affirmative action making changes in the senior level of government. Bob Pilot, one of the most senior people (he had been assistant commissioner and he was deputy minister of the executive council in 1984) was packed off to Ottawa.

I let it be known that the elected people were in charge. We didn't want a single civil servant around who could be seen as the strongest person in government. I also took over chairmanship of the executive council, a position always held by the commissioner, who now has no role in day to day government. In law, he is still chief executive officer of the federal government. He still serves a sort of formal function. John Parker has a role as a lieutenant governor.

Sibbeston lost no opportunity to assert his authority. In 1986 the GNWT held a picnic in Vancouver to reward the staff of the NWT pavilion at Expo 86. Both Sibbeston and Parker were present, but Sibbeston made the speech of thanks as head of government. He pointedly mentioned the "ambassadorial" function of the commissioner and said Parker was only an emissary between the GNWT and Ottawa.

Sibbeston's quite deliberate slights of Parker were part of a familiar pattern wherein ambitious newcomers push old office-holders out of the seats of power. There might have been social incidents if it hadn't been for the fact that the government leader was being guided in his new role by Parker himself.*

The transition of power was, in spite of minor social incidents, a long-term process that had proceeded from the early days of Hodgson to the end of the Parker regime in 1989. When Parker retired, he was succeeded as commissioner by Daniel L. Norris, the regional director of the Inuvik region and a Métis actually born in the Delta.

Norris's appointment had deep symbolic value, but he also had

---

*In 1987 I asked Commissioner Parker whether he had been deposed as CEO of the NWT. He said the transfer of power had been planned by himself and by Stuart Hodgson and was totally voluntary. Parker firmly said that whatever Sibbeston claimed, the commissioner retained all of his executive and legislative powers under the NWT Act and could, if he so chose, resume control of the GNWT whenever he felt like it. He admitted, however, that such action would not be advisable politically.

twenty-seven years of steadily rising service through the federal and territorial governments. Agnes Semmler had been a symbolic and token appointment as deputy commissioner. Now Norris was fully equipped to step into the shoes of Parker – ironically, at a time when real power was being transferred from the commissioner to the territorial assembly.

Norris represented so many factors in the North's changing history. His family had established a trading post thirty-five kilometres southwest of the site of Inuvik in 1932 and later became storekeepers in Aklavik. He graduated from an Alberta high school, and when the GNWT came into the Inuvik region, he joined it from the Department of Northern Affairs and National Resources. In 1985 he was the first native to be appointed a regional director.

Thus, only twenty-six years after the all-powerful commissioner ceased to be a full-time Ottawa mandarin, the most visible job in the Territories was held by an indigene.

~

As early as 1987, Sibbeston could claim with satisfaction that his government worked daily on a government-to-government basis with Ottawa. Asked about the commissioner's legal function as the most senior official, reporting directly to the DIAND minister, Sibbeston said: "I deal directly with the minister – but not very often." Asked about federal cooperation, Sibbeston said: "There's no difficulty on the political level. On the bureaucratic level, civil servants are still opposing devolution."

Sibbeston fired or forced into retirement a number of white deputy ministers, senior civil servants, and regional officials, replacing them with natives. Brian Lewis, long-time director of education and deputy minister, was abruptly fired and succeeded by a native. Sibbeston also reduced the authority of the directors of the five regions because "they had been mini-commissioners." Now, he said, they could only coordinate GNWT directives.

Jim Bourque, former president of the Métis Association, became deputy minister of renewable resources. Helen Adamache of Cambridge Bay, one of the outstanding NWT women and a member of the powerful Klengenberg clan from Coppermine, was named director of the Kitikmeot region.

Sibbeston's rise and fall exemplifies the subtle tensions always present in NWT government. The 140-year policy of the federal government toward the indigenous peoples had been ultimate assimilation. What has and is happening, however, is quite different. Sibbeston has said that along the Mackenzie, the Métis have always been leaders in the Indian communities and still preserve their strong ties of blood and culture with the Indians rather than the whites.

In the eastern and central Arctic, relations between kabloonat and Inuit have generally been good, and white traders often married Inuk girls and founded dynasties – the Klengenbergs in Coppermine, the Lyalls in Spence Bay, the Fords in Rankin Inlet, the Carpenters in Sachs Harbour, the Josses in Holman, the Firths in McPherson, the Thrashers in Aklavik, the Browers in Point Barrow.

Now that the NWT is in a transitional political phase, it is unlikely that any white person could go far without native ties. Gordon Wray, who is related to 180 members of one Inuit family in Baker Lake through his wife, believes that children of mixed marriages do well, absorbing the strengths of both sides. Wray says: "My culture would tend to be dominant in my children. They are more non-native than native. I think this would be true of most mixed marriages. My oldest child, who was born in Baker Lake, speaks Inuktitut, but my three youngest children, brought up in Yellowknife, have no Inuktitut."

Wray also said the white culture would be dominant even if the father was native and the mother white. His implication was that white culture today is extremely attractive to both whites and natives.

Dennis Patterson, in a similar social position, agrees with Wray that mixed-blood children tend to be successful. Speculating on the possibility that a new race of "true northerners" may be developing, Patterson says this may be a possibility, or at least a trend:

> I've counted twenty-five mixed families in Iqualuit alone [and] many native women are resisting marriage to Inuit because of the tradition of inequality between the sexes. The main factor in any family is adaptability and this helps survival in the mixed family. I think it's fortunate to have children who have mixed parentage. One of their grandfathers can show them how to build an igloo and hunt; the other can show them the world of Expo 86, the world of cities.

Wray and Patterson agree that children in the North are heavily influenced by television, radio music, discos, clothing styles. "The kids growing up now are incapable of talking with their parents in either language," said Patterson. "They're into punk rock, leather, and new wave music."

Such assimilation – if it is the wave of the northern future – is a far cry from the assimilation preached by Duncan Campbell Scott and other officials of the Indian Branch. Men like Patterson and Wray see it as an equal sharing of positive racial qualities. The NWT may be producing truly melded northerners for the first time.

~

Whether or not mixed marriage will solve the problems of the NWT, it is widely agreed that whites, Inuit, Inuvialuit, Métis, and Dene are learning to cooperate in government. James Wah Shee traces the political difficulties back to the 1950s and 1960s when "neither the Dene nor the whites nor the Inuit had any political rights at all." He says the Indian chiefs had no voice in their own government – but neither did the northern whites. All were equally under the control of Ottawa:

> When we started the Brotherhood we had to interpret and explain to our people and to the rest of the world. First of all we even had to get recognition of our right to make claims. We were aware of the evolution occurring in the Legislative Council, which originally involved only whites. Ultimately, the aboriginals had to participate in elected government as soon as it was available.

Wah Shee was caught personally in the middle of early misunderstanding and interracial bickering. He was the one who hired the white advisers, and he said in 1987:

> Any organization needs advisers. We needed consultants and lawyers when we were starting to approach our land claims. We had no experience dealing with many of the problems. The problem with the white advisers was that basically they were university intellectuals who were using aboriginal rights as an intellectual exercise, an experiment for their theories. Some of the individuals were so indoctrinated in their ideologies that they insisted we had to follow these views including refusing to participate in political institutions. The advisers were wrong for that period of time: we needed realists who were practical.

Wah Shee believes that the native organizations reassessed their position by 1979 and have been realistically working with the GNWT ever since. He thinks the partnership has been profitable.

Jack Sigvaldason, the white editor in Yellowknife, says: "I've always said if people from the south – journalists, the clergy, politicians, anthropologists – would leave us alone we could work out our own problems. From now on, the future will be decided in the NWT by northerners and nowhere else."

ARCTIC SNAPSHOT 4

TV INTERVIEWER: Do you think the Fort Smith Indians will be able to handle the problems of pipelines, considering the bad example of Alaska?

ROGER BRUNT: Certainly not! Most white people can't handle the 20th century! You know, there's guys going around hijacking planes and jumping off buildings and getting divorced and getting on drugs and going to jail. And that's after 2,000 years of practice!

Epilogue

Before the Fall: Eden Lost

The Human Beings reached the shoreline about midday when the sun was at its highest, well above the horizon. The ancient rocks weren't much higher than the rough ice of the ocean, and there was a small, low island a mile or so out. The sun was almost directly behind the People and their sleds.

The Leader climbed the highest rise and spent a long time looking over the land and sea. He and his brothers and uncles had spent five days on the hunt and it had been successful. The *komatiks* were loaded with *tuktu* meat, and the *kinmikmat* were straining and whining, eager to get back to camp and be fed. The Leader examined the rough sea carefully, looking for the dark heads of *ugyuk* and the flashing movements of Nanuk. His youngest brother saw the home camp first – a dozen *iglus* in the shelter of a low cliff beside a narrow cove.

It had not been a bad winter, and the sun rose higher every day. A hunter could take satisfaction in having led his people through without a single girl baby being left out to freeze. When the seals had disappeared, the men had gone inland after the caribou and had found them browsing on lichens in a sheltered *swale*.

The Leader was not much given to introspection. He knew some things were true because they were obvious to any observant creature. He knew and respected – almost loved – the cunning ways of Nanuk. He knew how to find his way across the ice to *ugyuk*, the seal, and where to look for *tuktu*, the caribou. He knew how to make snowglasses and how to build a *komatik*. And he knew that he was one of the only Human Beings in the world. The Human Beings were few but enough for this land. Only the Human Beings knew how to live with and use all of the other creatures. A sensible Human Being, an Inuk, knew that only he – and the other natural creatures – could survive here.

To be sure, there were the Dog People of the south, the *kinmikiut*, inferior beings springing from the mating of a Human Being with a *kinmik* bitch.

There were other stories the Leader had heard in camp from the grandfather of the eastern Human Beings, the Netsilik Inuit. The grandfather said that his grandfather (or one from before that) had seen creatures who might have been a cross between Human Beings and Nanuk the Bear – tall as Nanuk and white, with long white or yellow fur all over, including their muzzles.

These Nanuk people had come to the far-off eastern coast in the summer, when there was no ice, in vast *umiaks* that captured clouds and used them to make the winds drive them across the open sea. Like Nanuk they were fierce and treacherous, the grandfather said, and killed some of the Human Beings. In the end, the People had driven them back to their *umiaks* and they had departed. It was said they still lived across the sea on the shores of the great ice mountain.

The tales were told and retold in the long dark of winter when the People waited out the blizzards in their snowhouses. The tales only reinforced the People's knowledge that the Human Beings were unique in the world. What did it matter that there were inferior mongrels living on the far-off edges of the world, beyond the *tuktuat* and the *umingmat* and the *ugukat*? The mongrels were no threat to the Human Beings because they were unable to live for long on the ice, or even on the land in winter. If they came again, the People would help them survive, for that was their way, and then these lower species would go away again as they always had before.

If the mongrels, half-breed foxes or half-breed bears, snapped at the People, they would be killed. It was as simple as that.

The plain truth was that the Human Beings belonged here and no outsider did.

The ... spirits ... had created this land specifically for the Human Beings. The evidence was overwhelming: why else would all these creatures be so designed for the well-being of one another? Human Beings had no proper fur of their own, but the caribou and the seal and the muskox and the fox and the wolverine gave their skins for the benefit of the Human Beings.

Everything lived for the benefit of everything else here in the homeland of the Human Beings. The *tuktu* and the lichens were themselves eaten by wolf and brown bear and Human Beings. The seals ate fish and were eaten by Nanuk and by the Human Beings. It was evident that some great Hunter beyond the People's Land, Nunavut, had designed it for all creatures.

So, clearly, the mongrels were not suited to nor capable of living in this beneficent place. It belonged to the People and their friends.

It would always belong to the People because they, and only they – along with the wolves and the bears and the caribou and the muskox and the seals and the whales and the walruses – belonged here.

How could anyone challenge that? So it had been from the time of the first Human Beings and so it would continue until the sun finally went below the worn rocks of the tundra and rose no more, bringing eternal darkness to the entire world of Human Beings.

It was time to go.

The Leader of the Human Beings shuffled ahead a few steps and took a final look across the frozen sea. Now he could see behind the small island and he discovered a vast *umiak* with broken antlers frozen into the ice. It was as big as the grandfather had said. Bigger! Around it were moving black dots: bear people? seal people? whale people?

It didn't matter: tomorrow he and his sons would visit them and offer *muktuk* ... perhaps the mongrels would have interesting food or toys to exchange.

It didn't matter. The bear people (whale people?) might survive this winter. If they did they would sail their *umiak* away and be gone forever.

It had always been so. It always would be so. Only the Human Beings were fit to survive here.

After the Fall: Thoughts on Burnout

Caroline Anawak spoke to the author in Yellowknife in 1987. These are her words.

... They've run out of steam, they've run out of patience with their lifestyles; they've just run down like old clocks.

I remember one particular meeting of the National Indian Brotherhood. All the presidents were sitting around a table waiting for a meeting to start with time to kill. George Manuel started off with a little joke about how – "Well, I guess I'll be a bachelor these days; my marriage of twenty-eight years just went kaput; the lady doesn't want me anymore; she's tired because I'm travelling; the family's getting older and they're off on their own and she's getting involved and things are going – Well, I'll just have to deal with it."

At which point they all went around the table and said: "You, too?

Oh, us too! Our marriages are on the skids, broken up." ...
Somebody started hacking and coughing and said "Gawd! I have this
cold, can't shake it! The last two years I've had nothing but colds;
you're hacking away; you're coughing away; you've got pneumonia
or flu, you can't throw off."

It went around the table and everybody had their little flurry of
talk: how about that? ... And then the girl came in and sat down and
talked about smoking: the air was blue in the room and they were all
talking about their addictions; some were talking about hangovers;
then it was back to marriage, and at the time only James [Wah Shee]
and Harold Cardinal were still married. Harold said he'd tried to
avoid that syndrome: he left his office in downtown Edmonton and
drove out to Sherwood Park, quite a long drive, his wife and kids
were parked away out in the suburbs and he said, "I do that on purpose; I don't want the Indian Association or any poor people I deal
with all day coming out after supper to my little apartment; nobody's
going to pay the $15 taxi ride to go out there and I can live that kind
of life." He looked like he was the one who'd found the solution, and
James was the other one.

None of them had any idea of what they were really talking about:
what had happened to them as leaders: that they'd burned out. They
couldn't shake the disruptions of living patterns, their health, their
marriages and the kind of ongoing instability was making them go
kaput and they could see everything blowing up all around them.

At the end of that year Harold's marriage was gone and James and
I were to split up a year later. So the marriage patterns of two dedicated, involved people who tried to make it by keeping the office out
of their daily life, didn't work any better than the rest. Harold and his
family could have been on Mars, the distance was so vast from home
to office and political reality. It didn't matter. It was burnout. That
was what the pressures of leadership did to people.

Appendix

The Dene Declaration

The Dene Declaration was passed unanimously by 300 delegates to the second annual joint general assembly of the NWT Indian Brotherhood and the Métis and Non-Status Indians Association in July 1975 at Fort Simpson.

We, the Dene of the NWT, insist on the right to be regarded by ourselves and the world as a nation.

Our struggle is for the recognition of the Dene Nation by the Government and People of Canada and the Peoples and Governments of the world.

As once Europe was the exclusive homeland of the European peoples, Africa the exclusive homeland of the African peoples, the New World, North and South America, was the exclusive homeland of aboriginal peoples of the New World, the Amerindian and the Inuit.

The New World like other parts of the world has suffered the experience of colonialism and imperialism. Other peoples have occupied the land – often with force – and foreign governments have imposed themselves on our people. Ancient civilizations and ways of life have been destroyed.

Colonialism and imperialism is now dead or dying. Recent years have witnessed the birth of new nations or rebirth of old nations out of the ashes of colonialism.

As Europe is the place where you will find European countries with European governments for European peoples, now also you will find in Africa and Asia the existence of African and Asian governments for the African and Asian peoples.

The African and Asian peoples – the peoples of the Third World – have fought for and won the right to self-determination, the right to recognition as distinct peoples and the recognition of themselves as nations.

But in the New World the native peoples have not fared so well. Even in countries in South America where the native peoples are the vast majority of the population there is not one country which has Amerindian government for the Amerindian peoples.

Nowhere in the New World have the native peoples won the right to self-determination and the right to recognition by the world as a distinct people and as nations.

While the native people of Canada are a minority in their homeland, the native people of the NWT, the Dene and the Inuit, are a majority of the population of the NWT.

The Dene find themselves as part of a country. That country is Canada. But the Government of Canada is not the Government of the Dene. These Governments were not the choice of the Dene, they were imposed upon the Dene.

What we the Dene are struggling for is the recognition of the Dene Nation by the Government and the peoples of the world.

And while there are realities we are forced to submit to, such as the existence of a country called Canada, we insist on the right to self-determination as a distinct people and the recognition of the Dene Nation.

We the Dene are part of the Fourth World. And as the peoples and nations of the world have come to recognize the existence and rights of those peoples who make up the Third World, the day must come and will come when the nations of the Fourth World will come to be recognized and respected. The challenge to the Dene and the world is to find the way for the recognition of the Dene Nation.

Our plea to the world is to help us in our struggle to find a place in the world community where we can exercise our right to self-determination as a distinct people and a nation.

What we seek then is independence and self-determination within the country of Canada. This is what we mean when we call for a just settlement for the Dene Nation.

The Métis Declaration

In July 1980 the Métis Association passed its own Declaration of Rights at Fort Good Hope.

We the Métis people of the NWT do declare that we exist as a national entity. While it is true that our nationalism does not take the form of a nation state, it is sufficient to define us as a distinctive people. While it is true that we are descendants of the Dene of the NWT, we are also descendants of other nationalities. As such we have evolved as a people that are distinct from both groups.

From the newcomers to Canada, we inherit democratic rights as citizens of the nation state that they have established. As such we declare ourselves as loyal citizens of Canada. From our Dene ancestors, we inherit legal rights that are owed to us by the nation stated. As such we declare that we are possessed of the legal concept known as Aboriginal Rights.

Therefore we declare our desire to enter into negotiations with the Government of Canada to bring our Aboriginal Rights into a substantive form. We further declare that it is our desire that these negotiations should lead to our recognition as Métis people.

BIBLIOGRAPHY

PRIMARY SOURCES
Major Interviews (on Audio Tape)

Former NWT Commissioners

Gordon Robertson, 1953–63 (also deputy minister)
Ben Sivertz, 1963–67
Stuart Hodgson, 1967–79
John H. Parker, 1979–89

Former Federal Ministers Responsible

Alvin Hamilton, 1957–60
Jean Chrétien, 1968–72
Bill McKnight, 1986–88

Dean A.W.R. Carrothers, chairman of the Carrothers Commission, 1965–66

NWT Members of Parliament

Gene Rheaume
Bud Orange
Wally Firth
Thomas Suluk
Ethel Blondin-Andrews
Tach Anawak

Native Leaders

James Wah Shee, former president, NWT Indian Brotherhood
Georges Erasmus, former president, Dene Nation
Nick Sibbeston, former GNWT government leader
Herb Norwegian, former vice-president, Dene Nation
Charles Overvold, former president, Métis Association
Rick Hardy, former president, Métis Association
Richard McNeeley, former president, Métis Association
John Amagoalik, former president, ITC
Tagak Curley, first president, ITC
Nellie Cournoyea, co-founder COPE, GNWT government leader
Agnes Semmler, deputy commissioner, NWT; co-founder of COPE
Edna Elias, head of GNWT Language Services
Suzie Husky, Inuvik town councillor
Ann Hanson, CBC, Iqualuit
Jonah Kelly, CBC, Iqualuit

Bill Lyall, Inuit Cooperatives Association, Cam Bay
Joe Ohokanoak, mayor, Cambridge Bay
Alan Mahaugak, TFN negotiator
Larry Tourangeau, Métis Association
Roy Goose, Inuvialuit Communications Society, Inuvik
Rosemarie Kuptana, president, Inuit Tapirisat of Canada
Louie Goose, Inuvialuit broadcaster
George Tuccaro, CBC Métis broadcaster

NWT Government Ministers and Officials

Judge Jack Sissons
Judge William Morrow
Mr. Justice W.W. DeWeert
Mr. Justice John Parker, Whitehorse
George Braden, first government leader, GNWT
Dennis Patterson, government leader, GNWT
Gordon Wray, cabinet minister, GNWT
Tom Butters, cabinet minister
Don Stewart, former Speaker, GNWT legislature
Robert Macquarrie, former Speaker, legislature
David Searle, former Speaker, legislature
Gary Mullins, former assistant commissioner, NWT
Brian Lewis, former deputy minister of education
Bobby Cowcill, former Kitikmeot region director
Ray Creery, former senior GNWT official
Mush Mersereau, former senior GNWT official
Will Drake, senior GNWT official
Mike Pontus, senior GNWT official

Communications Authorities

Austin Curley, CBC
Bob Rhodes, CBC
Jack Sigvaldason, News of the North
Cindy Clegg, journalist
Peter Puxley
John Bayly

Business Leaders

Bob Blair, Nova Corporation
Peter Bawden, Peter Baden Drilling
Jack Gallagher, Dome Petroleum
Charles Hetherington, PanArctic Oil
Lindsay Franklin, PanArctic Oil
Pat Carney, Arctic Gas

Elders

Chief Jimmy Bruneau, Fort Rae
Chief Andrew Stewart, Aklavik
Chief Hyacinthe Andre, Arctic Red River
Chief Tadit Francis, Fort Simpson
Chief Charlie Abel, Old Crow, YT
Pete Baker, Yellowknife
Paul Kaeser, Fort Smith
E.J. (Scotty) Gall, Yellowknife
Norman Ford, Rankin Inlet
James Kavana, Cambridge Bay

Contacts

Correspondence or conversation

Mr. Justice Tom Berger
Father René Fumoloe, OM
Hon. Warren Allmand

PRIMARY RESEARCH

Indian Act, 1951 and 1978

DIAND documents entitled Indian Acts and Amendments, 1868–1950

Amending acts, statutory orders and regulations and other related contemporary legislation to 1978

Berger Commission hearings in Inuvik, Yellowknife and Toronto

NWT Executive Council, Council or Legislative Assembly sessions in Inuvik and Yellowknife, 1964, 1972, 1975, 1979, 1987

GNWT Archives, Yellowknife

Arctic Institute of North America Archives, Calgary

Government of Canada Archives, Ottawa

DIAND Archives, Ottawa

Yellowknife Public Library

Prince of Wales Northern Heritage Centre, Yellowknife

News of the North/The Yellowknifer, files, Yellowknife

Nova Corporation Archives, Calgary

"Arctic" Magazine files

University of Alaska Reference Library, Fairbanks

Government of the Yukon Territory Archives, Whitehorse

NWT Council Minutes

Indian Brotherhood/Dene Nation Annual Reports (1972–86)

GNWT Annual Reports (1968–86)

Minutes, Western Constitutional Forum covering meetings in Ottawa, Iqualuit and Yellowknife

PUBLICATIONS

Berger, Thomas. *Northern Frontier, Northern Homeland.* Toronto: James Lorimer, 1978.

———. *Village Journey.* New York: Farrar, Strauss, Giroux, 1985.

Boas, Frans. *The Central Eskimo, 1888.* Toronto: Coles Publishing Co., 1974.

Bevan, Bryan. *Elizabethan Seamen.* London: Hale, 1971.

Braden, George. "The Emergence of National Interest Groups in the NWT 1969–75." M.A. thesis, 1976.

Brody, Hugh. *The People's Land.* Harmondsworth: Pelican, 1975.

Brower, Charles D. *Fifty Years Below Zero.* New York: Dodd, Mead, 1963.

Brown, George, and Ron Maguire. *Indian Treaties in Historical Perspective.* Ottawa: DIAND, 1979.

Camsell, Charles. *Son of the North.* Toronto: Ryerson, 1954.

Carrothers, Dr. A.W.R. *NWT Government Development Report.* Ottawa: Queen's Printer, 1966.

Chrétien, Jean. *Straight from the Heart.* Toronto: Key Porter, 1985.

Davis, Mark, and Zamis, Mark. *The Genocide Machine.* Montreal: Black Rose Press, 1977.

Davis, Richard C., ed. *Rupertsland – a Cultural Tapestry.* Waterloo, Ont.: Sir Wilfrid Laurier University Press, 1988.

DeCoursey, Duke. *The Yellowknife Years.* 1986.

The Dene Nation. *Denendeh: A Dene Celebration.* Yellowknife: The Dene Nation, 1985.

De Voto, Bernard. *Across the Wide Missouri.* Boston: Houghton Mifflin, 1947.

———. *The Course of Empire.* Boston: Houghton Mifflin, 1952.

Diabaldo, Richard. *The Government of Canada and the Inuit.* Ottawa: DIAND, 1985.

DIAND. *Constitutional Provisions in Relation to Indians.* Ottawa, 1970.

Dickason, Olive P. *Canada's First Nations.* Toronto: McClelland & Stewart, 1992.

Drury, Charles. *Constitutional Development in the NWT.* Ottawa: Queen's Printer, 1980.

Eayrs, James. *In Defence of Canada.* 3 vols. Toronto: University of Toronto Press, 1964, 1965, and 1972.

Eyre, Kenneth. *Custos Borealis: The Military in the Canadian North.* Ottawa: DIAND, 1981.

Finnie, Robert. *Canada Moves North.* Toronto: Macmillan, 1947.

———. *CANOL.* San Francisco: Taylor & Taylor, 1945.

Freuchen, Peter. *Peter Freuchen's Book of the Seven Seas.* New York: Simon and Shuster, 1957.

———. *Book of the Eskimos.* Cleveland: World Publishing Co., 1961.

Fumoloe, Rene. *As Long as This Land Shall Last.* Toronto: McClelland & Stewart, 1973.

Grant, Shelagh D. *Sovereignty or Security?* Vancouver: University of British Columbia Press, 1988.

Gray, Earle. *Super Pipe.* Toronto: Griffin House, 1979.

Guillemin, Jeanne. "The Politics of National Integration – Comparing the US and Canada." *Social Program Journal,* vol. 25.

Handbook of the North American Indians. Washington, D.C.: Smithsonian Institution, 1981.

Hodgson, Stuart M. *Goals of the Government of the NWT.* Yellowknife, 1974.

Hunt, Barbara. *Rebels, Rascals and Royalty.* 1983. Reprint. Vancouver: Library Services Branch, 1987.

Iglauer, Edith. *Denison's Ice Road.* Toronto: Clark, Irwin, 1974.

Jacobs, Carl. *Inside the Pipe.* New York: First Books, 1979.

Jenness, Diamond. *Eskimo Administration.* Arctic Institute, 1962–67.

Keenleyside, Hugh. *Memoirs.* Toronto: McClelland & Stewart, 1981–82.

Lopez, Barry. *Arctic Dreams: Imagination and Desire in a Northern Landscape.* New York: Scribner, 1986.

Lotz, Jim. *Northern Realities.* Toronto: New Press, 1970.

Lysyk, Kenneth, et al. *Report of the Alaska Highway Pipeline Inquiry.* Ottawa: Supply and Services, Canada, 1977.

McGinniss, Joe. *Going to Extremes.* New York: Knopf, 1971.

McPhee, John A. *Coming into the Country.* Toronto: McGraw-Hill Ryerson, 1977.

Moorehead, Alan. *The Fatal Impact: An Account of the Invasion of the South Pacific, 1767–1840.* London: H. Hamilton, 1966.

Morrison, William R. *Under the Flag: Canadian Sovereignty and the Native People.* Ottawa: DIAND, 1984.

———. *Survey of the History and Claims of Native People of Northern Canada.* Ottawa: DIAND, 1985.

Mowat, Farley. *People of the Deer.* Boston: Little, Brown, 1952.

———. *The Desperate People.* Boston: Little, Brown, 1959.

———. *Tundra.* Toronto: McClelland & Stewart, 1971.

Newman, Peter C. *The Company of Adventurers.* Markham, Ont.: Penguin, 1985.

———. *Caesars of the Wilderness.* Markham, Ont.: Viking, 1987.

O'Malley, Martin. *The Past and Future Land.* Toronto: Peter Martin & Assoc., 1976.

Page, Robert. *Northern Development.* Toronto: McClelland & Stewart, 1986.

Paton, Richard. *New Policies & Old Organizations, Can Indian Affairs Change?* Ottawa: Centre for Policy and Programs, Carleton University, 1986.

Peacock, Donald. *People, Peregrines and Arctic Pipelines.* Vancouver: J.J. Douglas, 1977.

Pitseolak, Peter. *Pictures Out of My Life.* Montreal: Design Collaborative Books, with Oxford University Press, 1971.

Price, Ray. *Yellowknife.* Toronto: Peter Martin, 1967.

Pryde, Duncan. *Nunaga: My Land, My People.* Edmonton: M.G. Hurtig, 1971.

Ross, P.D. & Partners. *Report on Organization of GNWT.* 1971.

Stacey, C.P. *Arms, Men and Governments.* Ottawa: Queen's Printer, 1970.

Stefansson, V. *The Friendly Arctic.* Macmillan, 1921.

Swayze, Carolyn. *Hard Choices: A Life of Tom Berger.* Vancouver: Douglas & McIntryre. 1987.

Titley, E. Brian. *A Narrow Vision: Duncan Campbell Scott and the Administration of Indian Affairs in Canada.* Vancouver: University of British Columbia Press, 1974.

Tobias, Leonard. *Canadian Indian Policy 1918–1939.* Ottaw: DIAND, 1985.

Watkins, Mel. *Dene Nation, the Colony Within.* Toronto: University of Toronto Press, 1977.

Zaslow, Morris. *The Opening of the Canadian North, 1870–1914.* Toronto: McClelland & Stewart, 1971.

INDEX